Communication Theory for Christian Witness

Charles H. Kraft

Revised Edition

ORBIS BOOKS

Maryknoll, New York 10545

The Catholic Foreign Mission Society of America (Maryknoll) recruits and trains people for overseas missionary service. Through Orbis Books, Maryknoll aims to foster the international dialogue that is essential to mission. The books published, however, reflect the opinions of their authors and are not meant to represent the official position of the society.

This edition published by Orbis Books, Maryknoll, New York 10545.
Printed in the United States of America.

Library of Congress Cataloging-in-Publication Data

Kraft, Charles H.
  Communication theory for Christian witness / Charles H. Kraft. —
Rev. ed.
    p. cm.
  Includes bibliographical references and index.
  ISBN 0-88344-763-0 (pbk.)
  1. Communication—Religious aspects—Christiantiy.   I. Title.
BV4319.K73   1991
261.5'2—dc20   91-36213
                                                          CIP

Dedicated to

two sets of parents:

Mine — Mr. and Mrs. Howard R. Kraft
Wolcott, Connecticut

My wife's — the Reverend and Mrs. J. Milton Bowman
Lansing, Michigan

My parents have given me life and much more. My in-laws have given me a wife and much more. I seek hereby to honor them by passing on to others some portion of what they have passed on to me combined with some portion of what I have done with their investment in me.

Contents

Preface to the First Edition

We take communication for granted. That's the problem. Communication happens largely unconsciously, like the shining of the sun, or the plumbing system in our home, or the circulation of blood in our body. We don't even notice such vital systems until they break down. Then we say, "I just can't understand what happened!" Often, though, when things break down it is because we have not cared for them properly.

Such breakdowns in any given vital system are not, however, surprising to those who understand how that system works. For they have a kind of operator's manual, a set of procedures concerning how the system does what it does and how to fix it when it doesn't function properly.

This book is intended to be a short operator's manual for Christian communicators, for many of us seem to have little understanding of how the communicational system works. We are anxious to use that system for Christian purposes but often don't know the cause when things go wrong. In fact, we seldom know what is happening even when things go right.

Communication is always going on whenever and wherever there are people. To live is to communicate. Everything we say and do, every mannerism, every facial expression, the way we sit and stand, the way we dress, everything about us that is interpretable by others communicates something. The question is: How well do we control these activities so that what others receive is reasonably close to what we intend?

When we attempt to communicate, we reach out to other people across whatever gap separates us from them. This may be a comparatively small gap, as between members of the same family, or a very large gap, as between members of widely different societies. At the very least, there will always be differences in the life experiences of those who participate in communicational events. Frequently, then, the participants will possess additional gap-widening characteristics, such as differences in sex, social class, age, educational background, occupation, subculture, dialect, and the like. Often such differences affect less visible factors, such as trust and openness, that strongly influence communication at the deepest levels.

If effective communication is to take place, such gaps need to be bridged. Such bridging may be done by those who receive messages, the receptors. And this is regularly done by receptors who are highly motivated to receive what even poor communicators are presenting. But not all who hear the Christian message are so motivated. Frequently, it is necessary for communicators to build the bridge nearly all the way to the receptors if they are to have any assurance of being understood. Expert communicators need to know how to build such bridges.

As with all human behavior, things don't just happen. There are rules, patterns, and principles according to which the communicational process proceeds. When these rules are obeyed, the process ordinarily goes well. When they are disobeyed, things ordinarily do not go well. What are the patterns? How can we discern and follow the rules? Are there examples that can be followed? These are what this book is about.

The subject is communication, with a focus on the effective communication of Christian messages. God is the Great Communicator, and as Christians we have opened ourselves to him both as receptors of his messages and as co-laborers with him in communicating those messages to others. For some reason he has involved us in the process of getting out the messages for which he came and gave himself completely. How well are we carrying out our part of the task?

In this volume I seek to communicate to you the dynamics of the communication process. I want you to ask the above question in the light of the considerations raised in the following chapters. And if you interpret according to my intent, you will at least have gained insight into (a) the rules and principles according to which effective communicational transactions take place and (b) certain of the ways in which God has employed these principles to communicate his messages.

This book, therefore, will work from two points of reference: the Bible and contemporary communication theory. I will look to the theory to shed light on the communicational dimensions both of what we do and of what God does (as presented in the Bible). God's communicational activity, then, can provide us with a model to imitate and methods to be guided by. For he has revealed not only the messages to be communicated, but how to communicate them effectively for those receptors who have the interpretational skills to "hear" what he is saying in this regard.

My hope is that this book will function as a basic manual on communication for those actively involved in communicating the Christian message, whether in a professional or nonprofessional capacity. I attempt to offer a balanced treatment of communication theory and practice from a perspective that observes and analyzes God's use (and, therefore, endorsement) of these same principles. I aim to present the material simply without being simplistic, accurately without being technical, and comprehensively without being cumbersome.

I pray that the reading of this book will result in your being able to (a) gain a clearer understanding of the dynamics of the communication process, (b) see the ways in which God has employed these humanly discernible communicational patterns for his purposes, (c) develop the ability to analyze your own past and present communicational activity in terms of these categories, and (d) go on to improve your skills as a communicator to the end that the meanings intended by God may be channeled more effectively through you to those to whom God has called you.

I am a teacher of career missionaries, presently specializing in intercultural communication. I have training in anthropology, linguistics, and theology and have focused both in my missionary service (in Nigeria) and in my academic life on the problems related to effectively conveying the Christian message to those of other societies and languages. Though the focus of this book is on communication within English-speaking contexts, you will note the great relevance of insights from cross-cultural experience to the problems encountered in more familiar settings.

I would like to express my gratitude to a number of people who have helped me with this project. Among them are the audiences on which I tried out various portions of the material. These ranged from classes at Fuller and Ashland seminaries to lectures to my School of World Mission colleagues and to members of the Academy of Evangelism. Individuals whose help has been invaluable are my wife, Marguerite, my graduate assistants, Ross Bensley and Paul Muench, secretaries Ken Slenkovich, Ken Wollard, Joan Sizoo, Sabita Bensley, Jennifer Dillaha, and Betty Ann Klebe, Drs. E. Thomas and Betty Sue Brewster, who let my secretaries and me use their word processor and coached us in its use. Thanks also to Fuller Seminary and my faculty colleagues for a quarter-long sabbatical, during which I was able to complete the first draft.

A word should be said about the terms used for those who receive communication. I ordinarily refer to these as *receptors,* even though this term seems to imply that those receiving the communication are fairly passive. Occasionally I use terms such as *respondents, interactants, participants, audience, receivers,* or *hearers.* Either *respondent* or *interactant* would be preferable to *receptor* as the general term, since they nicely point to the fact that those who receive communication are active in the process. But they "feel" too technical, so I have chosen not to use either very often. *Audience* would be a possibility but provides no advantage over *receptor.* The remaining three terms are so imprecise that they constantly require modifiers. Even though *receptor* is mildly technical and connotes too much passivity, it is my usual choice as the least objectionable of the available terms.

Preface to the Revised Edition

It is a pleasure to be able to put a revised edition of this book into print. I am very grateful to Orbis Books for making it possible. The first edition received a gratifying response both from reviewers and from those who used it in and out of classrooms. And several of those who taught from it commented that the book met a need not filled by any other.

Though much of this edition is only slightly changed, there are several new features. Chapter 1 is completely new, filling a gap not addressed in the first edition. Chapters 4 and 5 constitute a new arrangement and expansion of the material in the previous chapter 3, which was too long anyway. And chapter 9 has been well worked over to correct and expand some of the shortcomings of the corresponding chapter (7) in the first edition. So there are twelve chapters in this edition, rather than the original ten, most of which are re-edited versions of the original chapters.

One additional change that those who used the first edition will notice is that I have abandoned the practice of alternating masculine and feminine pronouns chapter by chapter. This was an experiment that I feel did not work well.

As this new edition goes forth, I bless you in Jesus' name with greater ability to communicate God's messages as clearly and effectively as Jesus did.

1

Intimacy with God the Father

A Personal Word

The attitude you should have is the one that Christ Jesus had. (Phil. 2:5)

"Come with me, and I will teach you to catch men." (Matt. 4:19)

In these last days he has spoken to us through his Son. (Heb. 1:2)

As one who specializes in the communication of Christianity from society to society, I am increasingly fascinated by what the Bible shows us concerning how God communicated. Over the years as I began to learn more and more about communication, I noticed I was beginning to see the Bible from a new perspective, a communicational perspective. I was beginning to ask different questions.

Whereas previously I had studied the Bible with my primary aim being the discovery and appropriation of its teachings, I now started asking questions concerning how these teachings had been communicated to their original recipients and how they are now being communicated to us. And whereas I had been fascinated in a general way with the incarnation of God in Jesus Christ, I now began to focus especially on the communicational dimensions of that miraculous entry of God into human life.

Not that I had ceased to be concerned with the teachings of the Scriptures. But now there was the added dimension of curiosity as to how these teachings had gotten into the minds and hearts of the recipients and the example thereby provided for the contemporary communication of God's messages. Verses such as Philippians 2:5, in which I had already been very interested, began to take on added meaning as I considered the communicational implications of the attitude of Jesus Christ.

Likewise with Matthew 4:19. Learning to communicate is of the essence if we are to learn to "catch" human beings. Could it be, I began to ask, that the communicational dynamics of Jesus' interaction with his disciples formed the very basis of his relationship with them? And would not the way he interacted with others be intended to teach them how to communicate? Should we not, then, study both the activities of Jesus and his underlying attitude for clues concerning how we should communicate?

It has been my growing conviction that the communicational dimensions of the case studies recorded in the Bible are as much to be regarded as examples for us as are the more explicit teachings. Thus, when Jesus says, "Follow me," and Paul says, "Imitate me," we can and should imitate their communicational example as well as every other aspect of their lives.

For generations, we who have sought to communicate God's Word have looked to the Bible for our *message*. I am afraid, though, that we have seldom looked to the Bible for our *method*. I have become personally convinced that the inspiration of the Bible extends both to message and to method. My aim in this book, therefore, is to elucidate a scriptural method for getting God's message across—a method I claim is God's method and recommend that we follow as we seek to get his messages across.

Though I believe this is the approach we see from the very beginning of the Bible, it will be the example of Jesus that will be in primary focus. God, of course, has communicated with humans through others (Heb. 1:1). But Jesus was his method par excellence (Heb. 1:2)—the best communicational bridge God ever produced.

By way of application, note God's problem in reaching human beings across the gap between his abode and ours. We may illustrate this problem as follows:

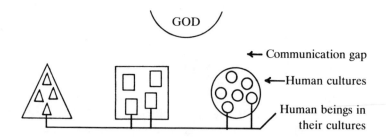

Figure 1. The Communication Gap between God and Human Beings

The problem is: How can an infinite, sinless, omnipotent God traverse the communication gap between himself and finite, sinful, weak human beings? The answer lies in an analysis of scriptural data showing how he actually solved the problem. Ultimately, of course, God himself "became a human being" (John 1:14; Phil. 2:7) to cross that gap once and for all. But an analysis of the rest of Scripture (e.g., pre-Christ) is also instructive.

We, then, are called to communicate the good news throughout the world (Mark 16:15; Matt. 28:18-19; Acts 1:8). But there are communication gaps between persons in the same society and even larger gaps between persons of different societies.

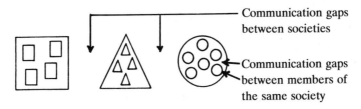

Communication gaps between societies

Communication gaps between members of the same society

Figure 2. Communication Gaps between Human Beings

How, then, can we learn to traverse the communication gaps between human beings? By imitating God's example. In what follows I seek to analyze his example to better enable us to imitate it.

Gaps and Bridges

Every communicational interaction involves a gap and a bridge. A communicational gap always exists between human beings and those who seek to interact with them, whether they be other humans or heavenly beings. To cross such a gap, a communicational bridge is needed. We who specialize in communication theory spend much of our energy seeking to understand how communicational bridges are built and how to cross them. Such insight needs to be applied to our understanding of how God gets his messages across to humans.

A bridge has two ends. There is the entrance end and the exit end. *And the bridge must be connected well at both ends.* I once saw a bridge that was constructed halfway across a wide river. It sat that way for nearly forty years before somebody figured out how to connect it on the other side of the river. For forty years, then, the halfway bridge sat useless, even though it was well connected at one end.

Any would-be communicator must be connected well at both ends of the communicational bridge. For, as we will see later, the communicator is the bridge over which the communication takes place. The end where the message is originated (which may be either within or outside of the communicator) we call the "source" or "communicator" end. The end at which the message is interpreted by another person we call the "receptor" end.

The chapters that follow will focus primarily on what goes on at the receptor's end of the bridge. We will not focus in those chapters on how communicators arrive at the content they seek to get across. The analysis and applications, then, will be designed to help us follow Jesus' example in his relationship to his human audiences.

At the source end of the bridge, however, it is important to understand how Jesus, our model, received the content he communicated. We therefore devote this introductory chapter to a consideration of his relationship to God, the Source of the messages he sought to get across. As we go along we will note how we can and should follow his example.

Jesus, the Son

From the very beginning God has shown himself to be a communicating God. He has never ceased to send messages to his creatures. In doing so, he has used several methods (e.g., dreams, angels, a burning bush). But he seems to prefer working through human beings to reach other humans. Thus, when he unveiled his ultimate method of communication, it turned out to be a Human Being, his Son (Heb. 1:2). His supreme choice of method is the One he calls his Son.

A son is a member of the family and thus in a relationship with his parents that cannot be dissolved. This relationship exists whether or not the son pleases the father. The son was brought up in the father's home and learned quite unconsciously to behave like his father. For genetic reasons, a son even looks like his father. And because of their close contact in the home, he acts like his father.

But even a father-son relationship needs tending if it is not to deteriorate. A son needs to spend time with his father. If, either by the choice of the father or that of the son, such time is not spent, a son can grow away from his father rather than more like him. Sons who refuse to listen to and obey their fathers are called unfaithful.

This is how Adam behaved, most of his descendants, and, eventually, the people of Israel God chose as his very own. They wandered away from their Father, refusing to listen to and obey him. The first Adam failed the faithfulness test (1 Cor. 15:45-47). And, though many of his descendants were faithful, many others turned their backs on their Father and left him. In Jeremiah 3:19-20, God laments concerning Israel:

> Israel, I wanted to accept you as my
>   son and give you a delightful land,
>   the most beautiful land in all the world.
> I wanted you to call me father
>   and never again turn away from me.
> But like an unfaithful wife,
>   you have not been faithful to me.

Jesus, however, the second Adam, modeled what our relationship with the Father is supposed to be. He was a faithful Son, one who spent time with his Father. By inheritance, like all humans, he participated in the image and likeness of God (Gen. 1:26). And by association, he came to reflect "the brightness of God's glory," attaining even to "the exact likeness of God's own being" (Heb. 1:3).

In becoming a man, Jesus agreed with God the Father to put aside his divine attributes, never to use them in his human state (Phil. 2:6-8). As the second Adam, then, he modeled true sonship, totally as a human being, both winning the victory over Satan and providing an example that we can imitate. He was tested (Heb. 4:15), taught obedience (Heb. 5:8), and made perfect (Heb. 2:10) as a human son, passing the faithfulness test that the first Adam had failed. His example, not that of the first Adam, is the one to follow.

Jesus' Intimacy with the Father

Jesus passed the test, not on the basis of his inheritance, but on the basis of his behavior as a human. He carefully established and maintained the kind of intimate relationship with God the Father that humans are meant to live in. Proper sonship requires intimacy. But intimacy takes work. So Jesus worked at maintaining intimacy with the Father. Though as a human he was separated from the Father by the vast communication gap that exists between God and humans, Jesus regularly took time from his ordinary duties to go away and be alone with his Father. It was his habit to "go away to lonely places, where he prayed" (Luke 5:16; see also 6:12; 9:18, 28; 11:1; 22:41).

When the term *pray* is used for what Jesus did during these times with the Father, what does it mean? We usually employ that word mainly for the activity of *asking* God for things. I doubt, however, if that is how Jesus spent most of his time with the Father. I suspect that the time was spent more relationally, perhaps discussing the events of the previous day and the plans for the next. Might much of the time have been spent simply relaxing in the Father's arms? Whatever they did, we can be sure that *they were cultivating their relationship and "feeding" their intimacy.* They were tending closeness at the "God end" of the bridge so that Jesus would have the authority he needed to minister effectively at the other end of the bridge. As will be seen below, both intimacy and authority are "with God" types of prayer, as opposed to the "to God" types.

Jesus' relationship with the Father was one of total dependence. His statement to this effect is, "the Son can do nothing on his own; he does only what he sees his Father doing" (John 5:19). Jesus lived his life and conducted his ministry totally under the Father's authority. He did not allow himself to do anything on his own authority (John 5:30). Though he had the right to be equal with God the Father, he took the position of a slave under the Father's authority (Phil. 2:7). He seems to have agreed with the Father to not use his inherent divine powers during the time he was on earth (see Wagner 1988:113-27). Thus he did no miracles before the Holy Spirit came upon him at his baptism (Luke 3:21-22). From that point he was able to "work the works" of his Father (John 9:4 KJV) as a full human being totally under the power of the Holy Spirit.

In submission to the Holy Spirit, he paid careful attention to what the Father communicated to him, speaking only what he heard him say (John 8:26, 28, 38) and teaching only what came from him (John 7:16). In obedience, he worked the Father's works (John 5:17), did what he saw the Father doing (John 5:19-20), and demonstrated what God is like through his deeds (John 10:37-38; 14:11), always pleasing the Father in the things he did (John 8:29).

We Need the Same Intimacy

In these ways Jesus modeled for us what our relationship with the Father should be. For *we, like Jesus, need to be connected tightly at the God end of the bridge to receive our instructions and authority.* For us, as for Jesus, it is this intimacy with the Father that gives us the authority to do the works of God. The power to do what God instructs us to do, then, comes to us, as it did to Jesus, from the Holy Spirit.

When Jesus began his training program, he chose twelve, saying, "I have chosen you *to be with me.*" Only after they had spent time with him could he "*also* send [them] out to preach . . . [with] authority to drive out demons" (Mark 3:14-15). He even promised that they would do what he himself did and more (John 14:12), presumably by cultivating the same intimacy with the Father that he had modeled.

The first step, then, for the apostles toward God's approach to communication both by word and deed was to develop an intimate relationship with the source of their authority. When Jesus left them, he told them to wait until the Holy Spirit's empowering (Luke 24:49; Acts 1:4) so they could do the work God intended for them. A major part of that work was to be witness — communication — to the world on the authority of Jesus and under the power of the Holy Spirit (Acts 1:8).

And it is likewise for us. *If we are to be effective in doing the works of Jesus, we must be close to him,* "for [we] can do nothing without [him]" (John 15:5). Whether the work we do is verbal or demonstrates power, the messages we carry across the communication bridge from God to humans can only be from God if we, the communicators, are connected to him and receive those messages from him.

So the only adequate starting place for those who would communicate God's messages in God's way is to develop an intimate, dependent, listening, and obeying relationship with God. Which brings us to our next question, How does this happen?

Six Types of Prayer

As suggested above, what Jesus did when he prayed may be more (or less) than usually comes to mind when we speak of praying. For the term *prayer* is used to label several different types of activity. I will here discuss six of them, though I believe that Jesus used only five of the six types.

We may classify these types of prayer in various ways. I will label the first way "with God" and "to God":

With God	**To God**
Practicing Intimacy	Gratitude Prayer
Taking Authority	Confession Prayer
	Asking Prayer
	Intercession

A second way of labeling them might be to relate them to the communication bridge. Three of them seem to function *at the God end of the bridge:* Practicing Intimacy, Gratitude, and Confession prayer. *Crossing the bridge* happens during Asking Prayer, in the sense that receiving what we ask for gives us something to carry across the bridge. *At the human end of the bridge,* then, the battle necessary to bring the freedom for people to receive communication from God is fought through Intercessory Prayer and Taking Authority.

Let's look at these elements and their importance to the tasks of communication in more detail.

1. I believe the most important of the things we refer to as prayer is what I term *practicing intimacy*. This is the activity of simply being with God, inviting him to come and be present with us. As suggested above, I think this is what Jesus usually did when he spent the night with his Father.

I believe this is the "rest" Jesus promised when we come to him with our burdens (Matt. 11:28). I suspect the disciples experienced it many times when their talking with Jesus was over for the day and they simply relaxed in each other's presence. Perhaps it was their need of such relaxation accompanied by being ministered to by God that prompted the Master to wash their feet in the midst of the confusing events of his last hours on earth (John 13:1-17).

Though we find it difficult to understand why Jesus, the Creator, would serve his creatures like this; perhaps we, like Peter, need to receive this kind of communication at the God end of the bridge if we are to continue to be his disciples (John 13:8). For it is for our own good and in order to learn to imitate Jesus at the other end of the bridge that we need to experience both the intimacy with and the service he experienced from the Father at this end.

We often spend the whole of our solitude with God talking, with little or none of it spent listening. A pastor friend of mine pictures the average prayer as a telephone conversation where one person talks and talks and then, before the other can say anything, hangs up the phone. When we practice God's presence by relaxing with him, we allow him opportunity to express himself to us in a way that doesn't happen when we are engaged in talking.

As I practice this kind of intimacy with Jesus, he often shows himself to me in a picture, sometimes hugging me or putting his arm around my shoulder. Sometimes we sit, sometimes we walk together and enjoy each other's presence. He communicates love and care to me, just as he did with Peter when he ministered to him—and, I believe, just as the Father communicated to Jesus in those times he spent alone with him. He treats me as his dear child (1 John 3:1), restoring and refreshing me as he did with David in Psalm 23.

Sometimes God allows me to simply *feel* his presence without any visual images. When I ask him to come, he often simply brings what feels like a sweet heaviness and a holy hush. At times like these, any noise or movement seems to be an intrusion. Sometimes, though, there is little or no feeling. But I know that when I ask God to come, he really does come.

I often experience this kind of intimacy accompanied by music in a worship setting. When we sing to God, he often responds by allowing us to feel that sweet heaviness. Singing ordinary hymns usually doesn't do this for me. Singing my love and commitment to God in the forms of contemporary worship music, usually with my eyes closed, however, frequently seems to take me right into God's throne room.

By practicing intimacy (whether or not we call it prayer), we connect tightly with God, the Source of the messages we seek to carry across the bridge to those on the other side. This kind of experience is crucial for those who would communicate like Jesus. It is probably this kind of prayer that Paul had in mind when he said, "Pray at all times" ("without ceasing," KJV, 1 Thess. 5:17).

As with Jesus, practicing intimacy is also the basic connection that enables us to represent God at the human end of the bridge. Crossing over that bridge, then, there are several types of prayer that enhance life and witness at the human end. Among these are:

2. *Gratitude prayer.* Paul commands this kind of prayer when he says, "Be thankful in all circumstances" (1 Thess. 5:18). Gratefulness to God is a kind of worship and, therefore, connects with the practice of intimacy. This is to be our attitude at all times, no matter what our circumstances.

Those who live in a posture of gratefulness both connect with God and communicate one of the major benefits of that connection to the people they relate to. Circumstances will not always be good to us. But the assurance of knowing "that in all things God works for good with those who love him" (Rom. 8:28) makes a difference to us and potentially opens up opportunities for communication to others.

When things go well, we know and proclaim that God is the author. And we thank him. When things happen that we don't understand, we know that God is behind the scenes ready to work with us for good (Rom. 8:28). So we thank him. And even when the enemy attacks us, we are assured that God sets the limits (Job 1:12; 2:6). So we thank him. We can have the same attitude David had when, though he often found himself in difficult circumstances, he said things like: "I will always thank the Lord; I will never stop praising him" (Ps. 34:1). Gratitude prayer is important both to the life and to the witness of anyone who is close to God.

3. *Confession prayer* functions to make clean the person who crosses the communication bridge. Jesus did not need this kind of prayer, but we certainly do. Through confession we acknowledge our deficiencies and disobediences in keeping with 1 John 1:9 and accept God's pardon.

Though it is a fact that we need to continually recognize and confess our failings, we are not to dwell on them. We are, rather, to focus on the God who has lovingly accepted, forgiven, and welcomed us into a relationship with him (Rom. 5:6-11). Knowing who we are in the freedom thus experienced enables us both to live and to communicate with Kingdom authority. The freedom from sin available in Christ also becomes an important part of the message we are to carry across the bridge to others.

4. *Asking prayer* is the most common kind of prayer here in focus. As those commissioned to work at both ends of God's communicational bridge, we stand at one or the other end asking our Father either to send something across to us or to give us something to take across to others. Our intimacy with God, based on our faith-relationship with him, gives us permission to come boldly into his presence (Heb. 4:16), knowing that we will be well received there.

Furthermore, Jesus says, "Ask and you will receive, so that your happiness may be complete" (John 16:24). This intimate relationship with God the Father means that we can make requests related to any aspect of our lives. We are, however, commanded to pray as well for the communicational goals of the Kingdom (Luke 10:2).

5. As members of God's Kingdom in intimate relationship with the King, we are a part of Jesus' army. This means we are expected to fight the enemy (Eph. 6:12). One of the major ways in which we do battle is via *intercessory prayer*. Other warriors need help at the human end of the bridge, and we are to bring their needs to God. In this way, according to rules we don't fully understand, we are privileged to cooperate with God in releasing those for whom we intercede from the power of the evil one.

We are to intercede for everyone (1 Tim. 2:1; Eph. 6:18). Among the multitude of scriptural examples concerning intercession are Abraham's intercession for Sodom (Gen. 18:23-32); Moses' intercessions for Pharaoh (Exod. 8:12, 30-31; 9:33; 10:18) and for the Israelites (Exod. 32:11-13, 31-32; 34:9; Num. 11:11-15; 14:13-19; 21:7; Deut. 9:18-20; 10:10); Jesus' intercession for Peter (Luke 22:32), for the disciples (John 17:9-19), and for all who would come to faith in him (John 17:20-23); and Paul's intercessions for the people he ministered to (Rom. 1:9-10; Eph. 1:16-19; 3:14-19; Col. 1:9).

Paul connects intercessory prayer with the use of the armor God gives us to fight the Devil (Eph. 6:18-19). It is to be used on every occasion according to the leading of the Holy Spirit (Eph. 6:18). Intercession would seem to play a major role in freeing people from the enemy so that they can receive the communication God seeks to get across to them. It also supports those who battle the enemy.

6. At the human end of the bridge, buttressed by the empowerment of intercessory prayer, we are to engage in the same kind of *taking authority* that Jesus demonstrated. Technically, I don't think taking authority should be called prayer. For in it we posture ourselves *with* God, speaking on his behalf against those things he leads us to speak against.

Like Jesus, we speak authoritatively against demons and diseases (Luke 9:1). For Jesus gave his disciples authority and power over such beings and entities, commanding them to preach and heal (Luke 9:2) and then to teach their disciples all that he taught them (Matt. 28:20).

Jesus did not use prayer types 1-5 when he ministered to people. Rather, he asserted his authority as a representative of the King and *commanded* the result to happen. Jesus thus demonstrated the Father (John 14:9) by using his authority and power to show the Father's love. And he promised that we would be able to do the same (John 14:12).

This authority issued from Jesus' intimacy with and obedience to the Father and provided the basis for his communication as a human. It is, likewise, the basis for the incarnational witness about which the remainder of this book speaks. Jesus was tightly connected to God at one end of the bridge and to humans at the other. So must we be if we are to communicate God's messages in his way.

The Point Is

Communication requires that there be a message, one or more people to whom that message is directed, and a messenger to take the message across whatever gap exists between the source of the message and the intended receptor(s). This book will elaborate on each of those elements in the communication process.

The Bible sets forth some additional requirements for those who would communicate on God's behalf. Among these are a divine source and/or divine endorsement of the message plus divine empowerment of the messenger(s). Jesus, our model, limited himself to saying and doing what he heard the Father saying and saw the Father doing (John 8:26ff, 5:17). To maintain this standard, he received empowerment from the Holy Spirit (Luke 3:21-22) and continuously maintained an intimate relationship with the Father.

At the end of his career on earth, he promised his followers that they would do as he did (John 14:12) and commissioned them, saying "As the Father sent me, so I send you" (John 20:21). To communicate his messages, we are to imitate him.

2

What Does God Want Communicationally?

At the beginning God expressed himself. (John 1:1, Phillips)

All these things happened to them as examples for others. (1 Cor. 10:11a)

As the Father sent me, so I send you. (John 20:21)

Imitate me, then, just as I imitate Christ. (1 Cor. 11:1; see also 1 Cor. 4:16; Phil. 3:17)

God's Communicational Goals

"At the beginning God expressed himself" is the way J. B. Phillips translates John 1:1a. How did God do this before human beings were on the scene? We don't know for sure. But the Bible's picture of the creating God represents him as creating through speaking. He is shown as a communicator from the very beginning. "Let there be light" (Gen. 1:3b); he said, "Let there be a dome to divide the water" (v. 6b); "Let ... the land ... appear" (v. 9b); "Let the earth produce" (v. 11b), "Let lights appear in the sky" (v. 14b); and finally, "And now we will make human beings" (v. 26b).

But making human beings wasn't his final activity; it was just the beginning of the story of a communicating God. Did he speak to himself before he created human beings? We don't know. But he does seem to have certain goals to be achieved at the end of the bridge.

1. *God wants a relationship with the human beings he created.* Again, we don't know why. Why would he want to relate to the likes of us after all we've done to deserve his rejection? But the Scriptures picture God as having a compelling drive to relate to his creatures. This, apparently, constitutes his communicational agenda. Effective communicators need to have a clear agenda, a clear understanding of what they intend to get across.

The establishing and maintaining of a relationship with his creatures seem to be paramount among God's goals.

He didn't have to go after Adam. He could have let Adam just spin off into whatever. But one of the first scenes after the Creation is God coming across and calling to Adam, "Where are you, Adam?" Nor did he have to rescue Noah and his family. And even if he did, he might have done it a good bit less personally. Nor did he have to cross the bridge to communicate with Abraham, calling to him in Ur, "Get up, get out, start living your culture for me," calling him into a relationship.

Likewise God reached out to Isaac, to Jacob, to Moses, to Joshua, to Eli, to Samuel, to David, to Isaiah, to the disciples, to Paul, to Augustine, to Francis of Assisi, to Luther, to Calvin, to Wesley, to you, to me. Abraham got to be called "God's friend" (James 2:23b) and David "the kind of man [God] wants" (1 Sam. 13:14b). God's relationship with Job pleased God (Job 1:8ff.), and God interacted constantly with his creatures as worthy partners in relationship with him. He frequently commanded (Gen. 1:28b; 17:1b), he comforted (Ps. 23:4b; Isa. 49:13b; 52:9b), he implored when he could have turned his back (Hos. 14; Matt. 23:37), he even changed his mind when people responded to his warnings (Jer. 26:3; Jon. 3:10).

And in Jesus he modeled the closest kind of person-to-person relationship. Jesus crossed the bridge and stayed, even becoming touchable, hearable, observable, rejectable in horizontal relationships with his creatures. Incredible, but true. This leaves us asking, "What kind of God is he, anyway?"

2. *God reaches out to us to elicit a response to which the whole relationship is keyed.* People whose response is passive don't please him, nor do they relate to him very well. God wants us to relate to God and elicits our response to maintain or correct the relationship. With Adam the vehicle was a question. Did he not know where Adam was? Of course he did. He asked the question, not to obtain information, but to elicit Adam's response to their broken relationship. By asking, "Where are you?" God was really asking, "Adam, do you really know where you are and what it means to be behind that bush?"

God was and is looking for a response to spark a relationship with his creatures—an incredible thing! And God rewards such response richly, both in time (Heb. 11) and in eternity (John 10:28). It's to be a long-term relationship—long-term and deep, not like the casual relationships that we Americans so often pass off as friendships. He wants with us the loving, growing, expanding, trusting, close relationship that he had with Jesus, that Jesus then modeled with his disciples when he invested the short time of his ministry in twenty-four-hour-a-day interaction with the Twelve.

God expects our relationship with him to include a three-way commitment. The first element is our response to his commitment to us. As the Head of the church, Christ commits himself to us, his body (Eph. 5:24-25). We, in turn, are to respond by committing ourselves to him, our head. The second is that as members of a body, God desires that we commit ourselves to each other (1 Cor. 12:12ff.; Eph. 5:21). And last, God intends that we share his commitment with the world at large (John 20:21).

A major goal of God, then, is a relationship with us, his creatures. Response and commitment are basic to that relationship as are faith, love, trust, growth, and service. But how does God communicate his desire for such a relationship across the great gulf that lies between himself and his creatures? How can he assure that messages from an infinite, sinless communicator will be perceived accurately by finite, sinful receptors? His goal is a relationship, but a major obstacle is the communication gap between us and him. So he has a third goal.

3. *God wants to be understood.* Like all would-be communicators, he wants to be interpreted in such a way that his intent is understood correctly and responded to appropriately by his receptors. So he comes all the way across the bridge into our language, culture, and human form. He enters the world of time and space, of relativity, of sin. As I will attempt to prove below, God employs the principles and rules of his creation to put across his messages to his creatures.

Many seem to forget that God wants to communicate for the sake of being understood. They seem to assume that he simply wants to impress us, to be admired by us, to generate awe and respect in us. There is, unfortunately, much in the way the church and individual Christians present him that gives the impression that God desires a distant admiration from humans, an admiration based on his impressiveness, rather than desiring understanding based on relational interaction.

Is this not the impression made on those who experience antique church buildings, music, worship forms, language, and the like? There is a lot of Christian ritual that is very impressive, but what does it communicate? Does it communicate what God wants to communicate? Or does it communicate something else? There are many sermons that are homiletical masterpieces. But they often communicate more about the expertise of the preacher than about God. There is much church music that can lift at least certain people to the skies. It is very impressive, and the performers are to be greatly admired. But the message communicated by such impressive fare often seems to bear very little resemblance to that of the God who spoke to Adam in "the cool of the day" (Gen. 3:8b RSV) in ordinary human language and who came to Galilean peasants as a baby who grew up to be a carpenter and a teacher. *The message of the true God hardly ever comes in impressive vehicles* (1 Kings 19:11-12). The impressiveness is in the content of the message, not in the forms in which it is couched.

Yet Christian communicators often elicit a response like that of the young man who pointed to the preacher and said, "That man is saying all of the right things, but he isn't saying them *to* anybody." He is impressive but unrelated to his hearers. "He doesn't know where I am, and it would never occur to him to ask." He is distant and unconcerned, far out-of-date, and both unable and unwilling to bridge the gulf between us (Kraft 1979a:279).

But notice the message embodied in God's choice of language. The New Testament was not written in classical Greek but in what is called "Koine" Greek. And what is Koine Greek? Polished? Not at all. Impressive? No. Precise? Certainly not in a technical sense. Communicative? Yes, there's the word for it — a vehicle that allowed God's messages to flow through it to ordinary people at the human end of the communication bridge. Koine Greek was the language of the ordinary, unlettered citizen of the first-century Greco-Roman world. Now, what about a God who comes (we would say, "comes down") into that kind of language? Why is he doing it? He could have used classical Greek or, better yet, ancient Hebrew to impress people. But he didn't. He used the ordinary language of the ordinary people he wanted to reach — in order to be understood.

The principle here is that *language serves the communicational purpose best when it calls least attention to itself.* What happens when *you* (for example, a midwestern American) listen to somebody who has a thick central European accent or uses a lot of technical language? You find yourself distracted. Your focus is constantly drawn to the way the person says the words rather than to the content he or she is trying to convey. Very often that's tiring. You know you can understand most of what is being said if you want to, but you just get tired. Your mind gets tired and you tune out.

Next, reflect a bit on the topics God dealt with. He could have spoken impressively (as many preachers do) about any number of things that he alone was interested in. Think of the discourses he could have produced on, say, theology or the intricacies of the Creation or the specifics of his relationship with angels and demons. And he would have said "all the right things" but not said them *to* anyone (except perhaps a few theologians).

Instead, he deals with topics of pressing relevance to his hearers, topics that usually relate to needs that are both real to his interactants and perceived to be important by them. Whether it's a flood from which to escape (Gen. 6:13ff.), the desire for an heir (Gen. 18), seeking release from Egypt (Exod. 3ff.), Israel's desire for a king (1 Sam. 8), a man's blindness (Mark 10:46ff.), or the need to look after a destitute mother (John 19:26-27), God concerns himself with the concerns of his receptors.

God wants to be understood when he communicates his desire for a personal relationship with human beings. To accomplish this, he has developed and implemented a strategy, a strategy that we can learn from once we respond to it.

God's Strategy

Our subject is: What does God want communicationally? We've now identified at least certain of his goals, his agenda. These we seek to respond to by committing ourselves to God. Then, as those committed to him, *we need to go on to participation with God in implementing these goals.* This leads us to seek to discover and imitate God's communicational strategy. For if, as I contend, God has not only acted but has revealed the principles on the basis of which he has acted, we who seek to serve him faithfully can ill afford to ignore this part of his revelation.

In dealing with God's communicational strategy, I will be focusing on convergences between what God seems to have done (as presented throughout the Scriptures but supremely in Jesus) and the principles that communication specialists would recommend in similar situations. There are a great many such convergences. This fact, I believe, confirms both a great many of the insights of contemporary communication theory and the contention that God usually abides by the communicational rules he built into his creation. If this be true, we can and should imitate God's example.

What follows makes explicit some of these principles as demonstrated in God's activity (especially in Jesus) and sets the stage for their further elaboration in the chapters that follow.

1. First of all, we recognize the loving nature of God in his communicational activity. To love is to seek the best for the recipient at whatever expense to the source. *To love communicationally is to put oneself to whatever inconvenience necessary to assure that the receptors understand.* We call this "receptor-oriented communication." This is God's approach and should be ours.

There are several dimensions to loving, receptor-oriented communication that we see demonstrated in God's approach toward achieving his goals. Among these is the *respect* that God shows toward his receptors and toward the context in which he finds us. It is nothing short of amazing that the God of all the universe would choose our familiar turf, our way of life, our language, our total frame of reference rather than his own to be the context within which he interacts with us. In adopting this approach he shows *trust in his creatures* and makes himself dependent on and *vulnerable to us.*

The term *frame of reference* refers to the culture, language, life situation, social class, or similar all-embracing setting or context within which one operates (see chapter 10). Such a setting provides the perspectives in terms of which one interprets all of life. Receivers automatically interpret communication from the perspective of their own context. They are, however, able to adjust to people presenting messages within another frame of reference they have learned, much as they can grasp an accented version of their own mother tongue. Such adjusting is, however, a very demanding kind of activity, often causing the receptor to get tired and give up attempts at understanding.

Communication that results in the receptor interpreting accurately what the communicator intends ordinarily requires that both participants be a part of the same frame of reference. There are two immediately available possibilities. First, the communicators may designate their frame of reference as that within which the communication will take place. People and governments often use power to do this. In this case, the receptor is required to make all the adjustments by learning the communicator's frame of reference. Or, second, the communicator may designate the receptor's frame of reference as that within which the communication will take place. In this case, the communicator makes all the adjustments by learning and employing those symbols that are familiar to the receptor. The interpretation, then, that makes communication possible will take place according to the rules of the designated frame of reference.

As mentioned above, the person with the most power ordinarily designates the frame of reference to be used. God could, therefore, have designated his frame of reference as that within which his communication with human beings would take place. This would mean that he would designate his language and his culture (if he has one) as that to be used in his interaction with people. We would, then, have to learn that language and culture in order to understand God. We would be required to do the adjusting, becoming dependent and vulnerable, and the communication would take place on God's turf.

Instead of asserting his right to require us to operate within his context, though, he designated *our* frame of reference, *our* familiar turf, as that within which the communication would take place. He, therefore, has had to do all the adjusting, allowing us to be the ones on familiar ground. It is an indication of his love, acceptance, and respect for us and a mark of his receptor-orientation that he has chosen our frame of reference rather than demanding that we use his. In so doing he built a bridge all the way across from his frame of reference to ours.

The principle in focus here is illustrated throughout Scripture and made explicit in at least two places. In Philippians 2:6-7, Jesus is spoken of as one "who, being in very nature God, did not consider equality with God something to be grasped, but made himself nothing, taking the very nature of a servant, being made in human likeness" (NIV). The apostle Paul endorses the same principle in 1 Corinthians 9:19-22. He, like Jesus, became a part of the group he sought to win in order to be correctly understood by them. He became a Jew to the Jews, a Gentile to the Gentiles, weak to the weak, rich to the rich, "so that by all possible means I might save some" (NIV).

In adopting the receptor's frame of reference, God entrusts himself to us, becoming dependent on and vulnerable to us. It is *our* life he lives, *our* food he eats, *our* homes in which he sleeps, *our* difficulties that he shares, *our* emotions that he feels. He employs *our* language and culture to get his ideas across to us, agreeing to the meanings that we attach to those symbols.

So the first thing we learn concerning God's strategy is that *God is receptor-oriented, seeking to reach his receptors by entering their frame of reference* and by participating in their life, in order to be maximally intelligible to them. He thus employs the most basic principle of effective communication, receptor-orientation, a principle we must learn to imitate.

Unfortunately, a large number of Christian communicators seem to ignore this principle. Too often we who are church leaders demand that would-be receptors learn a new vocabulary in order to understand what we are saying. Thus the majority of adjustment is on their part. We assume that they should learn our language, our customs, come to appreciate our kind of music, come to our places of worship at our appointed times, adopt our life-styles, associate with our kind of people.

This, of course, was what the early Jewish Christians assumed concerning the Gentiles. It is the approach that has come to be known as the heresy of the Judaizers. It was natural for them, and seems natural for us, to assume that those customs in terms of which God has met us are to be normative for all whom God meets. The Jewish Christians required circumcision and conversion to Hebrew culture as a precondition to Christian faith. Frequently, we who have power in the church in our day also require our own equivalents of these customs as preconditions for conversion.

In the discussion recorded in Acts 15, we see that the early church took a position against requiring converts to convert to Hebrew culture in order to be Christians. Such cultural conversion was judged to be contrary to God's will in that day. It must be so judged in this day as well (see Kraft 1979a:339-44). Instead, we, with God, must regard any frame of reference as adequate both as a vehicle for communicating the gospel and as a vehicle for response to the gospel.

2. A second characteristic of God crucial to his communicational strategy is *his personalness.* He does not, as we often do, seek either to love or to communicate impersonally. Rather, God *identifies personally* with his receptors. As a person God *interacts* with and becomes vulnerable to his receptors. Finally, *God becomes the message.* When God sends, he sends persons. When he comes, he comes as a person. Incarnation—personal participation in the lives of his receptors—is his constant method. And as in all life-changing communication, the person (whether God himself in Christ or another person as God's representative) is the major component of the message conveyed.

It is *as a person* that God met Adam, Noah, Abraham, Isaac, Jacob, Joseph, Moses, Joshua, Samuel, David, Elijah, Isaiah, and all the rest. It is as a human being, *a person,* that he came in Jesus Christ (John 1:14). Incarnation, coming as a human being, is part and parcel of God's communicational strategy. It was neither to angels (Heb. 2:16) nor as an angel that he came but *as a person,* one who shared our flesh and blood, our weakness, one who could thus be understood within the limitations of human beings.

As a person, then, he is a God who interacts with other persons. He opens himself to two-way communication. He takes the questions of human beings seriously, giving himself not only to us but to our concerns. He is concerned as a loving person is concerned, not with abstract matters, but with the concrete realities of our daily lives. When he comes in Christ, he spends his time with people, not as God above them, but as a human being among them. He even accommodates to the definition of personhood held by the social group to which he came. Had he become a Pharisee, he never would have won the peasants. But he defined himself as a peasant, and though losing many of the Pharisees, he effectively reached the group to which he came.

It is because God's aim is relationship that the means of communication must be so personal. A nonrelational message, such as a news broadcast or a mathematics lesson, is quite appropriately presented in an impersonal way. Information designed simply to increase knowledge can effectively be lectured about. But communicators who seek to present a message recommending a relationship must model the relationship they recommend if their message is to be effective. *Thus, communicators of Christianity are a more essential part of the message they communicate than a communicator of nonrelational kinds of information* (see chapter 6).

Jesus said, "Come to me" (Matt. 11:28a). Paul said, "Imitate me" (1 Cor. 11:1; see also 4:16; Phil. 3:17). Such statements are not mere arrogance. They are, rather, clear recognitions of what it takes to communicate a relational message.

How different it often seems in contemporary church communication. So often the preacher as propagator of information has replaced the relational pastor. The lecture (we call it a sermon), an efficient means of presenting sizable amounts of information, has replaced the participation-centered worship that characterized the early Christian churches. How different might things be if we learned to imitate God's strategy?

3. The God who is receptor-oriented and personal takes pains to see that *his messages are presented with a high degree of impact.* To do this he (a) develops high credibility with his receptors, (b) demonstrates, not just speaks, his messages, (c) deals with specific people and issues, (d) leads his receptors to discovery, and (e) trusts those who respond to do the right thing with his messages.

Jesus chose to lay aside the respect he could have rightfully demanded as God to put himself in the position where the only respect he would have was that which he earned as a man. To be able to communicate effectively, one needs to establish one's credibility. Jesus established his credibility as a human being among human beings. This is one aspect of God's communicational activity that was hard to establish before God came as a man. We see Abraham and David and many other heroes of the faith relating to God as if he understands, as if he had established credibility with them. But the more popular impression of God may well have been the kind of attitude that many of us have toward rich people who speak as if they knew what poverty was.

When, for example, members of the Kennedy family speak of poverty, one may question what they know about a condition they have never experienced. Likewise, it is common to regard God as one who is beyond understanding what our life is like, beyond feeling what we feel, lacking the ability and even the right to speak knowledgeably into our situation.

But when Jesus came and experienced life as we experience it, even going beyond us in his suffering, he earned the right to speak into our frame of reference. He attained a position of credibility similar to that of the Kennedys when they speak of personal and family tragedy. Whereas we might question the Kennedys' credibility when the subject is poverty, no one can question their credibility when they speak about family tragedy. Nor can we any longer question God's credibility when he speaks into human situations. For he has been a human being. He has sat where we sit. He has wept in the same kind of circumstances that make us weep (Heb. 4:15). He has earned the right to our attention by participating with us rather than pontificating over us.

Assuming that a communicator is both a worthwhile person and has a worthy message to communicate, the major barrier to credibility is the human habit of *stereotyping*. For all we know wealthy persons may have a great deal of worthwhile insight into the poverty problem. But our stereotyped perception of such persons leads us to predict that their background renders their views suspect in this area. Likewise with God—unless God does something radically unexpected (from the perspective controlled by the stereotype) to demonstrate that the predicted situation is not correct, the stereotype will continue to be a powerful barrier.

"Gee, you don't act like a professor," a student once said to me. I had done something unpredictable in terms of that student's perception of professors. I had treated her as a human being (not as a stereotyped student) and was concerned with more of her life than she expected a professor to be. So she reacted with the above expression of the impact my concern had on her. In the process, she granted me a credibility not ordinarily granted to those who fit better into the stereotype.

In Philippians 2:8 we read that even after Jesus became a man, he further humbled himself. He could have become a stereotyped religious professional, one who, though he had the form of a human being, really acted more like God. He had a right to demand our respect, to be preserved from our human difficulties, to lecture at us rather than to discuss with us, to deal only with his preferred topics rather than to take our topics seriously, and to use the power of God for political or personal purposes rather than always to help people. But he broke out of the stereotype, acting in a way that was quite unpredictable to those who expected him to act in terms of the stereotype. He even preferred to be called Man—"Son of Man" equals human being (see LaSor 1961:42; Kraft 1979a:304). As a human being he became very credible, very believable, very worthy of our respect, admiration, and commitment.

It is unfortunate that many of us who claim to follow Jesus do not imitate him at this point. We like the titles *Reverend, Teacher, Doctor, Pastor, Parent,*

Christian too much, with the status and position that go along with them. Yet such positions and titles often isolate us communicationally from those to whom we are called to minister. How, then, should we relate to such stereotypes? Each title, each position, each honor we attain becomes for us a communicational barrier between us and those who have not attained such. Imitating God's approach to communication requires that we turn our backs on such in order to earn credibility with those to whom he has called us.

As a credible witness to the Father, then, Jesus chose to demonstrate rather than simply to talk about the subjects he treated. He said to Philip, "Whoever has seen me has seen the Father" (John 14:9). He himself was the demonstration of who the Father is, what he does, and how he does it. He knew what communication specialists tell us—*the best way to get something across is to demonstrate it.*

When agriculturalists go out to teach some new technique or to win farmers over to the use of some new variety of seed or livestock, they set up "demonstration farms" or plots. The people they seek to convince are often hardheaded and feel they have a lot to lose if they adopt something new and it fails. So winning them over is done through demonstration rather than through words alone. If the farmers can actually see that the new seed produces a greater yield or the new breed of cattle grows larger or produces more milk, they will adopt them.

To prove that God is love, Jesus demonstrated love. He showed that God is concerned for the downtrodden by demonstrating that concern. He showed forgiveness. He also showed how to use God's power in the cause of love. He also showed how to relate to Satan, the Pharisees, and other enemies. He demonstrated patience, perserverance, strength in temptation, meekness, holiness, how to pray, how to serve, and all the other characteristics we as Christians need to learn in order to live a godly life. *He also demonstrated how to communicate God's messages in life and word.*

In behaving credibly and demonstrating what he taught, Jesus was concerned for specific people, approaching them with messages relevant to their needs. He did not simply speak general messages to general audiences. It is God's way to be specific. Whether it is God's seeking after Adam, his call of Israel, the giving of the Ten Commandments, his calling of Samuel or Isaiah or the twelve disciples, or the specificity of Jesus' life in a Galilean village and his ministry in a small Mediterranean country, or Paul's addressing of his letters to specific congregations, it is characteristic of God to relate to specific people with specific messages.

The nature of the Bible also portrays this characteristic of God. The Bible is a collection of case histories, recording specific personal encounters within specific socio-cultural contexts. Were it merely a human product it might well have become a textbook-type presentation of general principles. As it is, though, the Bible provides a clear indication of God's commitment to specificity in communication.

God's specificity and relevance are regularly displayed in Jesus' inter-actions with people as recorded in the Gospels. It is typical of Jesus to start with a person's felt need, often as a launching pad from which he moves to dealing with a more important need. Note, for example, how specific he is to the paralytic (Matt. 9:2-8), to the Samaritan woman (John 4), to the disciples on the road to Emmaus (Luke 24:13-27), to blind Bartimaeus (Mark 10:46-52), to the rich young man (Mark 10:17-22). Interestingly enough he starts, not with Scripture (his concern), but with the needs of those with whom he interacts (their concerns). It is only with Satan and the Jewish leaders who quoted Scripture at him that Jesus starts with Scrip-ture. And even then he was simply starting where they started. I wonder what changes we would make in Christian witness and preaching if we imitated Jesus at this point?

This aspect of God's strategy raises a question for us: How specific are we in our communicational interactions? Our American educational pro-cedures tend to focus on the importance of developing and passing on broad generalizations. We seem to assume that if people learn generalizations, they will themselves be able to apply the principles in specific instances. I wonder, though, if this is not a misguided assumption. It seems that people understand better and learn more effectively if they are presented with specific applications of the principles from which they can derive their own generalizations.

Many contemporary communicators have, however, learned the lesson of specificity. They have learned that illustrations from real life, either their own or someone else's, put the point across more effectively than gener-alizations and nonspecific explanations of the points they seek to make. Jesus' examples were of this nature, even though many were merely true-to-life rather than the actual life experiences of real people. But he was careful to insure that his illustrations related to their life, their interests, their experience — not simply to his.

Yet it is a fact that God doesn't necessarily make things easy for his receptors to understand. He, rather, entices us, leading us to discovery rather than insulting our intelligence by predigesting his messages and lay-ing them out on a platter in a form that is fully obvious. He acts and speaks and then allows us to struggle with what these actions and words mean. When we have discovered the meaning, it is truly ours and has a greater impact than if he had done it all and made it easy for us.

God's method is to lead people, as Jesus led his disciples, to discover who he is (Mark 8:27-30) rather than to simply tell them who he is. God's method is to raise questions that have to be wrestled with rather than simply to provide answers that have little value because they come too easy. And he is apparently more concerned that we exercise our creative powers to arrive at meaningful answers than that we all come to the same answers. He seems to respect us and our ability as learners more than contemporary educational techniques would seem to when they encourage teachers to merely develop and pass on their conclusions rather than to help students struggle toward their own understandings.

We can illustrate this aspect of God's approach with numerous passages of Scripture. "Who shall I tell them you are?" asked Moses. "The one who is called I AM," replied God (Exod. 3:13-15). Was not this enigmatic reply inviting the Israelites to discovery? Nor does God provide Job with a pre-digested, "straight" answer concerning his suffering. And poor John the Baptist in prison is left to sift the evidence to discover whether or not he had given his life for the right cause (Matt. 11:2-6). Jesus spoke in stories and metaphors (parables) *not to obscure but to challenge,* not because he wanted to be difficult but because he respected his hearers and wanted them to learn deeply. Peter is left to discover the meaning of Jesus' words to him on the beach (John 21:15-19) and, later, the meaning of the vision on the housetop (Acts 10:9-17). And the church and individual Christians down through the years have had to discover (with the assistance of the Holy Spirit, John 16:13) the answers to countless problems. God doesn't pamper us.

Are we discovery-oriented in our communicational efforts? Or are we given to predigesting what we would teach and expecting everyone to adopt whatever party line we feel to be appropriate? Perhaps God's way is better than ours.

But God even goes further in his communicational strategy by trusting his receptors to do the right thing with his messages. As we will learn in the following chapters, the ultimate decision concerning what is communicated is up to the receptors. Receptors create what they think the communicator intended. God, of course, knows this. He also knows the receptors' limitations. Nevertheless, he trusts us enough that he depends on us not only to understand what he communicates but to take responsibility in his cause.

In his ministry, we see Jesus accepting and trusting his disciples even after James and John had asked for special privileges, Judas had left, Peter had denied him, and Thomas had doubted his resurrection. He still turned his whole ministry over to the eleven. His ministry was theirs as well as his. He called them friends, those who participate in the planning and organizing of the ministry, rather than slaves who simply take orders (John 15:15). He did not leave them without help, for he gave them the Holy Spirit, but he sent them forth to "do even greater things" than he had done (John 14:12b).

And it is through this acceptance and trust that perhaps the most impactful part of God's communication comes. I believe that, humanly speaking, a good bit of the transformation that we see in Peter's life was mediated through the trust that Jesus communicated to him on the beach (John 21). And Peter's is but one of a long series of transforming trust relationships between God and human beings. Note the trust that he placed in Noah, in Abraham, in David, in each of the prophets. He gave them all a task to do and trusted them to do it (with his help). And each one grew as he creatively responded by taking responsibility in a work that was both God's and his.

How trusting are we in our communicational activity? God, who has much more right than we, seems to resist the temptation to dominate his receptors. And while there are disappointments to be sure, this approach also produces giants of the faith.

Are we specific, life-related, and demonstration-oriented in the topics we deal with when we attempt to speak for God? Or are we general, historical, learned, even impersonal, showing off our abilities rather than using them to communicate God's messages in his way?

Our listeners have stereotyped expectations both of how we will relate to them and of how we will talk. Such stereotypes will be based on how others like us have performed. *We can either conform to the stereotype and function with little, if any, credibility or imitate Jesus in being receptor-oriented and personal in seeking to earn the kind of credibility and respect that the stereotype could never give.*

How Should We Then Communicate?

The Scriptures provide us with communicational models to imitate. We see there a God who refuses to stay on the other side of an enormous communication gap. He seeks a relationship with us that will elicit from us a commitment to himself and his cause. To bring this about he develops a strategy to assure that he will be understood on our side of the gap. In this strategy he is receptor-oriented, entering our frame of reference in a trusting, dependent, even vulnerable manner to show his love, acceptance, and respect toward us in a way that we cannot misunderstand. God is personal and identifies with us by incarnating himself, becoming himself the message he sends. Furthermore, God assures that his messages come with impact. He develops high credibility, demonstrates what he says, deals specifically with his receptors and the issues that concern them, leads his receptors to discovery, and trusts them to carry on the cause.

This is all exemplary for us. He has shown us how we should communicate. Let us seek, then, to communicate for God in his way.

3

Ten Myths Concerning Communication

The sermon was horrible! It was on the subject of preaching. The preacher contended that preaching is God's ordained means of getting his message out to humanity. Jesus came to preach the gospel, he asserted. Paul had abandoned all other ways of communication to give himself to the "foolishness of preaching" (1 Cor. 1:21). And down through the ages, God has seen fit to spread his kingdom throughout the world via preaching.

The speaker never saw fit to define what he meant by preaching. Nor did he seem particularly concerned to illustrate his points from the Scriptures, though he claimed to be preaching from them. It wasn't even clear to me why he was telling his audience so forcefully that preaching is the God-ordained method of communicating the gospel. Did he expect all of us to become preachers? Or was he afraid that if preaching were demeaned he would lose his job?

That experience caused me to reflect on what I now rate as the second-worst sermon I have ever heard. It was on the Word of God. It seems, if we can believe this other preacher, that there is some kind of magic in the Word. It has a life of its own. We simply speak it forth, and it miraculously draws people to God all by itself. We mustn't do anything to it, like try to communicate it or make it relevant. It already has everything in it that God wants there, and we only tamper when we try to do anything with or to it.

I wish this man was right. I wish that all we had to do was to open our mouths, quote Scripture, and watch people flock to Christ. But that is not what we see going on. Instead, we see sincere, dedicated, highly motivated, faithfully praying ministers of the gospel frequently bearing precious little fruit. Or sometimes they bear fruit, but have no idea how it happens. Meanwhile, not a few scoundrels are quite successful at winning people to very questionable causes.

Let's see if we can get a better perspective on these and certain other myths frequently believed by Christian communicators. In the remainder

24

of this book we will deal in greater detail with the communicational understandings that give the lie to these myths.

Myth 1: Hearing the gospel with one's ears is equivalent to "being reached" with the gospel.

Romans 10:14 speaks of hearing in relation to proclamation on the one hand and to belief on the other. But many Christians seem to have a far too simplistic view of what is involved in the hearing that leads to a faith response. They often seem to equate the hearing that denotes simply listening with the hearing that denotes understanding. Thus they often give mere presentations of unadapted information in church vocabulary to unbelievers with the belief that this will automatically, magically win them. Such techniques as "street-corner" preaching and superficial uses of mass media such as radio and literature (even among nonliterates) are among the preferred techniques of such people, for they work on the assumption that if we can simply get all the world's peoples within earshot of the gospel, the whole world will soon be evangelized.

Yet simple hearing with the ears and intelligent understanding (hearing at a much deeper level) are quite distinct kinds of activity. And unless the hearers are already quite positive toward the message, deep-level understanding requires persuasion, a kind of communication not easily accomplished via such superficial uses of media. Those not already convinced or at least open to messages presented in a hit-and-run fashion by strangers who show greater commitment to the information they have to share than to the people with whom they share it. For such people usually turn them off or tune them out.

Such facts speak to the *need for person-to-person, long-term communication of the gospel message* as the norm, with more limited and specialized use of other vehicles such as mass media. Public communication (e.g., lecturing, preaching) and mass media (e.g., radio, television, literature) are effective when the receptors feel a great need for the message that is presented. When there is no such felt need, research has shown that those who listen are almost exclusively those who are already positive toward the message (Engel 1979:22). *There is, therefore, no magic in the media, since understanding lies far deeper than exposure.* God's basic method is incarnation.

Myth 2: The words of the Bible are so powerful that all that people need to bring them to Christ is to be exposed to hearing or reading the Bible.

We cannot lightly ignore the concern expressed here. The Bible is inspired. It is the Word of God. And as such we want to be careful to treat it as the special revelation that it is. But we dare not allow our respect for the Bible to devolve into superstition and idolatry. The fact that it is inspired should not be interpreted to mean that it is magical or that we can use its words as formulas that convey spiritual power in and of themselves. This is the attitude of pagan superstition, not of Christian reverence. We must never forget that the words and concepts of the Bible are but channels through which the inspired messages of the Holy Spirit flow. Those channels are not to be worshiped or regarded as possessing magical power in and of themselves.

When I reflect on my own early Christian experience, I note this magical attitude in myself. There were occasions when I would reflect on unsuccessful attempts at witness and conclude that the reason for my lack of success was the fact that I had not quoted the Scriptures word perfectly, i.e., so that every word from the King James Version was in its proper place as it came out of my mouth. Usually my mistakes were trivial and in no way resulted in any significant change in the meaning of the verse. But somehow I had assimilated the attitude that since those words in and of themselves possessed the power to convert, my failure to quote them with total accuracy had somehow broken the spell and led to my lack of success.

Such an attitude may be extreme, but there are many Christians, both professional and lay, whose reverence for the exact words, often of a particular version of the Bible, is somewhat akin to what I have described. Typically, such people are somewhat suspicious or even skeptical of the need for explanation, interpretation, and communication of the Bible. They commit themselves to literal Bible translations on the assumption that a literal translation is more accurate because it is less interpretative. They often have a preference for exegetical preaching on the assumption that exegetical preaching is always more biblical than, say, topical preaching (in spite of the fact that Jesus was always topical). In witnessing, they endeavor to quote as much Scripture as possible, on the assumption that the more of God's Word they can use and the less of their own words, the more likely they are to get a positive response. They are often keen to get printed Bibles out to the ends of the earth even without personal witnesses to interpret them to the receptors, on the assumption that God's unaided Word is sufficient to win the multitudes to Christ.

Their motivations are entirely laudable. But though God sometimes works through his Word alone, his primary vehicle is still people who in word and deed interpret that Word. There is no magic in words themselves, even scriptural words. And quite often those words, concerning other people at other times, need to be handled by a Spirit-led communicator if they are to be understood properly by the receptors. It is, I believe, inappropriate for Christians to avoid their responsibility in the communication process on the assumption that God will do it through his Word alone.

Likewise with respect to translation, the translator who attempts to avoid interpreting only interprets badly. For a translator, like all other communicators, is responsible for building the communicational bridge all the way from the source to the receptor. And for this purpose translators must translate *into* the receptor's frame of reference every bit as much as they translate *from* the source text. See chapter 9 for more on translation as communication.

Many who believe this myth contend that the Bible is *automatically* relevant. They say we do not need to make it relevant. Though such a statement is accurate when referring to the Bible's potential, it ignores the crucial fact that *often something that is potentially relevant is perceived by the receptors as irrelevant* and is, therefore, misunderstood and frequently simply rejected. I take the position that, though the Bible is potentially relevant, God desires that his people give themselves to communicating in such a way that the Word is also *perceived as relevant at the receptors' end*.

Myth 3: Preaching is God's ordained means of communicating the gospel.

The word *preach* brings to mind one person (the preacher) monologuing while the listeners sit silently. Whatever the original intent of the New Testament words translated "preach" (see below), this image is the primary meaning for large numbers of people. Our custom of preaching is rooted in the church's adoption of the European university lecture (slightly adapted) as the central focus of its communicational activity, especially since the Reformation. Though monologue oratory was widely used and highly honored in Greek society and, therefore, used in church contexts since early times, it was apparently during the Reformation that Protestants replaced the mass with a monologue lecture (the sermon) as the central feature of the worship service.

The present place and nature of monologue homilies in Protestant worship are thus of relatively recent origin (Grieve 1962). But our standard English translations of the Scriptures, by using the words *preach, proclaim,* and their derivatives so frequently (some two hundred times), mislead us into thinking that this method has been chosen by God as virtually his only ordained method of communication. Are we not commanded to preach? Didn't John the Baptist, Jesus, and the disciples communicate mainly through preaching? The Scriptures do not show that they did. For their view of communication was much broader than the concept most English speakers attach to the word *preach*.

Something very misleading has happened that relates first to the way the early Christians used certain Greek words and then to a tradition that has developed among Bible translators and interpreters.

1. It became the custom of the early church to employ the Greek word *kerusso* and its derivatives as the preferred label for their attempts to communicate the gospel. This word, like many of the words the early church used, did not originally cover every kind of activity to which they applied it. *Kerusso* originally referred mainly to the announcing that heralds or town criers did as they moved from house to house and from town to town making the kinds of important announcements for which we today depend on radio and television (see Kittel 1967:683-718). The word was chosen by the early

Christians and used in an expanded way to refer to a much wider range of communicational activity. It included monologue lecturing but was also used to label interactions that were mainly dialogical, as long as the focus was on the communication of the gospel. It is an interesting confirmation of this fact that John, perhaps sensing the limitations of this word, consistently uses the word *witness (martureo)* in its place.

Since words derive their meanings from the things they are used to label, we should seek the biblical meaning of *kerusso* by studying the contexts in which it is used (see Barr 1961). When, therefore, we find Jesus, John the Baptist, Paul, and others presenting the gospel largely via dialogue, we should recognize that the term often used to label their activities has a broader meaning than that suggested by our word *preach*. Although the proclamation or announcement of something important is usually in focus when *kerusso* is used, the method (i.e., whether monologue or dialogue) is not in focus as with our word *preach*. Rather, the focus of *kerusso* is on the fact that the source is other than the speaker, as with a messenger.

2. The use of the terms *preach* and *proclaim* as virtually the only translations of *kerusso* and several other Greek terms suggests, then, the failure of translators and other biblical interpreters to find in English a term that adequately represents the range of meaning covered by the original terms. In present-day English, at least, such a term is readily at hand in the word *communicate*. I would, therefore, contend that in most of the places where it is clear that the broad presentation of the gospel is intended by such Greek terms as *kerusso*, it would be more accurate to translate it "communicate."

For example, Mark 16:15b should read, "Go throughout the whole world and *communicate* the gospel"; Mark 13:10, "The gospel must be *communicated* to all peoples"; Matthew 26:13b, "Wherever this gospel is *communicated* all over the world, what she has done will be told in memory of her"; Galatians 2:2b, "The gospel message that I *communicate* to the Gentiles"; Galatians 1:23b, " 'The man . . . is now *communicating* the faith that he once tried to destroy!' " Indeed, one can open a concordance to the words *preach* or *proclaim* and nearly always obtain a better rendering by replacing them with *communicate*.

Perhaps this is laboring the point. Perhaps. But when even learned people (such as those cited above) are misled and as a result mislead others into believing that God endorses the "foolishness" (1 Cor. 1:21b) of the monologue form of presenting the gospel, something is badly amiss. Paul is referring, of course, not to the foolishness of the cultural form translated *preaching*, but to the content of the message that many regarded as foolish (see the TEV and NIV translations of 1 Cor. 1:21b).

It is simply a damaging myth that supports our tradition of preaching. It is based on the one hand on the historical fallacy that this is the way the early church did it and on the other by inadequate translation that gives the impression that monologue preaching is God's intended way of getting his message out. There is no magic in this (or any other) method. Jesus himself much preferred personal, interactional communication that encourages immediate feedback and, if necessary, adjustment of the message to assure greater relevance.

Myth 4: The sermon is an effective vehicle for bringing about life change.

Many Christians, both pastors and the members of their congregations, feel that the purpose of the Sunday morning sermon is to bring about major changes in the hearers' lives. Pastors are trained to understand that they should put large amounts of time into producing good content that they can deliver during the Sunday morning sermon time. Their constant prayer is that through their efforts the lives of their parishioners will be significantly changed for the better. Parishioners, too, often come with the expectation that they will be exposed to new, potentially life-changing insight. Yet the expected very seldom materializes, for there are other factors at work.

In communication, as in all of life, events can be analyzed at two levels: the level of the ideal or intended function and the level of the actual function. Pastors and people often intend that lives be changed through sermons. But factors such as the setting in which the sermon is delivered and the limitations of the monologue method very often conspire to keep it from functioning as the participants intend. Instead, since the sermon is presented as a part of worship ritual, it tends to function in that context as but one (important) part of this "ritual of consolidation." The fact that monologue presentations are poorly suited to stimulate significant life change mitigates against the intended function turning out to be the real function. Instead, the very valuable function of consolidation and mutual sharing of the same experience by like-minded people becomes the major function of the sermon part of the worship service as well as all of its other parts.

I do not regard this as a bad thing. If, however, the expectations of those who participate in such activity are quite different from what actually goes on, there can be serious consequences. Take, for example, the pastor who is oriented primarily toward the preparation and delivery of fine sermons at the expense of seeking extensive and intensive personal relationships with his parishioners. He may, in keeping with the way he has been taught, expect that such an emphasis is the God-ordained way to lead (or drive) his hearers into Christian maturity and be disappointed when very little change occurs in them. Such disappointment leads many to question their calling. It is not, however, the calling that should be questioned but the adequacy of the vehicle employed to achieve the intended goal. As I seek to demonstrate in the following pages, monologue preaching, though useful for certain purposes, is too frail a vehicle to adequately carry life-changing messages.

What often happens with monologue preaching is that sermon-hearing becomes a spectator sport in which the actual functions served are quite different from those aimed at. Though the stated goals refer to persuasion and instruction, what often goes on is more similar to a musical or an athletic performance in which the preacher prepares and practices during the week to perform competitively on Sunday. The real function served, then, may become the winning of the favor of the congregation expressed via compliments on the sermons, continued attendance (rather than leaving for another church), and the attracting of additional attenders (usually those who have left other churches).

Such congregations are every bit as much spectators as those at musical or athletic performances. However, most of the spectators are "regulars," and this makes a difference. For they are regularly life-involved with each other and with the pastor in at least this one small portion of life. This enhances the feeling of solidarity with the pastor and other members of the congregation that they experience throughout the worship service. Others, however, may feel that they are merely spectators watching someone else's game (a feeling that, unfortunately, is often contributed to by other aspects of the worship service as well). For these, especially, personal contact outside the church context is crucial. Neither group, however, is much changed as a result of the sermons they hear.

The Sunday morning sermon functions as a reinforcement of things largely already agreed upon by the group. A wise pastor can use the sermon to remind, to strengthen, to challenge concerning commitments already entered into. Any hint of competition for an oratorical prize should be avoided in favor of more participatory verbal and nonverbal activities designed to cultivate interaction rather than simply observation. Such interaction reinforces commonality and group identity and thereby contributes to the growth of the congregation both corporately and individually. Pastor and people move and grow together, though usually very slowly.

Sermons should not leave people unfed or even unchallenged. But pastors who expect much radical change as a result of sermonizing alone are likely to be quite disappointed. *A psychologist or other agent of change (e.g., Jesus) would not attempt to change lives via lectures that stifle feedback and minimize the ability of the communicator to make specific responses and adjustments to the receptors. Neither should church leaders.* As in many other areas of life, our traditions can seriously hinder our effectiveness.

Sermons should function as important parts of the participation of pastor and people in their joint struggle toward Christian maturity, even as the rest of the worship service does. When, however, people are to be reprimanded or otherwise challenged to make radical changes in their behavior, communicational techniques other than the sermon need to be employed. Interpersonal and small group interactions are much more effective for this purpose. Indeed, it is in such interactions that people are often prepared to make dramatic responses at times when a sermon has been delivered (e.g., Sunday morning or in an evangelistic meeting). This misleads the uninformed to believe that it was the power of the sermon that elicited the response, when in fact it was something that happened in personal interaction previous to the sermon itself.

In what follows I will argue that Christians should use a multiplicity of forms of communication (as Jesus did), chosen according to their appropriateness in each given situation. A monologue approach is thoroughly appropriate if one wants to present a body of cognitive information in a fairly short period of time to a fairly large audience for the purpose of raising their awareness or increasing their knowledge in any given area. But a monologue approach is very poorly suited to either changing people's opinions or leading them to make significant changes in their lives. With this latter purpose in mind, Jesus employed what I'll call a "life involvement" (i.e., discipleship) methodology (see chapter 4 and Kraft 1979b).

Myth 5: There is one best way to communicate the gospel.

Many people believe that there is a single best way to communicate the gospel. Indeed, many may be reading this book with the aim of discovering what that best way is. As Americans, we seem particularly prone to fads in this regard. D. James Kennedy develops a plan that is successful in Ft. Lauderdale, Florida, and before long a large number of other pastors are trying to imitate it. Many groups seem to be successfully using radio. So other groups begin to imitate them by starting their own radio programs. Preachers with certain characteristics seem to draw large crowds, so others begin imitating their preaching style. Billy Graham develops a certain style of evangelism, and before long, it seems, every evangelist in the country has adopted the same style. But many discover that the communication style that they have imitated is not as successful for them in their situation as it was for the originator in the original situation.

The problem is, I believe, that people and situations are different enough that no single style is going to be appropriate for all people in all situations. Professional communicators should learn a multiplicity of styles and techniques that can be applied to the proper groups at the proper times in the proper places. Many communicators are like television repairpersons who are only able to use a single tool. Imagine a repairperson coming to your home, examining your set, and leaving because it requires the use of a wrench but they could only use a screwdriver. Many of us are like that in our approach to communication. We can only use a single method, no matter what the situation or who the audience.

Many Christian communicators are like the person of whom it was said, "Since his only tool is a hammer, he sees every problem as a nail." Many can preach effectively but are not very good in interpersonal relations. These may become preachers but fail at being pastors. Some can communicate fairly well as long as they control the topics of conversation. But they are lost if receptors begin to ask questions that relate to their own agenda but not to that of the communicator. Such people are forced to take a catechetical approach to Christian witness. That is, since they are only able to answer certain questions, they must first teach the receptor to ask those questions they can answer. They are like sales clerks who have memorized their sales pitch but if interrupted must go back to the beginning and start over again.

Those who communicate God's messages should, however, be like repairpersons who both have and know how to use a toolbox full of tools. They should be able to study any situation and use the appropriate tool or technique. If, then, they find themselves in situations that demand approaches different from whatever they did last time, they will be able to adapt.

Jesus models this kind of approach to communication very well. If we go from chapter to chapter of the Gospel of John, we find him always starting with a subject and a technique that are appropriate to his receptors. His constant principle seems to be to adapt to the requirements of the situation and to the felt needs of his hearers. He is not tied to a single method or to certain specified places and times. Adaptability is the name of the game.

Myth 6: The key to effective communication is the precise formulation of the message.

Many would-be communicators pay primary attention to the technical preciseness, accuracy, and truthfulness of the words and phrases they use to construct their messages. Yet the choice to use precise, technical language, especially with popular audiences, usually increases rather than decreases the possibility of misinterpretation. The drive toward preciseness does not take account of the fact that much of what goes into effective communication is outside the control of the communicator.

It is the receptor who has the final say concerning what is communicated. And the key is the impact the message makes on that person, regardless of the technical accuracy of the presentation. This fact explains why many very well constructed messages result in a great deal of misunderstanding. Yet many would-be communicators seem far too little concerned with person factors, those things that affect how the receptor will interpret the message.

Precise language is the language of a particular in-group such as theologians or other academics. And those not in that group are likely to misunderstand or misinterpret when such language is used. Such is the typical response of non-seminary-trained hearers to the sermons of countless pastors who have not yet learned to exchange their seminary language for that of the people they seek to minister to. The Bible, however, shows that God employs down-to-earth language. There is very little technical language used in the original Hebrew and Greek.

The biblical texts have suffered greatly at the hands of scholarly translators who, probably because they are unaware of this principle, have tended to represent nontechnical biblical words in technical English. Words like *conversion, redemption, sin, repentance,* and even *church* have become technical words in English, though the scriptural words they translate are not technical. It is to correct this error that the communicationally aware translators of the Good News Bible, Phillips' New Testament, and the Living Bible have gone against church tradition and sought to render the nontechnical language of the biblical manuscripts with equivalently nontechnical English.

God's way is to use ordinary, highly communicative language to convey spiritual truth. This fact is a part of the nature of the Scriptures. The word commonly translated *convert,* for example, is the ordinary Greek word for *turn.* Likewise, the word translated *repent* is the ordinary Greek word referring to changing one's mind or attitude. Such ordinary words used with proper elaboration and illustration have a far better chance of being interpreted correctly by nonspecialist audiences than do technical words. With this in mind, then, the effective communicator strives to couch the message in the vocabulary that is likely to be most accurately interpreted by the hearers.

Truly effective communicators are more concerned with "preciseness" in the way people respond to their messages than with the preciseness of their vocabulary. They, therefore, prepare carefully but with a very different emphasis than those who aim at technical preciseness. *They concern themselves with person factors more than with the impersonal, structural, and linguistic factors in message construction.* They are constantly conscious of and oriented toward the impression their messages make on their receptors.

Myth 7: Words contain their meanings.

Often underlying the kind of attitude we discussed under Myth 6 is the assumption that it is a part of the nature of words to *contain* their meaning. Words are regarded as more or less like the boxcars on a freight train. They have goods inside them and can be connected at both ends to other words that likewise carry specific meanings. Thus a sentence gets built up like a freight train by connecting cars together. And meanings are deciphered by examining the contents of the words that are strung together.

The problem with this approach to understanding language is that *a given word may have different meanings to different groups of people.* And these meanings depend on how the members of the group agree with each other concerning the proper use of the words. Some years ago, for example, an agreement developed among American youth that the word *cool* should be used when a person wants to show a positive attitude toward someone or something. Americans of older generations had no such agreement. Their agreement was to use other words (even, sometimes, *hot*) in such contexts. In listening to young people who used the word *cool,* older people had to learn to translate by equating it with their preferred word in such contexts—if they hoped to understand what the youth were saying, that is.

Another example would be the differences in meaning attached to so-called *four-letter words*. In certain groups, the use of such words is interpreted as normal and natural. In other groups such words are regularly used, but only when people want to say something in as forceful a way as possible. In still other groups (including evangelical Christian groups) the meaning conveyed by the use of any of those words at any time would be extreme vulgarity and total inappropriateness, no matter how agitated the user might be. Linguistically, there is no difference between these words and the other words of our language. But at the person level—that is, socially—there are important differences of meaning for nearly all groups. This would not be true if words carried their meanings like boxcars.

Such illustrations, and there are many others, point to the fact that *meanings are attached to words (and other symbols used in communication) by people rather than being inherent in the words themselves.* Meanings, therefore, remain the same when people continue to use words in the same way. Meanings are changed, then, when people decide to use words in different ways. *Word meanings are a matter of social agreement, not of anything inherent in the words themselves.*

This fact becomes clear when one studies the etymology and subsequent history of any given word. The fact that meanings do not fluctuate wildly points to the power of such social agreements. Indeed, within a given community, the range of variation covered by a given word can often be delineated quite precisely because of the power of these agreements supported by strong cultural conditioning. It is, therefore, social agreements that maintain the constancy of word meanings just as it is social agreement that brings about change in word meanings.

This insight adds to our understanding of some of the problems related to preciseness of vocabulary dealt with above. *For a word's preciseness is directly related to the tightness of control over the agreement concerning its meaning held by the community that uses it.* Smaller communities, such as those sharing a narrow technical specialty, are able to keep tight control over the vocabulary they use in their area of specialization.

Terms that are used more widely, particularly if used by a variety of different groups, tend to be less precise. This is why *the preciseness of a word is usually proportional to how widely it is used.* Thus, while preachers may find it quite appropriate to use a technical theological vocabulary within a community of theologians, it is inadvisable for them to do so outside that community. Those who have studied in theological institutions where it is quite appropriate to use such vocabulary must learn to communicate cross-culturally when they leave that community if they are to be understood.

For words are like darts or arrows that prick people in order to stimulate a response by assigning the socially approved meanings rather than like boxes that contain their meanings. The meanings assigned by the hearers are, then, those of the community of the receptor rather than those of the communicator's community, if communicator and receptor belong to different groups. See chapter 7 for more on this subject.

Myth 8: *What people really need is more information.*

We often assume that what others really need in order to become Christians is more information. If they only knew what we know about God and Christ, we say, they would certainly become Christians. So our job is to get them more facts.

The problem with this myth is that there are plenty of people who have enough information to become Christians who still refuse. Even Satan and demons have enough information to repent and turn back to God, but they refuse (James 2:19). Certainly their basic problem is not a lack of knowledge and information. Nor is such a lack the major reason why people reject the gospel.

Some, indeed, fall into the category of persons blinded by Satan (2 Cor. 4:4). We are told that one of Satan's activities is to keep people from understanding the truths of God. This activity of Satan is especially obvious in situations where there is a good deal of demonic activity. In such cases, the first step is authoritative prayer, followed by providing appropriate amounts of information and/or stimulus. That information alone saves no one. Furthermore, large numbers of people who have enough information do not believe. Their problem is more likely to be *either a matter of stimulus or a matter of will.* Many reject because they will to reject. Their self-will and refusal to respond to God motivate them against acceptance.

But many do not accept the gospel simply because they experience no adequate stimulus to motivate them to consider leaving their present allegiance for a commitment to Christ. Perhaps they have never experienced a relationship with those for whom the gospel made an attractive difference in their lives. But they know enough facts so that if they wanted to they could turn their face toward God in faith and be saved. For such people, and there are many of them in all parts of the world, *it is motivation that is the crucial problem, not lack of knowledge.*

One twist of this particular myth is the belief that only those who know and accept certain doctrinal facts can be saved. This position advocates a kind of *salvation by knowledge.* Many would require a fairly long list of essential doctrines to be believed in order for a person to be saved. Others would require a shorter list but, I believe, still put such knowledge in too high a position. Actually, I think the Scriptures indicate that saving faith requires very little knowledge, at least at the beginning.

Perhaps all that is necessary is indicated in Hebrews 11:6b: "Whoever comes to God must have faith that God exists and rewards those who seek him." The thief on the cross (Luke 23:39-43) is perhaps the clearest example of one who had precious little knowledge but who was soon to join

Jesus with God because he demonstrated the proper faith-response to what he did know.

My point is that as Christian witnesses our real job is not to convey large amounts of information, though frequently the proper type and amount of information at the right time can provide the stimulus required to bring about the decision advocated. Rather, we are to stimulate people to respond to the God they probably already have enough information about.

Myth 9: The Holy Spirit will make up for all mistakes if we are sincere, spiritual, and prayerful enough.

I sincerely wish this were so. But our experience is that we frequently find very spiritual people making incredible blunders and turning people away from the gospel, while many who are apparently misleading people are attracting large followings. Perhaps many believe this myth because they fail to distinguish between what God *can* do and what he *chooses* to do. God is omnipotent. This means he can do anything he wants to do. But throughout the Scriptures we see him deliberately restraining himself from using his power at many points when it might have been a better idea (from our point of view) for him to step in.

Why, for example, did he not simply step in and clear out the land of Palestine for his people? The Israelites experienced untold agony, temptation, and failure as a result of the fact that non-Israelites remained in the land. Why does God allow Satan and evil? Why does he allow suffering? Why, when he had the power to keep Jesus from being killed, did he not use that power? We don't know the answers to these questions, but we refuse to believe that God is limited by factors external to himself. It must be that for reasons that we cannot now understand God limits himself, deliberately choosing not to step in and exercise his power.

A myth like this one, however, assumes that God will step into communicational situations in which we are involved if we are only spiritual enough. And if he does not step in, we conclude that the problem is our lack of spirituality. I contend that this is not necessarily the reason.

I have tried to point out in the previous chapter how even God seems to abide by the rules for effective communication that he built into the Creation. I believe he expects us to abide by them also. Though he may on occasion step in and direct situations in such a way that they are not as bad as they could have been. And probably he often does this without our even knowing it. I don't believe this is his normal practice or one we can count on. I think he normally expects us to learn the proper techniques and to employ them in partnership with him so that when we do our job better, he is able to do his better.

Myth 10: As Christians we should severely restrict our contacts with "evil" people and refrain from going to "evil" places lest we "lose our testimony" and ruin our witness.

How carefully many churches teach their members to keep away from certain people and places lest their witness be harmed. There is, of course, a certain amount of truth in such warnings, particularly for immature Christians. But the basis for such warnings is *fear that our Christian commitment is so weak that we will be influenced by those around us to compromise our witness.* To maintain our "purity," therefore, we must associate primarily with those of "like mind" lest we be contaminated.

But such a practice imitates the Pharisees, not our Lord. For it was the Pharisees who were scrupulously careful not to go to certain places and not to associate with certain people. But Jesus said, "People who are well do not need a doctor, but only those who are sick" (Matt. 9:11-13). To be sure, Jesus was criticized for associating with the wrong kind of people. But can we seriously recommend the example of the Pharisees in preference to his own example?

I remember how shocked many of us were to hear a committed Christian lady make this same point by testifying that she no longer has time to go to Wednesday evening prayer meetings. For Wednesday evening is the time when her local Parent-Teacher Association meets. She went on to point out that she had nothing against the Wednesday prayer meeting. Indeed, she greatly enjoyed the fellowship and spiritual enrichment of those meetings. But they kept her from cultivating friendships with non-Christians. And she felt that God wanted her to be a witness rather than simply a person who soaks up spiritual nourishment.

Receptor-oriented communication of the gospel is a risky business, however, for it requires that we go where the receptors are and identify with them (though not participate in their sin) in order to reach them. We are to imitate Jesus in this regard, not the Pharisees. We are, like Paul, to become Jews to Jews, Gentiles to Gentiles, rich to rich, poor to poor, that we "may save some of them by whatever means are possible" (1 Cor. 9:20-22). And if our supposedly strong brethren criticize us for imitating Jesus by identifying with the weak and the lost, that is a spiritual problem that they will have to deal with.

Here at the beginning of our examination of communicating Christianity I have raised a number of what I believe to be myths widely held within the Christian community. My reason for doing so is to stimulate within us a spirit of introspection that asks: Do any of these fallacies characterize my ministry? If so, how do I overcome them?

Read on.

4

Person and Message

Three Communicational Situations

Situation 1: A church service. The pastor is in the pulpit to deliver his weekly sermon. He is dressed formally and stands sedately behind the pulpit on a platform at a distance from and elevated above the people he addresses. The members of the congregation are dressed formally and sit quietly and politely in rows facing him. They listen attentively and silently until he finishes.

The pastor's method is monologic — he does all of the talking. The setting is formal. The building is designated for the purpose. The time is also appointed. The pastor is paid to do what he does. Little, if anything, unexpected is done or said.

What is happening communicationally? Are the listeners really as passive as they seem? What will they take home with them from that experience? Will any of their lives be better or different because they have attended this church service?

Situation 2: After the service. Once the meeting is over, the pastor moves out of the sanctuary, and a dramatic transformation takes place. People get up from their seats and begin to move about. Whereas only moments before they sat silently, all eyes front, only the pastor talking; now people stand, move, talk to each other, shake hands, and even embrace as they move out of the sanctuary.

Many different conversations go on simultaneously. Some interactions are fairly formal, some less formal but still serious, some quite relaxed. There seems to be no rule that any person or group has to remain silent. There is obvious give-and-take dialogue in each grouping. The verbal interactions are most obvious, but much nonverbal communication is also noticeable.

Some people flit from one group to another, friendly but not much involved with any single group. Others fix their gaze intently on each other, communicating great interest in and enthusiasm for what the other is saying. Some seem to be avoiding each other's glances. A few seem to have been captured by someone from whom they would like to escape.

The pastor at the door has also changed his style. Now when he asks a question he expects an answer. He stands close to the people he is talking to. He listens as well as speaks. And the topics are quite different from those he addressed in his sermon. This is an informal communicational situation, and the rules for acceptable behavior are significantly different from those for the more formal preaching situation. The postures differ. The topics differ. The opportunities for receiving, correctly interpreting, and properly adjusting to feedback are much greater.

What is happening communicationally in this situation? It is obviously different from the one in the sanctuary. Does this mean that one situation is better than the other? If so, in what ways and for what purposes?

Situation 3: At home. Soon most of these people sit with their families at their Sunday meal. They have driven home from church, changed into informal clothing, a meal has been prepared, they have been called to the table, a prayer has been said, and now they sit eating and chatting. There is more silence here than in either of the previous situations. Many of the messages are transmitted by looks, gestures, and short verbal exchanges, though some of the verbalizations between parents and children are (like the pastor's sermon) intended to be persuasive.

Here there is close *life involvement,* the fine tuning that comes from knowing each other's habits and responding instinctively to them. There is some formality here—the blessing, the "Good meal, Mom," obedience to the rules for sitting and eating. There is even overt instruction for those in the family who have not yet developed the proper habits—"Wash your hands before coming to the table, Johnny" or "Use your fork, not your spoon, to eat your beans." And there are discussions of various topics, sometimes including the pastor's sermon. There is more variety here, less formality, less overt information passed between the participants except when instruction is given or reports made.

What are the communicational dynamics of this situation? It obviously differs from the other two situations at many points. Yet the same people are able to move from one situation to the other within a short period of time and to function well within each.

I will attempt in this chapter and the next to provide the kind of insight that will enable us to see beneath the surface of such communicational situations as these. Each is a valid kind of situation for certain purposes. Each, however, is poorly adapted to serve other goals. It is important that Christian communicators learn to use the techniques appropriate to each situation in such a way as to maximize their value as tools of communication.

A glance at situations such as these from a communicational perspective raises the question, What is actually getting across to the receivers? In each case the participants were overtly Christian. In each case messages were sent and received. Yet the structuring of the situations differed as did the intent of the participants, the amount and type of verbalization, and many other factors. How did such factors affect the messages sent?

In what follows I will contend that there are indeed differences in what comes across in different situations, even if the message is intended to be the same. I contend, furthermore, that the distinctions of the Christian message demand that we gravitate toward greater use of certain means and methods of communication and away from a reliance on others so that we do not risk serious distortion of the message itself.

Communicational Implications of the Nature of the Christian Message

It is extremely significant from a communicational standpoint that the message we are called to communicate is far more than a verbal message. As I pointed out in chapter 2, God's communication is personal rather than simply informational. He is thoroughly involved in his messages. For in a way that boggles our minds, *the God who brings the messages is the major component of the message he brings.* God brings us the message of love by personalizing that love. He brings us the message of truth by becoming truth (John 14:6). He demonstrates his relationship and commitment to human beings by becoming a human being, eternally committing himself to us by uniting with us.

Furthermore, *his goal is a personal relationship with his respondents.* It is relationship with him, not merely knowledge of him, that he seeks to stimulate. We interpret his communications properly when we understand and respond to his acceptance of and commitment to us. And the appropriate response is a living, growing, person-to-person relationship with him that is advocated as both the beginning and the goal of the response.

Christian life is a personal response to the God who is the message, not simply to the words that proceed from him. And that response, like life itself, begins experientially small. But from there it grows, it expands, it enlarges. Or we may liken it to love, again tiny at the beginning but always growing as long as it is cultivated. We who have gone along the road of love quite some distance may be tempted to look back at the beginning and to question whether that little thing we started with should in fact be called love.

Yet relationships and personhood are like this. They start qualitatively very important, participating in the same quality at the beginning as at the end. A small child and a grown adult both possess the quality called life. Young couples and older couples all experience the quality called love. The crucial differences lie between those who are alive and those who are dead, between those who experience love and those who have never experienced love.

God himself is the message, and we respond to a person. It is in relation to the person of God, not to some words about him, that we "live and move and have our being" (Acts 17:28). As with human communication at a much lower level, the most crucial dimensions are the results of life rubbing against life to produce and maintain life. *The ultimate Christian message is a person. And anything that reduces that message to mere verbalization is unworthy of the message.*

The analogy most commonly used by Jesus to depict his relationship with God is that of Son and Father. This is an analogy that depicts a person (the Father) in life involvement passing himself on to another person (the Son). Is it not significant that he did not call himself Preacher (as did the author of Ecclesiastes) or Teacher or Rabbi or even Prophet? Is it not significant that *the supreme typification of Jesus' ministry is, not that "he spoke to us," but that he "lived among us"* (John 1:14b)? Actually, most of what he said was not all that new. What he lived, however, has turned many worlds upside down (or right side up).

The basic implication of the nature of the Christian message is, then, that *the Christian message is a life message, not simply a word message.* I believe this fact has high significance for us who seek to transmit God's message to others. For *if the message is life, only life is an adequate vehicle for its transmission.* If the message is merely words conveying information, then words are adequate vehicles. It is worth asking, What happens to a life message if it is reduced to mere words conveying mere information? Is not the message itself changed?

If the message is pervasively personal, transmitted by persons from the person of God to other persons, the crucial characteristics of the response, as well as of the source and the channels, will be personal. And this is, in fact, what we see in Scripture. Among these personal characteristics demonstrated in Scripture are the following.

As noted above, *the primary aims of Christian communication relate to behavior, not simply to knowledge.* Whether we look at Adam in the Garden, the way Noah saved his family, the example of Joshua (Josh. 24:15), the way David got to be called the kind of man God wants (1 Sam. 13:14b), the example of the disciples, the injunctions of Paul, or any of the counterexamples (such as those of King Saul or of the Pharisees), it is clear that Christian messages concern behavior based on a faith relationship with God rather than on any amount of knowledge that may have been attained (see especially Rom. 1-2; Heb. 11).

When, therefore, the vehicles we use and the contexts in which we use them hijack this message, causing us to interpret the "faith which once and for all God has given to his people" (Jude 3) as a body of information rather than a type of behavior, we have exchanged the birthright of the gospel for a mess of pottage.

For the message concerns personal behavior, and it behooves us to employ those vehicles and contexts that most adequately convey it as personal and life-transforming. Since messages are not totally separable from the vehicles used to convey them, we must give solid attention to the vehicles we use. If we are to be accurately understood by our respondents, we who attempt to communicate Christian messages must make use of those vehicles and contexts that most appropriately convey them accurately and turn away from those vehicles and contexts that add to, subtract from, or otherwise distort the messages.

A further characteristic of this personal message is that *it is designed to dynamically move people in a certain direction rather than advocating that they simply attain a static position* (see Hiebert 1978; Kraft 1979a:240-45). That is, the direction in which receptors are moving seems scripturally to be more important than any position they might have attained.

The thief on the cross, for example, was saved because he was moving in the right direction (i.e., toward Christ) rather than because he had attained a righteous position. The Pharisees, on the other hand, were condemned in spite of the fact that they had attained a "righteous" position. For in their hearts they were headed away from God and Christ. Their behavior, as opposed to their knowledge, betrayed a commitment that was diametrically opposed to the saving faith-commitment that moves one motivationally and behaviorally in the direction of Godlikeness. *Our message recommends and our commitment requires growth.*

In this respect, we recommend what we are ourselves becoming by rubbing our life against the lives of others. The initiation and continuance of the life in Christ is faith-energized behavior that we practice, model, and recommend. A mere word message ordinarily has little ability to move people behaviorally unless they are desperate.

Another characteristic of the message implied by what I have been saying is the fact that *the cognitive content of the message is small in comparison to the behavioral outworking of it.* I believe the basic message of the Bible is encompassed in the statement attributed to Samuel Shoemaker, that we are to *give as much of ourselves as we can to as much of God as we can understand.* This message is illustrated over and over again, in context after context, in personal experience after personal experience throughout the Bible. Whatever knowledge people have, then, functions appropriately as a means to that end, never as an end in itself.

The focus is on faithfulness to God, not simply on cognitive belief concerning him. Faithfulness (rather than faith or belief) is the Hebrew and Aramaic concept behind the word often translated "faith." Throughout Hebrews 11, for example, it is the faith that automatically obeys that is in focus, not an intellectualized faith. We would be helped considerably if our translations indicated this. It was by his faithfulness that Abel offered a more acceptable sacrifice than Cain (v. 4), by his faithfulness that Noah constructed an ark (v. 7), by his faithfulness that Abraham obeyed (v. 8). And without faithfulness it is impossible to please God (v. 6). The personal call to personal commitment and faithfulness is the message we are called to communicate.

The personal message that it is God himself interacting with and through persons to bring about personal faith-response to and growth in relationship with him, then, gives rise to person-oriented characteristics. Such a fact must be constantly in focus as we attempt to faithfully communicate God, lest we be enticed into applying impersonal means to communicate a personal message.

As with God, *the person who communicates the Christian message is not only the vehicle of the message but the major component of the message as well.* We are thoroughly involved in what we seek to communicate. Our credibility, trustworthiness, and other personal characteristics in relation to our receptors are crucial to the messages we send. This fact puts identification at the heart of the Christian message as well as at the heart of the Christian method. Identification happens when the communicator identifies with the receiver within the latter's frame of reference for the purpose of effective communication. Jesus, practicing the most demanding form of identification — incarnation — became both a member of the group he sought to teach and the primary message of God to that group. So should his followers.

So Christian communicators are like Jesus, communicating both the message and themselves. As Christian communicators we are squarely in focus. We are on the line at every moment. And with life messages (as opposed to word messages), *it is impossible to effectively communicate to others something that we are not ourselves.* Yet we point them to ourselves as people on the way, rather than as people who have arrived. And that "on the wayness" is toward greater approximation to Christlikeness. Thus, though we do point people to ourselves, we also point them beyond ourselves. But the message is still life to life concerning life.

If this perspective is accepted, we come to see the pervasive informationalizing and intellectualizing of Christianity as nothing short of heresy. From where I sit, it looks as though the Bible makes most of the information that fills so much of Christian communications radically subservient to the need to stimulate people to more acceptable Christian behavior. And that kind of stimulus comes best through personal interaction, usually accompanied by word messages.

The personalness of the communicator must, however, be visible to the receivers if it is to be of any value. And this requires interpersonal contact outside of formal, talk-oriented situations. God's messages require *pastors,* those who interact as persons with their flock. God's cause has been badly hurt by a multiplicity of mere preachers, those who may perform that function quite well but may seldom really give themselves to (much less *for*) their flock.

"At the beginning God expressed himself. That personal expression, that word, was with God and was God . . ." (John 1:1, Phillips). God came in a person, not merely in one or more verbal or written utterances. Jesus was and is a pastor, a shepherd, who gave himself first to and then for his flock. And it is persons who gave themselves to their receivers that Paul pointed to as the ultimate letters that he and God had written (2 Cor. 3:2-3). With messages, then, as with the vehicles that convey those messages, we point to the crucial importance of persons in communicating Christianity.

Person, Goal, Motivation, and Means

An extremely important influence on any communicational interaction is exerted by the motivation and goal(s), whether conscious or unconscious, of the persons involved in it. When the person is seen as the major component of the Christian message, it becomes clear that motivation and goal are not intended to be hidden in Christian communication. There are certain goals and motivations forbidden to us if we are to properly represent the One who called himself "the truth" (John 14:6).

We are not, for example, to use methods of communication that do not "fit" our messages. As we will learn later, *the means of communication are interpreted as part of the message.* If, therefore, those means are perceived to mean something other than what is intended, our message will be damaged. Our receptors are likely to judge our motives and goals at least as much on the basis of their interpretation of our means as by what they think we say. If, then, receptors "read" our approaches to communicating with them as impersonal, uncaring, distant, condemning, or the like, they will probably assume that we intended to communicate those things.

I believe God wants us to be straightforward and transparent in our goals and motivations. If so, we need to consider goals and motivations in relation to both what and how we communicate.

Our motivations and goals may be conscious or unconscious. They are usually multiple. We need, then, first to work at becoming conscious of those beneath the surface and then to square them with the overall message we seek to communicate. This must be done in such a way that the total message will be perceived accurately by the receptors.

It is quite common for a message consciously intended by a communicator for one purpose to be perceived (often rightly) by receptors as really designed to serve another. Many an exhortation delivered in a fiery way, for example, has been rightly interpreted by the receptors as relating more to the speaker's problems than to theirs. Often, what is actually a speaker's anger over something in their own life gets directed toward others. Thus the gentleness of Jesus is often sacrificed on the altar of the unconscious motivation of the speaker.

Unconscious motivations can disrupt the intended message in any number of other ways as well. Such things as shyness, the need to be in control, impersonalness, or other defense mechanisms may mask fear of being discovered. These behaviors, stemming from unconscious motivations, of course, interfere greatly in the communication of Christian person messages.

Often we seek communicational interaction merely for the sake of the interaction itself. We are interactional beings and validly seek others out for this purpose. But many get in the habit of "talking just to hear themselves talk" and thus (often quite unconsciously) use people in communicational situations simply to serve their own ends.

Among other motivations we may include: to give or gain information; to get people excited; to persuade our hearers; to entertain; to play; to negotiate; or to compete. Indeed, probably any motivation for relating to people can become a goal of communication. Not that any of these are problematic in and of themselves. But intending one thing consciously and another unconsciously, or intending one thing and being perceived as intending another, can seriously mislead both others and ourselves.

For example, I know at least one person who never seems to contact his "friends" unless he wants to get them to do something for him. I don't know whether or not he is aware that this is his pattern. It happens often enough, however, that we suspect that his main motivation when he thinks of his "friends" is to use them for some purpose or other. This suspicion destroys for us any attempt on his part to communicate sincere interest in us.

I'm afraid I came across in a similar way to some of my Nigerian friends. Their requirements for friendship are much greater than ours in terms of the amount of time friends are expected to spend together. In discussion of our relationship one day, one of them said something like, "You whites are not friendly. You never spend any time with us." In response, I pointed out that I had spent several hours with them in the past few days—an amount of time I felt was adequate to indicate that I, at least, would qualify as a good friend. His response was, however, to the effect that such a small amount of time proved *his* point, not mine.

Messages and means intended to serve one purpose frequently get hijacked so that they actually serve another. One common occurrence is for a sermon, lecture, musical presentation, drama, or the like, supposedly intended to convey a message, to devolve into what is merely a performance.

By *performance* I mean the kind of presentation that consciously or unconsciously is aimed primarily at exhibiting the performer's abilities at the expense of whatever other messages might have flowed through the vehicles used. This use of the vehicles is, of course, interpreted by the receivers and does, therefore, communicate something. But what a performance communicates is often more, "Look at/Listen to me. Notice how able I am as a performer," than the expected content. Unless the source intended to simply perform, the original message is hijacked and replaced by another message concerning the performer's expertise.

A good communicator does perform. But such performance is used to enhance another message, not to hijack it. Performance, furthermore, is a legitimate activity when it is what is intended and expected. We gladly pay money to watch a good musical, dramatic, or athletic performance. Unfortunately, however, many churchgoers have come to consciously or unconsciously expect a performance by their pastor. And that is often what they get whether or not the pastor consciously intends it. When, then, it is performance (in this sense of the word) rather than communication that takes place in a church context (whether intentionally or unintentionally), the message communicated is radically affected.

The place of ritualized behavior in hijacking a communicator's goals and motivations also needs to be recognized. Ritual communicates something quite different from what one might expect if one simply focuses on the surface-level words and phrases. As I will point out in chapters 5 and 9, stylized and ritual communication is a very important and valid part of life. But when we participate in rituals (such as greetings and worship services) we dare not be unaware of the influence of the ritual nature of the context on the message conveyed.

Sermons, for example, are not free-floating communicational events. They are, rather, a part of a ritual of consolidation (the worship service) that serves well the vital function of confirming people in relationships and beliefs that they value highly. The ritualized nature of the interaction and the context in which it occurs usually do to the specific wording of sermons what the ritual nature and context of greeting interactions do to the specific words of greetings: they signal to the receptors that the real meaning of the interaction lies beneath the surface of the words themselves. Pastors should not, therefore, expect too much from their attempts to persuade via sermons. Other approaches better serve the goals of persuaders. We will look at these in the chapters that follow.

As mentioned above, it is likely that any given interaction will involve more than one goal or motivation. Would-be communicators, for example, may aim to persuade by means of the information they present. They may at the same time, however, be trying to impress someone. During the same interaction, then, they may deliberately seek to include interludes of entertainment to change the pace (often in the form of humorous stories). But, no matter how sincere and conscious they may be of their motives, they may from time to time fall prey to the unconscious desire to perform for their audiences. God often works through us anyway, but *by increasing our consciousness of such factors, we are likely to find ourselves more effective in our attempts to serve him.*

In addition to the possibility of multiple goals on the part of communicators, there is often a difference between their goals and those of the receivers. A communicator, for example, may seek to be persuasive, while the receptor's aim is simply to gather information or to watch a performance. Such may be the case when a media reporter attends a Billy Graham rally. Likewise, when Sunday sermons are perceived more as ritual than as persuasion, it is more likely to be because of the (unconscious) intent of the receivers than that of pastors who deliver the sermons. Pastors may, in fact, become very frustrated because they have been led (by people such as their teachers) to believe they have more control over the situation than is, in fact, the case.

Communicating Christianity with Impact

A crucial factor in communication is the kind and nature of the impact that a message has on the receptors. I use the term *impact* to refer to the impression that a communication makes on those who receive it. *Impact is a personal thing.* Different communicators are, therefore, able to convey essentially the same message with different impacts. Communicators can, furthermore, vary the impact of what they say and do by varying the message. Other factors, such as context and the internal state of the receptors, also affect impact.

Impact, like all else in communication, is subject to the interpretation of the receptor. There are, therefore, several principles, each relating to receptors, on the basis of which messages are disposed toward or away from greater impact.

The first principle may be labeled the *principle of acceptability.* The question to be raised in this regard is, Given the present perspective of the receivers, is this message acceptable to them? If not, what needs to be done to message code, content, treatment, or circumstance (see chapter 5) to make it possible for receptors to easily accept the message?

As will be pointed out in chapter 6, people have a range of tolerance. For some, this range is so wide that they are willing to accept almost any message on almost any topic from almost any communicator. But most people's range of tolerance will vary from topic to topic, communicator to communicator, and circumstance to circumstance. For these, communicators need to make judgments concerning the topics, the circumstances, and their own credibility with that particular audience. For this reason it is very difficult for most communicators to effectively address unknown audiences in unfamiliar settings on sensitive topics.

Nothing valuable can be communicated if the receptor tunes out the message. Whatever the communicators' goal, it is incumbent on them to at least start with material that is acceptable to the receptors and that will keep them listening. One frequently effective tactic is for the communicator to begin the presentation by making complimentary remarks concerning the audience.

Another, perhaps more effective, tactic is for communicators to give primary attention at the beginning to *presenting material that will establish their credibility in the hearers' minds* (see chapter 11). For if the credibility of the communicators is high, they will have the receivers' permission to deal with a wide range of subjects. But such credibility can be squandered if the communicator oversteps the permission given. It is often, for example, virtually demanded by conservative audiences that an outsider present a good bit of personal information, preferably in language valued highly by the receptors, before the message will be tolerated at all. There is what Mayers (1974) aptly labels "the prior question of trust" to establish before a hearing is gained. The first messages should, therefore, be messages concerning oneself aimed at winning the right to be heard by the particular group of receptors in focus.

I learned this principle once while doing a series of studies in a very conservative church. They suggested strongly that if I didn't begin using highly valued terms such as "the blood of Christ," I would not be listened to. What they were really asking was that I state my conservative credentials before they would regard me as credible. So I took some time to give testimony to my conversion, commitment, and growth in Christ, whereupon they listened to me gladly.

A second crucial principle for attaining impactful communication is the *principle of relevance.* Receivers constantly ask themselves the question, Do I need this message? Does it help me with any of the areas of life or thought with which I am struggling? Communicators must, therefore, ask themselves questions concerning the relevance of their content to their receptors. Unfortunately, too many communicators are found to be "scratching people where they don't itch." Though of high interest to themselves, their messages may be perceived by the receptors as irrelevant to most or all the needs they feel. It is unfortunate that not a few sermons fall into this category.

"But," many preachers will contend, "I am dealing with their *real* needs, not simply the needs they feel." A valid point. But it ignores the fact that people operate on the basis of *perceived needs* and *perceived relevance,* whether or not they have deeper needs that might overall be more important. It is, therefore, incumbent on an effective communicator to deal with need at the level at which it is perceived, patiently leading the receptors to perceive deeper needs not formerly recognized by them. Then, once they are aware of those deeper needs, the communicator can deal with them with greater assurance that the messages will be perceived as relevant.

In this way communicators can always be relevant even though at an early stage they may have been dealing with comparatively trivial needs. Attention to trivial needs is, however, only a starting point, enabling the communicator to enter the receptor's range of tolerance and to build credibility toward the time when it is appropriate to deal relevantly with deeper needs. *Being relevant is being wise, not superficial or simplistic, as some would have us believe.*

The statement is frequently made in some circles that the Bible *is* relevant, it does not need to be *made* relevant. There is a truth here. But that truth pertains only to the potential of the Bible, not necessarily to the receptors' perception of it. For if biblical content is presented in such a way that the receptors do not perceive it to be relevant, the verdict concerning the communication is that the Bible is not relevant to them. For *relevance is as relevance is perceived.* The language used to present the message may not be their language. It may be the language of another time or of another place, such as the theological classroom. Such language, though appropriate in other times and other places, hijacks a message that might otherwise have been perceived as relevant and induces a perception of irrelevance.

Too many sermons (both in the West and cross-culturally) have been delivered as if the preacher's homiletics professor were the intended audience rather than the needy congregation in front of them. These sermons are rightly perceived as irrelevant, regardless of the potential value of their content to that congregation.

A third principle for impactful message production is the *principle of specificity.* Receivers are much concerned with the relationship between the messages they hear and the life they live. A general message, such as *God loves everyone,* is, therefore, only of general interest to most hearers, especially when compared to a more specific rendering of that same message, *God loves you, John Smith.* There is a much greater likelihood that respondents will feel the need for a message if that message is presented as specific to their needs rather than as generally applicable to the needs of all humans or of some subcategory of human beings. This is one reason why individual counseling or pastoral visiting in the home has much greater impact than public communication such as preaching.

Even in preaching, however, it is often possible to be more specific than is ordinarily the case. We have a psychological mechanism that enables us to identify with other people, such as a speaker or a person within a story told by the speaker. Jesus made effective use of this characteristic by depending so much on true-to-life stories (parables) in his messages. Effective communicators, in recognition of this characteristic, ordinarily decrease the amount of information that they present in a given segment of time and increase the amount of illustrative material, particularly illustrations from human experience. Such experience may be their own, that of others, or, like Jesus, fictional true-to-life stories concerning typical human experience. Such treatment of messages enables the very personal thing we call communication to be much more impactful.

A fourth impact producer is *unexpectedness* or *unpredictability.* People enter into communicational situations, as into all other situations, with certain expectations. The persons involved, the place, the time, and other contextual factors, plus their previous experiences with all of these, lead them to expect certain things. If their expectations are fulfilled, their stereotypes confirmed, there is a dampening effect on the communication. In church, for example, people come to expect a certain code, a certain content, and a certain treatment. When their expectations are fulfilled, therefore, although they feel comfortable, the communicational impact of what goes on tends to be quite small. This is one reason why church-service communication functions better as ritual than as stimulus to change.

If, however, even in a familiar setting such as a church service, something unusual happens, it will be noticed and have an impact. Many people, accustomed to traditional church language, notice and are impressed by speakers who are down-to-earth in language, posture, casual attitude toward their achievements, nontraditional treatment of the topic, and the like. Such things are unexpected and out of the stereotype for communications that take place in that setting. Their messages are, therefore, impactful.

Not all impactful communication is, of course, helpful. A shady story told in the wrong context can have quite an impact but not for good. A church message concerning a biblical character presented in the first person, a dramatized Scripture reading, a dialogical or panel presentation of the Sunday message, a more personal treatment of biblical topics, and similar techniques can, however, because of their unexpectedness, considerably increase the impact of what happens on Sunday morning. For the concern of God and his servants is to communicate, not to preserve an archaic form of oratory on the assumption that God has endorsed preaching.

A fifth impact-increasing technique is to *increase the opportunity for one's receptor to discover insights and answers on their own.* There is a radical difference in impact between messages that we receive that are labeled "the property of someone else" and messages we can label "our own discovery." The latter consist of the insights to which we have come at least partly through our own efforts. The former consist of messages that have been predigested by someone else and presented to us in rather final form.

Those who communicate most effectively are those who are expert at leading people to discovery rather than at predigesting and cleverly presenting the results of their own efforts. Jesus was, of course, a master at asking questions in preference to giving answers. This enabled him to be a master at leading people to discovery.

Discovery-learning puts the focus of communication on the receptor's creativity, where it belongs, rather than on the communicator's cleverness in creating and "performing" messages. A communicator who focuses on leading receptors to discovery does indeed need to be clever, but it is a different kind of cleverness — receptor-oriented cleverness.

Such a communicator is more likely to stimulate than to entertain the receptors. This is the real aim of persuasive communication. Because church communication has so often focused on answers rather than on questions, Christian orthodoxy has been pushed in the direction of concern for commitment to creedal information rather than concern for creative, discovery-oriented, deeply personal interaction with God. Such interaction can be labeled "mine." Creedal information is always labeled "someone else's."

What Is the Message of All This for Us?

We always communicate something. But experience shows that what gets across is frequently more than, less than, or otherwise different from what we intend. In our quest to better control the results of our communicational efforts there is, however, some help. This chapter has been designed to raise to our awareness certain characteristics of messages and their relationships to persons. The aim of the chapter is, however, that we use this information to bring about improvement (if we need it) in our communicative efforts.

5

Message and Technique

Humans Are Quite Flexible in Handling Different Message Types

We regularly use expressions such as the following, either as responses (e.g., 1-3 below in response to "How are you?") or as statements. They constitute a variety of message types and tip us off to a variety of communicational situations. Our experience with such a variety of message types and the situations in which they function means, however, that we seldom misinterpret them.

"How are you?"

1. "Fine."

2. "I've had a horrible week! I was on my way to the doctor's and my car broke down. So I got there late. Furthermore, he told me that I need an operation. . . ."

3. "Who wants to know?"

"Don't look at me that way."

"I see that in every way you Athenians are very religious" (Acts 17:22).

"I can't get that song out of my mind."

"Who does that preacher think he is anyway?"

"Her life speaks so loud, I can't hear what she's saying."

"I've heard this message often from preachers. But coming from you, it sounds different."

"What right did she think she had to tell me what to do?"

Peter answered, "Lord, I am ready to go to prison with you and to die with you!" (Luke 22:33)

"Hallelujah!"

Characteristics of Messages

Having discussed the personal nature of Christian communication and introduced some of the external personal factors influencing messages, it is important to look at certain of the characteristics of messages in general. In this way we will set the stage for a more detailed discussion of the relationships between the nature of communication and the nature of Christianity.

There are four rather important general facts that every serious communicator needs to know about messages and message-sending.

The first fact is that *we cannot avoid communicating.* Any behavior that is observed is interpreted by those observing and, therefore, is received by them as communication. As Watzlawick et al. (1967:48) have said, "One cannot not communicate." Whenever there is interaction between persons, communication is inevitable. Whenever there is someone to interpret, messages are being received, whether or not those sending them are conscious of the fact that they are communicating. Perhaps it is not too much to say that for human beings, to live is to communicate. It seems that we cannot keep from sending messages, whether or not we intend to. We will further discuss the reasons for this in chapters 6 and 7.

Second, *when we communicate, we always send multiple messages.* Or, rather, receivers regularly pick up multiple messages when they interpret. Some of these additional messages may distort or even contradict the main message we are trying to send, as when the message of our life communicates something different than what we are trying to get across with our words. If all goes well, however, those other messages (technically called *paramessages*) will function to support, amplify, and otherwise assist in the correct interpretation of the main message.

In each of the illustrative situations at the beginning of chapter 4, everyone who attempted to communicate (including the preacher) sought to send the same main message. This message was, however, surrounded by a variety of paramessages sent via tone of voice, gestures, eye contact, space between participants, posture, attire, and the way the participants used their physical surroundings (such as pulpit, notes, Bible, furniture, and the like). Even the knowledge and experience receivers bring with them concerning the communicator, themselves, other participants, the setting, and life in general function to add paramessages to the communicational interaction.

These additional factors produce additional material to be interpreted by the receptors. These "additional" messages, then, either support or weaken the main message in the minds of the receptors. If, for example, the communicator shouts, "The building is on fire," but doesn't run, this action will likely be interpreted as contradicting the word(s) uttered. If, however, after shouting, the person runs to escape, the message of word and that of action will likely be seen as supporting each other.

Third, *messages, once sent, are irretrievable.* Unless the receptor does not hear us, we do not get a chance to send a corrected version of the same message before the message we have sent penetrates the other's consciousness. We often make mistakes in transmitting messages and often attempt to correct those mistakes by sending additional messages. But we can never take back the original message once it has been received and interpreted. It becomes, as it were, a permanent part of the record.

Sometimes in attempting to compensate for a message that we regret having sent, we apologize. This often results in the second message, the apology, having greater impact than the first, resulting overall in a much better communication than if the first message had been correct. In many cases, however, no matter what corrective messages we attempt to send, the respondent chooses to abide by his/her interpretation of the original message, and the communicational situation remains a disaster.

Fourth, it needs to be noted that *a message is a complex thing.* Whether it is a main message or a paramessage, it will be made up of several parts. For each message presented it is possible to describe: (a) the code or vehicle via which it is sent; (b) the content or information that is conveyed; (c) the treatment or style used by the communicator in structuring and presenting it; and (d) the relationship between the participants and its influence on the giving and receiving of the message. Each of these elements is interpreted by receivers and contributes to the overall result of the communication. If, then, the main message is to get through clearly, it is important that the fit between these message elements be appropriate both to the intent of the communicator and to the perceived needs of the receivers.

As pointed out above, there is a unique content to Christian messages in that they are *life* messages rather than simply *word* or information messages. This fact places restrictions both on the codes used to convey that content and on the way the content and code are treated. In our attempts to communicate the Christian gospel, for example, it is incumbent on us to use only those means that enable us to demonstrate what we recommend as we recommend it. Jesus refused to use a coercion code (e.g., with the rich young man, Matt. 19:16-22) or a warfare code (Matt. 26:52), since the means of transmitting a message becomes a part of that message.

There are many codes and treatments available to us. Among the codes are language, music, drama, ritual, and many others. These will be treated in the following pages (especially in chapter 9). So will the importance of treatment/style matters such as formality-informality, personalness-impersonalness, generality-specificity, lecture-discussion, and the like.

Message Types

It is important for communicators (and receivers) to recognize that there are many types of messages, several of which may employ the same vehicles (e.g., language, music, and so forth) but with quite different meanings. If, for example, the phrase "I'm fine" is used in a greeting context, the meaning is quite different from what that phrase would mean in response to a genuine request for information (see the example at the beginning of this chapter). This, in turn, is quite different from the meaning that phrase would have if it were spoken in a sarcastic tone of voice.

The first type of message I will treat may be called *stylized* or *ritual.* The "I'm fine" response functions as part of a greeting ritual, and the real (i.e., deep-level) meaning is something like, "I recognize your goodwill toward me and hereby return an expression of my own goodwill to you." Life is full of such stylized communication, and it usually goes well unless someone mistakes this type of message for another. As mentioned above (in chapter 3 in our discussion of myth 6), sermons and the other parts of worship ritual also function largely as stylized communication. The underlying (and very important) meaning of a sermon may often be phrased something like, "We are gathered here with people of like mind to share this presentation with each other as a symbol of our common commitment to God, to each other, and to this organization."

It is impossible to overestimate the importance of stylized communication. An abundance of such interaction and of the larger rituals of which it is a part contributes markedly to a psychological sense of security and belongingness in all societies, especially when the participants are members of the same group. Much of the communication in situations such as those cited at the beginning of chapter 4 was of the stylized type, even much of that which occurred after the service and appeared most spontaneous.

But suppose that in one of those interactions someone asked, "How are you?" seeking the stylized response but instead received a detailed analysis of the respondent's physical condition. It would be obvious to the questioner that the question had been misinterpreted. The misinterpretation was, however, *a misunderstanding of the type of message rather than of the words themselves.* The respondent had simply confused the cue designed to trigger a stylized response with one triggering a request for information. And this person responded with an informational answer rather than a stylized one.

A similar kind of upset often happens when the members of a congregation whose expectation is to participate in their usual ritual of consolidation are presented a sermon designed to upset and change them. Because of the external factors present in such a context (treated above and in chapter 10), such messages become incongruous and tend to simply irritate (or become performance) rather than to help. Other contexts should be sought for them.

Informational messages, secondly, are perhaps those most in focus in American society. Such messages have as their primary function the transmission of information for the purpose of increasing the receiver's knowledge.

There is a sense in which all communication involves the transmitting and receiving of information. All messages, therefore, convey some kind of information. But certain messages can be said to have the transmission of information for its own sake as their primary purpose. Among these are news broadcasts, lectures, statements in response to questions about time, place, weather, and the like.

American society is so given to the accumulation and transmission of information that we experience a bombardment through such vehicles as radio, television, newspapers, magazines, books, and lectures/sermons that has produced an information glut. We have been trained to value knowledge and information for its own sake to such an extent that we simply ingest it in whatever form it comes to us—whether or not we can see any actual or potential use for it. Our intake, therefore, far exceeds our ability to assimilate, producing a kind of intellectual indigestion. In places like school, church, and home, then, our focus is thereby often diverted from the concerns of living to the task of accumulating and storing as much information as possible.

The resulting problem is highlighted in the story of the farmer who was approached by an agricultural specialist with the question, "Wouldn't you like to know how to run your farm better?" "No," answered the farmer, "I already know much more than I can practice. When I catch up a little, I'll let you know." Perhaps the farmer's attitude was a bit extreme. Yet one wonders if we aren't often crippled in our behavior more by knowing too much than by knowing too little.

I believe that as Christian communicators we too easily fall into the culturally approved habit of simply trying to increase the amount of information stored in people's minds. We have been carefully trained in our educational institutions to value information for itself, and so we continue to dig it out and to pass it on as if God also subscribes to such a value. People, therefore, usually know much more than they can possibly live, yet they feel supported by the church in their belief that if they can only learn more they will be more blessed. We often seem to subscribe to the aims of the Athenians who "liked to spend all their time telling and hearing the latest new thing" (Acts 17:21b).

But God seems much more concerned with how information is used than with the mere accumulation of it. Messages from God, therefore, are more likely to be of types labeled persuasive or instrumental.

Persuasive messages, thirdly, are designed to win the respondent over to something such as a favorable attitude toward the communicator or the cause. Messages designed to persuade people to change their attitude, thinking, and/or behavior fall into this category. Such messages are usually most effective if based on a solid interpersonal relationship plus a felt need on the part of the receptor(s) for a new answer to a life problem.

Public persuasive communication often appeals to the receptors' emotions. Whether or not the receptors change in response to such messages is, however, usually more dependent on their relationship with and/or attitude toward the communicator than on the way in which the message is delivered. Given a positive attitude toward the communicator, public and mass media may be appropriate vehicles for bringing about changes in attitude. They are, however, usually less useful in bringing about changes in behavior beyond the changes in thinking. (For an excellent treatment of persuasive communication for Christian purposes see Griffin 1976.)

Instrumental messages, fourthly, are intended to get others to do or not to do things. They commonly involve requests and orders, either of which may be direct or indirect. Requesting someone to type a letter, shut the door, follow Christ, or stop sinning qualify as instrumental messages. So do prayers in which we ask God for things. Indirect instrumental messages are sometimes disguised as requests for information, as in the question, "Is it too hot in here?" when the intent of the questioner is to get someone to open a window. The Scriptures are, of course, full of both direct and indirect instrumental messages aimed largely at stimulating us to live up to the requirements of information we already know.

Messages about other messages, fifthly (technically called *metacommunication*), are another important type. Such messages are usually sent as paramessages via tone of voice (e.g., sarcastic, threatening, playful, excited), use of space (e.g., standing close to encourage friendliness), use of time (e.g., arriving early for an appointment to show respect), and the like.

One important type of metacommunication may be labeled *preventive*. Such messages are designed to cut off or prevent communication. Wandering eyes, disturbed looks, uncomfortable movements, certain hand gestures, a cool tone of voice, fidgeting, coughing, and the like are often the vehicles for such messages.

Sixthly, Christians need to be aware of the fact that messages can be empowered by supernatural beings. *Blessings* and *curses* (and their relatives, vows, spells and hexes) are messages that convey supernatural power to those at whom they are directed. The power they convey is beyond that of human agencies alone and is to be taken very seriously.

As Christians, we may follow the example of the heroes of Scripture and bless people knowing that when we do so God empowers these messages. There are several hundred examples of blessing in Scripture. The most common is the blessing of peace (Heb. *shalom*). Jesus used this blessing frequently. So did Paul at the beginning of each of his letters. When Jesus sent out his disciples to minister, he told them to bless with peace the homes in which they stayed (Luke 10:5). I have frequently blessed individuals and groups with peace and found that they felt the peace of God come over them at that time. Other common blessings in Scripture are grace, joy, mercy, love, and faith.

Cursing is also common in Scripture and is taken very seriously. A curse is the opposite of a blessing. It is a message that conveys negative spiritual power to the person cursed. We are commanded to respond to those who curse us by blessing them (Matt. 5:44; Rom. 12:14).

We can also bless other messages in Jesus' name (e.g., sermons, lectures, letters). Such "anointed" messages are thereby invested with God's power to convey more of God's intent than the human message alone could convey. Sermons can and should be so blessed. So can and should the communion elements (1 Cor. 10:16).

A counterfeit of this type of message is a kind of ritual message that we may label *magical*. A magical message uses special words, phrases, gestures, and the like assumed (usually unconsciously) to be invested with power in and of themselves to *compel* supernatural beings to be favorable toward the user.

Americans often think we are free from such "superstitious" attitudes toward the vehicles of communication we use. It is, however, difficult to explain in any other way the attachment of many Christians to archaic language (such as "thee" and "thou") and "vainly repeated" set phrases (such as "our gracious Heavenly Father," "the blood of Christ," and "Amen"). People very often develop magical attitudes toward praying and other worship ritual, regarding them as means of manipulating God rather than as means of submitting to him.

Such are the types of messages that communicators and receptors alike need to recognize and learn to use. Wise communicators will make sure they are in control of such understandings so that they may choose the most suitable message types to serve the intended goals. As should be clear from the above discussion, message types are not always used in isolation. Quite often a given communication will involve more than one type. Also frequently, a given message will combine more than one of the above functions in the same message.

Relating this material to that in chapter 4 concerning the impact of what we communicate, it is important to point out that the type of message has much to do with the impact it conveys. *Stylized messages seldom have high impact* unless contextual features, such as a greeting between people who have long been separated, or factors internal to the interactants, such as a constantly high level of emotional expression, condition the participants toward high impact. *Informative messages, likewise, are not expected to have high impact.* If, however, the information presented is startling or particularly relevant to the receptors, there might be considerable impact. *Instrumental and persuasive messages, on the other hand, can frequently have high impact,* as can any of the other types of messages, given the proper circumstances. The key principle in this regard would seem to be that the impact is likely to depend on the fit between the type and circumstance of the message. A communicator should not, therefore, expect too much by way of impact from a kind of message or circumstance that is not well suited to conveying such impact.

Audience Size and Type

It is not possible to present a "main message" in isolation from a wide variety of external factors that influence a message both as it is presented or as it is interpreted. These influences are such that one might question whether the "same" message presented in several different situations would indeed be the same message (e.g., the example at the start of chapter 4). Because of the pervasive importance of such factors, much of the rest of this book will be devoted to discussing their nature and influence. Whole chapters on the crucial position of receptors (chapter 6), the vehicles employed (chapter 9), and the influence of context (chapter 10) will highlight those important areas. In addition, numerous subsections of other chapters will focus on such things as the multiplicity of messages sent, the importance of the personal relationships between message senders and receivers, and the need for a good fit between message content, structuring, setting, and receptors.

Before we turn to those matters, however, we need to treat the relationship of message and technique to the size and type of audience being addressed. For the types of interaction in any communicational situation directly correlate with the size of the audience and the methods chosen. Such considerations are quite basic to the message as it comes across, though not ordinarily considered to be a part of its content.

The types of interaction may be pictured on a continuum from intrapersonal to media:

Intrapersonal → **Interpersonal** → **Small Group** → **Public** → **Media**

At one end of the scale is *intrapersonal* communication, in which one talks to oneself. Interaction between two people is *interpersonal*. When one or more communicators interact with several (roughly, up to twenty-five or thirty) receivers, we speak of *small group* communication. The term *public* communication is used to refer to situations (such as lectures and sermons) in which one communicator addresses a fairly large group. When extending devices such as radio, television, and print are employed, then we speak of *media* communication. Frequently the term *mass communication* is used to refer to either or both public and media situations.

Each of these labels points directly to an audience size and indirectly to a kind of interaction between the participants. *The kind or nature of that interaction itself becomes a part of the message.* Take, for example, a message such as, "I love you." If this message is spoken over television or radio to an unseen audience, it is understood quite differently than if it is uttered interpersonally to one's sweetheart. When a message is spoken to one person there is usually little doubt about the intent of the communicator to be personally involved with the receptor in such a way that the communicator's life will back up the words. When, however, the receiving group is very large and/or receives the message via electronic or print media, the receptors know they would probably not even be recognized by the sender of that message if they tried to get those words backed up with life-involvement behavior. This knowledge changes the message.

There is a sense in which *all communication boils down to interactions between two people.* When we talk to ourselves *intrapersonally,* the two persons may be seen as two parts of ourselves. When we talk to more than one other person, it is as if we relate to each one separately but all at the same time. In *small group and public communication,* this relationship between communicator and receiver is complicated by such factors as how well they know each other and spatial considerations like the size of the room, the arrangement of the seating, and the distance between communicator and receptors.

In *media communication,* the relationship may (as with interpersonal situations) be a one-on-one situation, but the interposition of the medium precludes personal contact except as the receiver personalizes the situation internally. This internalization process is particularly important in reading, due to the fact that the reader must play both the part of the receiver and that of the author as communicator. Readers conduct an intrapersonal conversation stimulated on the one side by the book and on the other by their personal reactions to what they understand the author to have written.

Each communicational event is conducted across a wide or narrow communication gap. This is the gap defined by the differences between the frames of reference in which each of the participants lives. Traversing it needs to be negotiated carefully, particularly if the subject of the communication is complex or the gap wide. Such negotiation often requires a good bit of give-and-take on the part of both communicator and receptors if the latter are to understand properly. Media, public, and, to some extent, even small group settings greatly hinder the give-and-take by reducing receivers' opportunities to request clarification. The use of media and/or the presence of a sizable group of receptors greatly increase the possibility that misunderstood messages will not be corrected.

In such ways, the audience size affects the nature of the communication. This, then, intrudes into the message. Effective communicators, as they attempt to fit message to circumstance, take audience factors seriously.

Communicational Technique

Effective communicators also use care in their choice of the communicational method or technique they employ. There are at least three methods that people use to interact communicationally with others. These relate closely to the interpersonal, small group, and public types of audience discussed above. In public communication, the technique employed is usually *monologue.* With small groups a *dialogue* or discussion approach is ordinarily most satisfactory. For very small groups or individuals the most effective is what I call *life involvement.* Each of these is valid for a given size audience and situation or for certain types of message in any situation.

But the communicator must take account of the fact that the audience interprets the method of presentation used along with the message delivered. *It is, therefore, possible for the method of presentation to interfere with the message it is counted on to transmit, particularly if there is a lack of fit between method, message, and situation.* This lack of fit is what Queen Victoria noted when she complained, "Mr. Gladstone always addresses me as if I were a public meeting." When speakers present a message to one person as they would to one hundred people, the message is in danger of being seriously distorted because of the inappropriateness of the method chosen.

Messages are most effective when there is a coordination between the goal of the communicator, the content of the message, contextual factors, and the kind and use of the methods employed. With respect to the three methods here in view, it is appropriate to ask questions concerning the way each of these factors fits with each of the methods.

Let us note, first of all, certain peculiarities of each of these three methods. As already mentioned, a *monologue* approach is appropriate for public communication to sizable groups. Typically such a situation will be fairly formal, will require that the receptors be seated in rows with the communicator elevated on a platform in front of them behind a podium or pulpit. The communicator will do all, or nearly all, of the presenting with little or no opportunity for feedback from the audience. The message will have been prepared beforehand and will undergo little or no adjustment during the communication process. The message will be designed to appeal to the audience as a whole rather than to any individuals or small groups within that audience.

In the normal (*"sedate"*) use of this method within WASP (White Anglo-Saxon Protestant) churches, the message will tend to be informational and predigested, seldom involving any modeling of behavior (except public speaking behavior) or discovery-learning. The amount of information that can be covered in a fairly short period of time is considerable via monologue—much more than with more personal methods. The credibility of the message tends to be rather tightly tied to the reputation of the speaker. *The audience is expected to be relatively passive* in its responses during the time when the message is being delivered.

The communicator may show excitement over the message and develop illustrations concerning its application to draw the audience into greater interaction. And such overt commitment, if coupled with verbal ability on the part of the communicator and felt need on the part of the hearers, can on occasion generate at least a change of attitude and perhaps some change in the behavior of the hearer. But this method in this setting strongly disposes the participants to see the message as primarily informational rather than motivational and the presentation more as a performance than as a real appeal for action. The members of the audience go away with their knowledge increased but usually find it very difficult to apply what is said in their lives.

In certain church situations (notably black churches and evangelistic rallies) a tradition exists that might be labeled *high-emotion monologue.* In these settings several techniques are employed that result in greater emotional involvement between speaker and audience than in the more sedate use of monologue described above. In comparison to the sedate monologue, high-emotion monologue will ordinarily be characterized by less information; more repetition; more audience participation; the use of a wider range of gestures, vocal variations, and bodily movements by the speaker (and sometimes by the audience as well); and more time to present the message. The major distinction between sedate and high emotion uses of monologue is in the much greater use by those employing high-emotion monologue of dramatic and interactional techniques designed to generate an emotional response.

Dialogical interaction, where there is constant give-and-take between the leader and the other members of the group, is much more appropriate when the group is small. A dialogue or discussion format is ordinarily much less formal than a monologue situation. It also requires a much longer time to deal with the same amount of information, since the information is more fully discussed and applied more specifically than is possible via monologue. Whereas in a monologue situation the reputation of the speaker is likely to be crucial, since the speaker is required to give so little personally to the audience in such a presentation, in dialogue, personal characteristics of the communicator carry more weight and reputation correspondingly less.

Receptors cannot be as passive in a discussion as they are in listening to a monologue, for there is considerable opportunity for feedback, adjustment by the communicator, and discovery-learning on the part of the receptors. Dialogue has, then, greater potential than monologue for influencing peoples' thinking and, via such changes, high potential for affecting other behavior as well. Receptors go away from a dialogue session not merely informed but with a sense of having grappled with some issues.

As a means of influencing the total behavior of receptors, however, there is no substitute for *life involvement.* In life involvement, communicator and receptors spend large chunks of time together in as wide a variety of experiences as possible. Children learn in the family via life involvement, as did Jesus' disciples in their day in, day out interactions with him. This method takes much more time to cover a given amount of information, but it is covered at a deeper level of understanding and application. Life involvement is highly informal and exposes to view much more of the total behavior of the communicator than either of the two previous methods. Furthermore, the likelihood of the receptor making the recommended behavior habitual is increased enormously, because behavior is modeled, discussed, and practiced over a long period of time and often adopted unconsciously. There is maximum opportunity for feedback and adjustment as well as for discovery-learning. It is no mystery why Jesus adopted this method of communication as that best suited to his goal of influencing the total behavior of his followers.

A chart that may help the reader to picture these details and some others follows. I reproduce it here from Kraft 1979b:44-45.

A TYPOLOGY OF APPROACHES TO COMMUNICATION

CHARACTERISTIC	APPROACH I (Monolog)	APPROACH II (Dialog)	APPROACH III (Life Involvement)
1. METHOD OF PRESENTATION	Monolog/Lecture	Dialog/Discussion	Life Involvement
2. APPROPRIATE TYPE OF MESSAGE	General Messages	Specific to Thinking Behavior	Specific to Total Behavior
3. APPROPRIATE AUDIENCE	Large Groups	Small Groups	Individuals or Very Small Groups
4. TIME REQUIRED FOR GIVEN AMOUNT OF INFORMATION	Small Amount	Medium Amount	Large Amount
5. FORMALITY OF SITUATION	Formal Dominant	Informal Prominent	Informal Dominant
6. CHARACTER OF COMMUNICATOR	Reputation Important	Personality Characteristics Important	Total Behavior Important
7. FOCUS OF PARTICIPANTS	Source Dominant (Message)	Message Prominent (Source-Receptor)	Receptor Prominent (Source-Message)
8. ACTIVITY OF RECEPTOR	Passive — Merely Listens	Considerable Mental Activity	Total Life Involvement
9. CONSCIOUSNESS OF MAIN MESSAGE	High (Both Source and Receptor)	Medium	Low (Perhaps Contradictory Verbal Message)
10. REINFORCEMENT AND RETENTION	Low	Medium	High
11. FEEDBACK AND ADJUSTMENT	Little Opportunity	Considerable Opportunity	Maximum Opportunity
12. DISCOVERY BY RECEPTOR	Little — Message Predigested	Considerable Discovery	Maximum Opportunity for Discovery
13. TYPE OF IDENTIFICATION	Source Identifies Primarily with Message	Reciprocal Identification with Each Other's Ideas	Reciprocal Source-Receptor Identification on Personal Level over All of Life
14. IMPACT ON RECEPTOR	Low — Unless Felt Need Met	Potential High on Thinking	Maximum on Total Behavior
15. APPROPRIATE AIM OF APPROACH	Increase Knowledge	Influence Thinking	Influence Total Behavior

There are two questions I would like to raise concerning these communicational methods. The first concerns the adequacy of each technique for serving the goals of Christian communication. The second concerns the adaptability of monologue, in particular, to goals that lie beyond the simple impartation of information or emotional arousal.

As for *adequacy,* the first question, I have stated previously above that I believe the major goals of Christian communication are person goals. They have to do with the development and growth of the receptors' commitment to God and changes in their behavior to make it more consistent with that commitment. The Bible seems to focus little or not at all on people's need for more information. Indeed, there are even indications that certain of those condemned in the Bible might have been better off with less information (John 9:41; 15:22; Luke 12:47-48). Yet the most prominent communicational vehicle in Protestant Christianity is the sermon — an information-oriented technique.

On the other hand, the technique that Jesus chose and that seems to be most effective in bringing about behavioral change seems to be widely neglected as those who define ministry and those who prepare for it focus on sermonizing before large groups. Does not the personal nature of our message demand that we be primarily concerned with pastoring rather than with preaching? Should we not, like Jesus, prefer personal interactions with groups of manageable size to less personal (often impersonal) performances before large groups?

The second question deals with the possibility of *adaptability.* Can monologue be adapted in such a way that it can be more effectively used to bring about behavioral change than would ordinarily be the case? The answer is, to some extent, yes. To do so, however, a communicator will need to use the method more personally and less oratorically with more attention to personalizing the message and less to its intellectual content. For both the sedate and the high emotion approaches to monologue easily devolve into rather impersonal, predictable ritual. Such a ritual, though often of value as reinforcement of the group's internal unity, usually has little effect on the lives of its members as they go from worship into the outside world.

The sedate monologue method seems to be based on the assumption that human beings are basically rational and intellectual. Information cogently presented in rational form is, therefore, assumed to be sufficient to motivate people to change and grow. Approaches designed to generate high emotion, then, seem to be based on the assumption that humans are basically emotional and, therefore, simply in need of being aroused to act on what they are already largely aware of. Neither assumption is likely to be accurate for more than a small proportion of any given audience. Communicators need, rather, to see their task more broadly.

Those now locked into either form of monologue can profit from examining their goals in relation to the considerations made explicit in the above typology. If, then, their goals are more like those best served by a life involvement approach, they should seek to modify their use of monologue in ways that will facilitate their true aims. Those whose ordinary approach is more sedate will probably increase their effectiveness by making such changes as decreasing the formality (number 5 on the chart above), sharing themselves more fully with the audience (6), presenting more specific, less general messages (2), decreasing the amount of information presented with a corresponding increase in applicational illustrations (4, 6, 7), seeking ways to involve the audience in the message (8), soliciting and adjusting to more audience feedback (11), increasing the ability of the receptors to identify with the communicator (13), and increasing the possibility for the receptors to discover the importance of the message for their lives (12).

In addition, such "sedate" communicators should take every opportunity to spend time participating with their receptors outside the formal situation. For pastors, this should mean visiting parishioners at home, at work, and wherever else is appropriate both in normal times and in times of stress (for more on this subject see Kraft 1979b: ch. 4; see also an especially good treatment of personalizing preaching in Chartier 1981).

High-emotion preachers, then, sometimes need to move in the opposite direction on the chart. They may need to move in the direction of greater informational content, the use of a greater variety of techniques to avoid the deadening effect of too much sameness, and a turning away from the tendency to merely perform, lest the communicator get in the way of the message. In addition, several of the above life involvement characteristics are frequently lacking even in high-emotion preaching and should be supplied. Such preachers, like their more sedate counterparts, should furthermore give themselves as fully as possible to meaningful interpersonal interaction with their parishioners concerning the latter's topics and on their turf.

For even high-emotion monologue is still monologue. And even though such a technique is focused more on emotion than on information, giving the preaching at least an appearance of informality and personalness, the stylization involved in such a method still distances communicator from receptor. This method, like sedate monologue, calls for additional person-to-person contact between the participants if its strengths are to be maximized.

Our conclusion is that either type of monologue can be adapted to some extent so that the impact is more like that of dialogue or even life involvement. But such adaptations can only go so far. It is best both to adapt one's use of monologue and to combine it with the use of dialogue and life involvement with the same receptors in contexts other than the Sunday morning meetings. The reasons for such combined usage of methods lie, of course, in the fact that people who are already interested and sympathetic (usually because of person-to-person contacts) are usually more open to monologic messages than are others. The way to keep this interest up, then, is to regularly interact with them in situations that are more personal and intimate than public communication allows for (see Kraft 1979b:43-60 for more on this topic).

As noted in chapter 2, I believe there is a reason why God chose interpersonal, life involvement communication as his preferred vehicle. Jesus could have invented microphones, loudspeakers, even satellite communication. I think, though, that to do what he wanted to do, the method he chose is the only way. For he sought in his primary ministry to thoroughly influence his receivers' behavior. Maximum life involvement, however, severely limits the size of the audience. When he had things to say to larger groups he, like we, had to turn to monologue (e.g., Sermon on the Mount and his Matthew 23 diatribe against the Pharisees) and settle for merely presenting information. It is instructive to note, though, that *life involvement was Jesus' preferred method and the monologue was a last resort.* Unfortunately, much church communication reverses Jesus' priorities.

What More Have We Learned about Messages?

We have surveyed message characteristics and types and have related these to audiences and techniques, all with the underlying assumptions concerning the personalness of communication developed in the preceding chapters.

Pointing to the inevitability of communication and the irretrievability of messages was a fairly sobering place to start. Yet it is better to know than to not know such information if we are concerned about learning to control our communication. Recognizing the different types of messages, then, helps us both as senders and receivers to identify the functional category into which a message falls. Since there is often a discrepancy between the intended type and the actual type, such knowledge should increase our ability to more frequently produce in actuality what we intend. We may then more effectively conform code, content, and treatment to produce messages that will have the desired impact within the context of our receptors. No less can be the aim of those who are called both to communicate and to be the messages of God.

6

The Key Participant:
The Receptor

The Receptor's Interpretation Is Crucial

The more we learn about the communication process, the more we become aware of just how crucial the receiver of the communication is to that process. Whether we are attempting to deeply influence people via interpersonal interaction or simply convey information via lectures or sermons, the receiver has the final say over what the results will be. It thus behooves us to learn as much as we can about what is going on at the receptor's end when we attempt to communicate.

Receptors are active, even when they seem to be "just sitting there." They are not simply passive recipients of whatever is sent their way. They interact in a *transactional process in which the results are negotiated* on the spot rather than predetermined. Nothing compels receptors to interpret messages in the way intended by the communicator, though mutual trust and goodwill help a lot. Building that trust and goodwill (or at least not squandering it) becomes, therefore, an important part of any effective communicational interaction. And such building is more likely if we understand and take full account of who and where our receptors are. There are many biblical passages that exemplify the fact that any given communication may have more than one interpretation, depending on who is doing the interpreting.

Note the variety of possible interpretations in the following passage from John 7.

After his brothers had gone to the festival, Jesus also went. . . . (v. 10a)

There was much whispering about him in the crowd. "He is a good man," some people said. "No," others said, "he fools the people." (v. 12)

The festival was nearly half over when Jesus went to the Temple and began teaching. The Jewish authorities were greatly surprised and said, "How does this man know so much when he has never been to school?" (vv. 14-15). "If a boy is circumcised on the Sabbath so that Moses' Law is not broken, why are you angry with me because I made a man completely well on the Sabbath?" (v. 23)

Some of the people of Jerusalem said, . . . "Look! He is talking in public, and they say nothing against him! Can it be that they really know that he is the Messiah? But when the Messiah comes, no one will know where he is from. And we all know where this man comes from." (vv. 25a, 26-27)

Then they tried to seize him. . . . But many in the crowd believed in him and said, "When the Messiah comes, will he perform more miracles than this man has?" (vv. 30a, 31). "You will look for me, but you will not find me, because you cannot go where I will be." (v. 34)

The Jewish authorities said among themselves, "Where is he about to go that we shall not find him? Will he go to the Greek cities . . . ? He says that we will look for him but will not find him, and that we cannot go where he will be. What does he mean?" (vv. 35a, 36)

Some of the people in the crowd . . . said, "This man is really the Prophet!" (v. 40)

Others said, "He is the Messiah!" (v. 41a)

But others said, "The Messiah will not come from Galilee!" . . . So there was a division in the crowd because of Jesus. (vv. 41b, 43)

Given the possibility of such multiple interpretations, what kinds of things do communicators need to understand about those who receive their messages? It will be helpful to recognize at least three background conditions that affect receptors (i.e., their needs, their reference groups, and their commitments), plus seven important activities.

Receptors Have Needs

Apparently, few if any human beings are completely and permanently satisfied with what and who they are. And no cultural system or life-style appears to provide answers for all of life's questions. Those problems perceived to be uncared for or inadequately dealt with by one's cultural system result in what are commonly referred to as "felt needs." Such needs may be felt at the surface level or at deeper levels. *Surface-level needs,* such as the needs for food, shelter, money, transportation, and the like, are usually easy for a person to articulate.

Deep-level needs, such as the needs for someone to care or for some ultimate cause to be involved in, though they may be felt very keenly, are, however, often beyond a person's ability to articulate or even to recognize. Wise communicators seek to discover those needs that respondents feel, particularly at the surface level, and to adapt their messages so that they perceive the message as relevant to their felt needs.

In Jesus' interactions with people, such as the rich young man (Matt. 19:16-22), blind Bartimaeus (Mark 10:46-52), and the Samaritan woman (John 4), each receptor articulates his or her felt need, and Jesus deals with it before leading that person to deeper perceptions of need. The disciples, likewise, since they had put themselves in a student-teacher relationship to Jesus, frequently expressed to him their felt needs in the form of questions. With Nicodemus, however, Jesus endeavored to raise to his consciousness a need that was either latent at a subsurface level or one of which he was totally unaware. Though he treated Nicodemus somewhat kindly, Jesus frequently resorted to more drastic measures to stimulate other Jewish leaders to recognize their needs (see, for example, Matt. 23).

In this area, as in all other areas of communication, we are dealing with what is perceived, no matter what other factors may be involved. That is, *we are dealing with the receiver's reality, no matter what the objective reality might be.* The communicator's strategy should, therefore, be to discover and deal with whatever the receptor perceives to be important and is willing to discuss, regardless of what the communicator believes to be that person's basic need. *The communicator must gain permission to enter the respondent's private space by dealing with what the respondent permits to be dealt with.* Only then, once the communicators' credibility has been established via a demonstration of their ability to deal with surface-level problems, can they venture to suggest that the receptors have problems of which they are not now aware and to deal with them. Communicators need to scratch where the receptor perceives that there is an itch before they will ordinarily be allowed to dig for deeper itches.

Sometimes, due to the intensity of the receptors' felt need or due to their response to such factors as the communicator's reputation, the respondents will give immediate permission for the communicator to approach them concerning fairly deep-level needs.

The normal process, however, involves (a) the identification of a felt need and the agreement by both interactants that it is indeed a felt need, (b) dealing with the felt need, and in the process (c) identifying and raising to the level of felt needs one or more deeper needs, (d) dealing with one or more of these, and (e) discovering and then dealing with one or more others as the process continues.

Felt needs are very personal, even those at the surface level. They are, furthermore, a matter of transaction and association between receptor and communicator. That is, a given receptor will only allow a given communicator to deal directly with those needs that the receptor deems appropriate to their relationship. It is for this reason that public- and mass-communication techniques are usually inadequate vehicles for either uncovering or dealing with felt needs—unless the receptors are desperate.

Felt needs are, however, the touchstones from which life change can be recommended and accomplished. And the Christian message is designed to change life. It is of paramount importance, then, for Christian communicators to recognize the importance of felt needs and to employ those communicational techniques that will result in stimulating receptors to effectively deal with them.

Within Christianity there are at least two major avenues by means of which this process takes place. The first is through sincere, concerned, loving, Spirit-led Christians ordinarily organized into groups called churches. Such churches are the most important vehicle through which God operates this process. A second avenue is open to the minority of the world's population who have learned to read well enough to respond to messages presented in written form — the Bible. God's written Word can at many times fill the communicator's role in this interaction.

Perhaps most often, though, at least where both literacy and freedom are widespread, some combination of these two kinds of vehicles will ordinarily be employed. The personal, casebook nature of the Bible, by the way, makes it a more usable vehicle in this kind of interaction than most books, particularly books written in a technical style (see Kraft 1979a:198-202 for a discussion of the Bible as a casebook). Textbooks, for example, are notably poorer at stimulating and dealing with deeper needs than are popular books that present details concerning how real people have coped with their felt needs.

Receptors Are Parts of Reference Groups

Receptors, being human, are not alone. Though many societies are more group-oriented than are Western societies, even individualistic Westerners considering a change of behavior will ask, *"What will people think?"* These "people" about whom receptors are concerned are the "significant others" who make up their "reference group." These are the people the respondent considers most important and, therefore, most necessary to please.

We all have reference groups consisting of relatives, friends, business associates, members of our social class, neighbors, church associates, and others in similar relationships to ourselves. These may often be quite distant from us geographically and may even be a figment of our imagination. But they exist in our perceived reality and are strongly considered when we contemplate making a decision for change.

Not infrequently, people are *influenced by more than one reference group*, sometimes in different directions and often at different times. Receptors in an evangelistic rally, for example, are often conditioned toward accepting Christ by virtue of their participation in a sizable group of positively disposed persons who are responding to the invitation. They respond because "everybody else" seems to be. Later, however, away from the influence of that reference group, their relationships with people of other reference groups may lead them to question and often to reject the decision sincerely made at the rally. Wise evangelists understand this phenomenon and attempt to assist new converts to quickly develop an allegiance to and participation in a local church reference group. Such a group is permanent enough to provide a matrix for continual encouragement and growth in the direction pointed to by the decision to change.

All this points up the fact that everyone is related to at least one group. Any change that an individual contemplates and/or carries out is, therefore, contemplated and/or carried out in relation to such groups. If one contemplates a change, one may well turn away from it in anticipation of a negative reaction by the reference group. Or one may make a change against the wishes of that group and later have to decide whether to go back on the change or to leave the group.

Groups ordinarily allow their members considerable leeway for change in areas that the group considers trivial. Changes made in values, allegiances, beliefs, and the like that are considered by the group to be crucial to their well-being, however, are a far different matter. Change in such areas will not ordinarily be allowed unless appeal is made to the opinion leaders of the group. They, then, may either lead the group to make the change together or give permission to certain of the membership to make it. Wise communicators take such group phenomena into account and appeal both to individuals and to groups with full recognition of their significance to each other.

Receptors Are Already Committed

As can be deduced from what has already been said, receptors do not operate in a vacuum. Not only are they parts of groups, they are *committed to those groups.* Furthermore, they have *values and beliefs to which they are committed.* When we appeal to people for commitment to God through Christ, we are not inviting them to move from a position of no commitment to a position of commitment. We are inviting them to move from one commitment to another.

We are, furthermore, requesting a change in their ultimate commitment. People have multiple commitments to persons, groups, values, beliefs, and many other things. They may, for example, simultaneously be committed to self, family, occupation, one or more friends, God, one or more organizations, a hobby, and a host of other material and nonmaterial things that they value. The question for Christians is, of course, Which commitment is the greatest? (Matt. 6:24-34; 10:37).

Implied in this question is the consideration of what is invested in each commitment. Some will invest a considerable amount of psychic energy in their commitment to self with a much lesser amount in their commitment to God. A message that suggests that they reverse their priorities might, therefore, have little chance of being accepted unless they become dissatisfied with the fruits of their existing priorities. If, however, they do not have a tenacious grip on their highest commitment, there might be more possibility of convincing them that it should be replaced by a commitment to God (unless, of course, this lack of profound commitment betokens an inability to commit deeply to anything). Wise communicators must take seriously such commitments and seek to present their messages in such a way that receptors are attracted to the option of exchanging their present primary commitment for the recommended one.

Many of the appeals Christian communicators make are directed toward leading receptors to replace or reorder certain of their present commitments. Those commitments are usually evident from observing the kinds of things or activities they devote their time and money to. In most cases appeals for such change are best directed toward the self-interest (or commitment) of the receptors. Even within Christianity, self-interest is probably the most important motivational factor. A person's felt need for greater meaning and/or success in life is perhaps the most vulnerable point in this regard—that is, if the person believes that greater meaning and/or success is a possibility.

A commitment to conservatism on the part of receptors can be a major obstacle. Many individuals and whole societies believe that the way things are is either best, inevitable, or unchangeable. Such persons and groups may be virtually impervious to suggestions of change for the purpose of gaining greater meaning or success. If so, some other felt need will have to be searched out and utilized. With such groups a perceptive communicator can often discover a way to build a change upon some tradition to which they are committed.

Other individuals and groups are committed to change for its own sake. This commitment can often provide a launching pad for the introduction of Christian values. It can, however, lead to flightiness and instability. Wise communicators need to learn to work with such values in order to assist people both to follow Christ more faithfully and to become more stable.

People think in terms of stereotypes. We stereotype people, messages, places, types of activities, and just about everything else that regularly recurs in our experience. These stereotypes, too, are a kind of commitment. They must be recognized and worked with and around if we are to communicate effectively.

Receptors' commitments, beliefs, and values, therefore, have much to do with what they will accept from a communicator, especially in the area of recommendations for change. (See Rogers 1983 for an excellent treatment of how to introduce change.)

Receptors Are Active

In addition to such background conditions that influence those who receive communication, we may point to several important activities in which they engage, even when they seem most passive.

The first is the activity of *interpreting*. All communication is bathed in the interpretations of the participants. In communicational interactions, receptors interpret everything that is said and done as a part of the message. Thus even such nonverbal things as the time and place of the interaction, the communicator's life, gestures, tone of voice, use of space, and the like, and even the receptor's past experiences with the communicator and/or with similar people all play very important parts in the way the receptor interprets the messages sent. For this reason, a given verbal message presented informally to an individual at home will be quite different from the "same" message presented formally in church from behind a pulpit.

Interpretation is clearly one of the most important activities engaged in by receptors. Communicators must do their utmost to ensure that everything they do in presenting a message will be interpreted by the receptors in a way that enhances their intended meanings. Not infrequently, factors of formality, impersonalness, insincerity, inappropriateness, and the like become part of the way a message is presented and result in the discounting of the message by the interpreters/receptors. Effective communicators learn to control such factors insofar as possible.

The interpretations of the receptors lead to the most important activity that receptors engage in, that of *constructing the meanings* of the messages they receive. Communication theorists have amassed a considerable amount of evidence to indicate that meanings do not lie in words or other symbols that we use but, rather, in the people that use them. Meaning is not transmitted from person to person but constructed by people on the basis of their interpretations of the words and other communicational symbols they receive. Receptors, therefore, are actively engaged at all times in constructing the understandings with which they come away.

The attachment of meanings to the symbols employed in communication is a creative kind of activity that receptors perform in keeping with whatever motivations they deem to be appropriate. A receptor may or may not choose to carry on this activity with the kind of motives that would be most favorable to the communicator. No matter what the message, receptors are likely to interpret it in accordance with the way in which they relate to the communicator. Such relational characteristics as friendliness/unfriendliness, personalness/impersonalness, informality/formality, intergenerational or interclass affection/antipathy, or any of a number of other factors become important building blocks from which receptors construct meanings. (See chapter 7 for more on this topic.)

A third important activity of receptors is the *granting or withholding of permission* for a communicator to enter what might be termed their communicational space. Since communication is a transaction, it proceeds only at the permission of the transactors. Communicators often discover that many of their best messages have fallen on deaf ears because the members of their audience have refused to grant them permission to be heard.

Such permission, as with all receptors' responses to a communicator's efforts, is often quite selective. A given receptor may, for example, not agree to accept anything that a given communicator says. Or the receptor may agree to listen to the communicator on certain subjects but not on others. Or the receptor may take a wait-and-see attitude, suspending evaluation until the communicator has finished before deciding if or what to accept.

It is as if people have a certain range of tolerance for people and messages they encounter. Any message that is to be permitted to enter a receptor's mind must fit through the opening provided by that range. We may illustrate as follows:

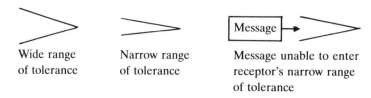

Wide range   Narrow range   Message unable to enter
of tolerance   of tolerance   receptor's narrow range
                                          of tolerance

Figure 3. Ranges of Tolerance

Such factors as the credibility of the communicator, the maturity of the receiver, the potential threat of the message, the acceptability of the language used, the place and time of the interaction, and even the mood of the receptor greatly affect the tolerance for a message. Jesus told the disciples, "I have much more to tell you, but now it would be too much for you to bear" (John 16:12). Apparently either their lack of maturity or the circumstances of the interaction (or both) affected their range of tolerance at that point. And Jesus was wise enough not to push matters beyond his hearers' limits.

The first priority for any communicator is to win and retain the permission of the receptors to enter their communicational space. Often small things such as the type of language we use, the type of appearance we make, whether we are personal or impersonal, the felt need on the part of the receptor for the kind of message we are presenting, and the like have a large influence on whether or not the receptor will give us the permission we seek. Having once granted that permission, receptors actively continue to grant or decide to withhold it either temporarily or permanently during the interaction.

Underlying much of the receptors' activity is the fact that they are *constantly evaluating everything that goes on.* As with interpretation, their evaluation extends to every aspect of the communicational interaction, whether personal, situational, or grammatical, whether internal or external to themselves. Receptors ask such questions as, Is this communicator worth listening to? Is this message of value to me? Is there congruence between the communicator, message, setting, language, and so forth? Does the communicator know what they are talking about? If I accept this message, what will it cost me?

The answers to these questions form the basis for the receptors' responses even more than the content of the message. Positive, negative, or neutral responses may have more to do with the paramessages the receptors have picked up than with the message we intended to get across. Things they perceive from observing us or from some factor of setting, timing, audience, or the like over which we may have little or no control can easily hijack what we intended. This fact again underlines the need for attaining as much congruence as possible between the verbal and nonverbal concomitants of a communicational event.

A very significant but perhaps deeper-level activity that receptors engage in is the activity of *maintaining their equilibrium.* Many find receiving certain kinds of communication so threatening that they develop rather elaborate strategies to minimize the risk. They will act as if they have all the facts necessary on that subject and either tune out if it is raised or provide themselves with a store of counterarguments, each prefaced with some such phrase as, "Yes, but . . ." The strategy of others is simply to ignore or forget anything that if taken seriously would require change and threaten their equilibrium. Such receptors feel compelled to somehow stem the flow of what they consider to be equilibrium-disturbing messages.

Along with the need for maintaining equilibrium comes the need for change and growth. Human beings, like all other living organisms, need growth, or they soon stagnate and die. This need for change is, however, perceived differently by different people. *For many, almost any change, especially in religious areas, is perceived as a threat to their equilibrium.* In the area they consider threatening, such people automatically reject any message that seems to require change on their part.

Others, though, will gladly accept almost any message recommending change. And in between are those who accept certain messages that require change and reject others. In general, probably the more psychologically secure receptors feel, the more likely they are to seriously consider a message that appeals for change. Such people often experience change as positive and growth-producing rather than as a threat. They, therefore, gravitate toward it rather than away from it.

The matter of equilibrium is closely related both to felt needs and to the relationship of the receptors to their reference group. It is felt needs that often seem to demand change while it is the relationship with the reference group that provides the major symbols of equilibrium. With regard to recommendations for change, then, the primary question that arises is, *What will accepting the recommended change cost me personally, socially, economically, and the like?*

It is extremely important for Christian communicators to understand that potential acceptors of the gospel message are asking this kind of question. It is likely that Christianity is more often rejected because the perceived cost is considered too high in relation to the perceived benefit than because the message is judged to be unworthy. In general, a person or group needs to be quite dissatisfied with a situation to respond favorably to a message perceived to require rather radical changes in such areas as personal, social, and economic life. In such cases the desire to maintain a known, though perhaps flawed, equilibrium usually seems to outweigh the desire to move toward an unknown, though perhaps attractive, change.

To overcome such inertia, the Christian communicator needs to discover what within the Christian message would be attractive to such people. In non-Western cultures, Western Christians have, unfortunately, usually focused on what has been emphasized within our traditions without much regard for whether or not these emphases were attractive to the receptors. Evangelicals, for example, have tended to emphasize doctrinal knowledge. Both evangelicals and non-evangelicals have focused on introducing Western institutions such as schools, hospitals, agricultural programs, and church structures.

A bit of research and observation tells us, though, that the major quest for most of the peoples of the world (increasingly including Westerners) is for enough spiritual power to provide them with freedom from and a measure of control over the vagaries of life. Others seek personal relationships, forgiveness, peace of mind and heart, relational harmony, or some other human or spiritual thing far more than the material and institutional "goodies" we in the West tend to focus on. Scriptural Christianity, however, usually seems to be more concerned with meeting the spiritual needs that they feel than with supporting our rather secularistic approach.

A sixth activity of receptors is the *production of feedback*. We use the term feedback to label the messages sent back from receptors to the communicators. When receptors produce feedback, they reverse the flow of messages so that each receptor becomes a communicator and the communicator becomes the receptor. Feedback can be used for all the purposes that any communication is used for, though it is often limited to the use of nonverbal techniques. Via feedback, receptors often encourage the communicator, ask for clarification, show excitement or lack of interest, or send a variety of other types of messages.

The feedback process is most effective in interpersonal and small group interactions and least effective in response to media presentations. In one-on-one situations, feedback may be so immediately and so actively presented that it may be more appropriate to speak of two communicators interacting with each other rather than to attempt to designate one as the communicator and the other as the receptor. In a public presentation, however, though the feedback is presented immediately, the lecturer/ preacher may so control the situation that the feedback is totally ignored and no adjustments are made in the presentation in response to it.

In media communication, any feedback is so delayed that it seldom reaches the communicators until after their presentations are over and can, therefore, have no effect on the presentation itself—though perceptive media communicators may alter subsequent presentations in response to feedback that comes via letters, telephone calls, or polls. Even with media presentations, though, there is plenty of feedback produced by the receptors. The problem is simply that the medium blocks the immediate transmission of that feedback to the communicators.

Feedback, like all communication, is subject to the rule that says meaning is the creation of the receptor. In this case, though, it is the communicator who is the receptor and who constructs meanings from the signals received. *Communicators may or may not even give permission for certain kinds of feedback to enter their perception,* for they, too, are attempting to maintain their equilibrium. And radical suggestions for change are especially unwelcome when a communicator is working from a prepared text. Wise communicators, however, are constantly on the lookout for even disturbing kinds of feedback and always ready to make adjustments in order to keep their presentations from simply becoming performances.

The smaller, more informal, and more homogeneous the group, the harder it is to ignore feedback unless, of course, the social distance between speaker and audience is great. The larger, more formal, and more diverse the group, the greater the diversity of the feedback and the difficulty for a communicator to interpret and do something about it. In public communication, communicators may easily misread the feedback messages or find that some members of the audience are sending one message while others are sending another. This sometimes leads a communicator to develop the habit of completely ignoring the feedback. This is a very damaging habit for those who seek to be effective public communicators, particularly if their presentations tend to generate a good bit of negative or lack-of-interest feedback.

Receptors who regularly send feedback but who are regularly ignored tend to develop a stance toward the communication and the communicator that is particularly damaging to the message. They develop a high frustration level that often leads them to disengage as completely as possible from the interaction, or to regard the lack of communicator response to the feedback as a part of the latter's strategy designed to prevent their assertions from being critically scrutinized. In either instance, the receptor is likely to stop caring about what is being said and done and to develop a negative evaluation more in response to the way the presentation has been made than to the content presented.

In public and media communication situations, receptors soon learn that sending feedback seldom does any good. They, therefore, restrain themselves automatically and often find themselves struggling to maintain their interest.

Finally, *once receptors have decided to receive the communication, they must decide what to do with it.* As with most of the previously treated receptor activities, this one is characterized by decision, choice, and selection. Receptors must decide whether to pay attention to the communication or to ignore it, whether to deal with it now or to try to store it for later, whether to try to remember it or simply to forget it. If they decide to ignore what the communicator is saying, they simply allow the latter to perform but do not take seriously what is being said.

Or, whether intentionally or by mistake, receptors may forget what the communicator has said. The message may seem important at the time it is presented but be driven from their minds by subsequent events. This is one problem that many students face in school as they move from class to class or that adults face in response to the information glut. We may be impressed with the information received in one situation but move rather quickly into another situation where we are confronted with equally important material that virtually forces us to forget the previous information. In such cases we may attempt to store the material either by means of memory or by using techniques such as writing or taping. In any event, ignoring, forgetting, or storing messages represent various answers to the question, What shall I do with the communication?

If the response is to accept the message, such *acceptance may be partial, total, or conditional.* Partial acceptance involves receptors in the activity of discriminating between those parts of the message they wish to retain and those parts they wish to reject. Total acceptance does not involve such discriminations. Conditional acceptance, however, sets up conditions that if met will result in the receptors' acceptance of the message but if not met will result in the receptors' rejection. Complementary to acceptance is, of course, rejection. *Rejection, too, may be partial, total, or conditional.*

In these and other ways receptors have at least as much to do with the outcome of communication as communicators. Indeed, it is likely that receptors actually have more control over the outcome than communicators. For this reason it is crucial that would-be effective communicators learn and make good use of information concerning those who will have so much to say about what the communicators attempt to get across.

How Do Receptors Make Decisions?

There is much to be said with respect to the ways in which receptors reach decisions. See Engel (1979, 1988) for a thorough discussion of what he calls "the spiritual decision process." In general, however, following Smith (1984) we may see the process as involving seven stages (see also Rogers 1983). These do not necessarily occur in sequence, however. Several of them occur at the same time.

1. *Awareness (knowledge).* Receptors need first to come to an awareness that their way of belief or behavior is not the only way. If they do not know that another option exists, they are unlikely to seek one. A communicator's first task is, therefore, to provide information and/or stimuli that will result in the receptors perceiving an alternative to their present commitment.

2. *Interest.* Knowledge of an alternative is not, however, sufficient in itself.

Receptors must be interested in a new option, or the decision will be to continue in the old.

3. *Evaluation.* Receptors must then evaluate the alternative with a view toward deciding whether it would be worth pursuing. Such an evaluation, as pointed out above, would involve an assessment not only of the contemplated course of action but also of the consequences of adopting that course of action.

4. *Choice.* Once the evaluation is made, receptors have to choose whether or not to pursue the new option. They then choose either to accept a new commitment or to reject all alternatives and to continue in their present commitment.

5. *Implementation.* They then proceed to implement their decision, whether this be a new option or a continuance of the old. Such implementation makes visible and tangible the choice that may have been made in secret.

6. *Readjustment.* Proceeding from that implementation is the necessity of readjusting all other aspects of the receptors' lives to accommodate the new commitment. Such readjustment affects both their thinking processes and the more overt aspects of their behavior.

7. *Reassessment.* The evaluation stage ordinarily continues even after a decision is made and a change implemented. Only at this point we label it "reassessment." Receptors test the change made, reflect on its appropriateness and adequacy, check it out to see if it is living up to expectations, and develop an awareness of their postdecision situation. On this basis, they choose either to continue implementing and readjusting or to follow some other course of action, such as going back to the old way or developing some intermediate option.

Wise communicators who seek to bring about change on the part of their receptors recognize and strategize in terms of these stages. They recognize, for example, that it is interpersonal communication that is most effective at stages 3 through 6. Media and public communication are of limited usefulness during those stages, though they may be quite helpful at bringing people to awareness and interest (stages 1 and 2) if people are listening. At stage 7, especially, but also at several of the earlier stages, it is important that there be a warm, caring fellowship of people who become the primary reference group for the decision-maker. This is one crucial function that the church is intended to serve.

The research that underlies the above seven-step analysis shows a very interesting relationship between the cognitive and affective elements in the process of decision-making (see Sogaard n.d.). Note that the primary ingredient of each step is an emotional response rather than an increase of knowledge. Indeed, knowledge plays a major part only in stage 1. And even there it serves an instrumental function, i.e., it is valuable only insofar as it contributes to the affective process of becoming aware on the part of the decision-maker. It is true that people need a certain amount of knowledge to base their decisions on. But the knowledge necessary as a basis for most decisions is neither great nor in short supply. *The major hindrances to the making of decisions, including those advocated by Christianity, are therefore matters of human emotion and will.*

Thus, when church communications focus primarily on contributing to knowledge (awareness), they are being partial at best and misleading at worst. Such failure to focus on bringing receptors through the decision-making process has resulted both in immature Christians and the misleading of many into believing that the absorption of information is more important than the alteration of behavior. Several of the following chapters (especially chapter 11) contain further discussion of these matters.

Becoming More Receptor-Oriented

If receptors are as important to the communication process as this treatment attempts to suggest, it is incumbent on Christian communicators to become more receptor-oriented than is often the case. As Engel has said, *the audience is "sovereign"* (1979:46ff.; 1988). One change that many of us must make in response to this recognition is to alter our thinking and behavior to take account of this fact. I have endeavored to show that Jesus was receptor-oriented. At this point I will suggest again that we study his model with the aim of imitating his approach to his receptors.

7

How Does Meaning Happen?

Paul and Barnabas Misinterpreted

In Lystra there was a crippled man who had been lame from birth
and had never been able to walk. He sat there and listened to Paul's
words. Paul saw that he believed and could be healed, so he looked
straight at him and said in a loud voice, "Stand up straight on your
feet!" The man jumped up and started walking around. When the
crowds saw what Paul had done, they started shouting in their own
Lycaonian language, "The gods have become like men and have come
down to us!" They gave Barnabas the name Zeus, and Paul the name
Hermes, because he was the chief speaker. The priest of the god Zeus,
whose temple stood just outside the town, brought bulls and flowers
to the gate, for he and the crowds wanted to offer sacrifice to the
apostles.

When Barnabas and Paul heard what they were about to do, they
tore their clothes and ran into the middle of the crowd, shouting,
"Why are you doing this? We ourselves are only human beings like
you! We are here to announce the Good News, to turn you away from
these worthless things to the living God." ... Even with these words
the apostles could hardly keep the crowd from offering a sacrifice to
them. (Acts 14:8-15a, 18)

This passage again illustrates the preeminence of the receptor's interpretation in the communicational transaction. Paul and Barnabas intended
"to announce the Good News." But their hearers interpreted their act of
healing as the conveyer of quite a different message, a message that led
them to offer sacrifices to these "gods" who had come to them. And it was
that message, not the one intended by Paul and Barnabas, that the people
of Lystra acted upon. What they "heard," based on their interpretation of
the apostles' activity, was the only message that got across, even though it
was quite different from the one sent.

How can such misunderstanding happen?

Where Is Meaning?

There are at least three theories concerning where meanings exist.

The first suggests that meaning is *in the external world.* That is, things *contain* their meanings and give them out to those who observe them. The assumption would seem to be that a mountain is a mountain, an accident is an accident, and those who observe carefully will come to the same meaning because there is only one real possibility. If, therefore, people should come to different meanings for the same external phenomenon, the reason lies in faulty observation and/or interpretation on the part of the observer.

A second theory suggests that *meaning rests in the symbols* (primarily linguistic symbols) in terms of which the reality that we experience is described. This theory as applied to language is referred to in chapter 3 as the "boxcar theory" of word meanings. It sees words, gestures, and other symbols invested with meanings in a manner similar to that in which a container is loaded with goods. A skilled interpreter can study the words and/or other symbols from which a message is constructed to discover what the meaning is. The primary task of literary (including biblical) analysis is, therefore, the impersonal process of studying the history of the words and phrases of which a given text is composed. These are considered to virtually have a life of their own. Differences in interpretation, then, are due to a lack of knowledge of the history of these "containers."

A third theory is more person-oriented than the other two. It contends that *meanings lie within people,* not in either the external world or the symbols in terms of which we describe that world. *Meaning is, therefore, a personal thing, internal to persons rather than a part of the world outside.* Messages, constructed of symbols, may come from outside a person, but the meanings attached to message symbols are attached or even created within the minds of the persons who receive them.

As noted in chapters 2 and 4, this is the theory ordinarily advocated by contemporary communicologists. They argue against the first theory that if external phenomena and events contain their own meanings it would be possible for anyone in any society to follow a single set of rules for interpretation and thereby to uncover the same meaning. This does not seem to happen, however, even when people of different backgrounds within the same society follow the same set of rules. Though there seem to be broad general rules, or at least predispositions, on the part of all people to classify external phenomena and events in particular ways (rocks and people, for example, are seldom regarded as basically similar), the more impressive fact is that people interpret phenomena and events according to patterns agreed to by the members of their group. And such interpretations differ, sometimes widely, from group to group.

Even within American society, for example, the meaning of a landscape, a sunset, or a flower is not always beauty. Native participants in many societies, though, consider it strange that an American would refer to either a landscape or a sunset as beautiful and little short of insane that we would lavish attention on anything as bothersome as a flower.

Perhaps they (or we) are simply wrong in our interpretations, and there is, in fact, an inherent meaning to each aspect of the external world. More probably, though, external phenomena should be looked on as data that do not demand any given interpretation. Their interpretation is, like beauty, in the eye of the beholder. And it is from such a human interpretive process, not from the phenomena themselves, that the meanings come.

The second theory, that meaning lies in the symbols by means of which we communicate, is subject to a similar criticism. There is divergence, sometimes wide divergence, in the way in which various people interpret the same symbols. There is, furthermore, change, sometimes great change, from generation to generation in the meanings attached to any given word, phrase, or other symbol employed for communicational purposes. *Though there are limits imposed on the area of meaning that any given symbol can cover, these limits seem to be imposed by the community who uses them rather than by something inherent in the symbols themselves.*

English speakers once agreed, for example, that the word "let" referred to "hindering" (see the KJV translation of Rom. 1:13 and 2 Thess. 2:7), whereas now they agree that it refers to "allowing." Likewise, within contemporary America some groups freely practice hugging and kissing between members of the opposite sex as an expression of concern, care, and love. Other groups, however, interpret such activity always as an expression of sexual attraction. It is necessary to distinguish between the data of experience (in this case the data are the symbols we use in communication) and the interpretation of that data. And meaning proceeds from the interpretation rather than being inherent in the data itself.

This point of view is well stated by Berlo (1960:175) when he says:

> *Meanings are in people,* [they are] covert responses, contained within the human organism. Meanings ... are personal, our own property. We learn meanings, we add to them, we distort them, forget them, change them. We cannot *find* them. They are in *us* not in messages. Fortunately, we usually find other people who have meanings that are similar to ours. To the extent that people have similar meanings, they can communicate. If they have no similarities in meaning between them they cannot communicate.

> If meanings are found in words, it would follow that any person could understand any language, any code. If the meaning is in the word we should be able to analyze the word and find the meaning. Yet obviously we cannot. Some people have meanings for some codes others do not.

> The elements and structure of a language do not themselves have

meaning. They are only symbols, sets of symbols, cues that cause us to bring our own meanings into play to think about them, to rearrange them, etc. *Communication does not consist of the transmission of meaning.* Meanings are not transmittable, not transferable. Only messages are transmittable, and meanings are not in the message they are in the message-users.

Meaning is the result of interpretation. And interpretation is the subjective interaction of one or more persons with a situation. What the situation means to the person is what that person comes away with from that situation. And persons attach their meanings independently of each other, though ordinarily in keeping with habits that they have learned to share with other members of their community.

We ordinarily interpret according to interpretational reflexes or habits that we have been carefully taught by our elders. This fact makes communication largely predictable between people of the same community. At times though, we (or others) interpret creatively rather than reflexively. For example, we may be disposed either because we are negative or because we are positive toward the communicator to "read into" what is being said something that is not intended. And this fact lends an air of uncertainty to an interpretation that otherwise might be quite predictable. In ordinary speech, for example, we expect and depend on reflexive interpretation. In humor, however, the communicator must often guide the receptor to interpret creatively if the latter is to get the joke.

Even without such creative guidance, the meanings we (as receptors) assign might still be quite wide of the mark intended by the communicator if the community of which we are a part habitually attaches different meanings to the symbols employed than is the case in the communicator's community. How many American women, for example, have been taken aback by being referred to in England as "homely." In order to counter their interpretational reflexes in such a situation, American women would have to know that the British use that word as a compliment with a meaning similar to the American "homey." A similar situation exists within U.S. society among members of groups who have opposite attitudes toward concepts like liberalism, socialized medicine, abortion, church, people of a given ethnic group, and a myriad of other topics.

The fact that we interpret reflexively has both a good and a bad side to it. The good side is that it *saves energy*. We do most of our interpreting with very little consciousness of the fact that we are interpreting or of the energy we may be expending in the process. We can interpret without thinking about it. On the other hand, the habitual nature of interpretation means that we frequently jump to conclusions without considering carefully whether they are at all likely to correspond with the intention of the communicator.

Learning to understand persons from another group is, therefore, a matter of learning the conventions in terms of which they attach meanings to the symbols they use. Once those conventions are learned the receptor/ interpreter has developed a second set of habits in terms of which to interpret. This set of habits can, then, be employed whenever interacting with any member of that communicator's group.

If the attachment of meaning is a matter of social habit, it is obvious that one's cultural training has an important influence on those interpretations. Subcultural groupings such as social class, family, occupational group, and others with whom one associates also have an important influence. Such groupings share certain values and reject others. A conservative group will, for example, tend to interpret similarly in areas touching their particular concerns. Any such group will, however, conserve energy by focusing in on certain key (token) issues while ignoring others that may ultimately be just as important to them. *Agreement is the crucial factor that leads members of a group to interpret similarly.* This is usually, though not always, rooted in training.

When we attempt to analyze a communicational situation, then, we need to ask what is going on interpretationally, what meanings are being attached to which items by which participants. What, for example, is the communicator's attitude toward the respondent? What is the respondent's attitude toward the communicator? And what is the attitude of either toward the message, the setting, the language, the style? The attitude of each of the participants toward each of these factors plus their interpretation of the messages will figure prominently in the way they attach meanings to the symbols employed.

Forms (Symbols) and Meanings

It is implicit in what has already been said that we are constantly forced to operate on two fairly distinct levels simultaneously. At the surface level, we are dealing with what scholars have traditionally labeled "forms" or "symbols." At a deep, personal level, then, are meanings based on interpretations. As we have noted, meanings are attached to forms/symbols by persons. *There is no interpersonal communication except via cultural forms/ symbols.*

The forms of a culture and its language are the elements of which it is made up. Many cultural forms are material items such as houses, trees, dogs, persons, chairs, automobiles, and the like. Many are, however, nonmaterial concepts such as wedding ceremonies, church services, families, words, customs of dressing, eating, sleeping, speaking, gesturing, and the like. The forms are the surface-level building blocks of culture. These are the visible and invisible things that are manipulated, invested with meanings, and interpreted by human beings according to conventions usually learned in childhood.

Cultural and linguistic forms are interpreted as pointing to meanings that lie beyond the forms themselves. Almost every form, however, can be used to point to more than one meaning, depending on the context in which it is being used, how it is ordinarily (habitually) used, how the community agrees it should be used, and/or how the interpreter feels toward it. A table knife, for example, is likely to be used (and, therefore, interpreted most often) as a part of an eating context. Yet, if it is being used to pry open a can or if it is being used as a weapon, the interpretation will be quite different. And even the ordinary (i.e., the conventional) meaning assigned to it may be quite different if the interpreter has some strong positive or negative attachment to the knife. "My knife" or "a knife like the one that someone hurt me with" can, for example, be attributed a meaning far beyond that of the simple symbol in its ordinary usage.

Furthermore, as mentioned above, any given form may be interpreted quite differently by different people (or even by the same person). Think, for example, of the multiple interpretations of a church service. The same set of forms is likely to be perceived quite differently by those who have used them for forty years than by those for whom this is the first time. Tired old Christians and enthusiastic new converts will probably interpret very little church activity in the same way. Hymns, sermons, or even announcements that are familiar to the one group may be considered quite novel (and interpreted either in a positive or a negative sense) by the other. Much that is easily intelligible to the older group may be quite differently perceived or even unintelligible to the younger group. I remember vividly the time when I handed the communion plate past my five-year-old son, then heard him tearfully ask, "Why can't I have any refreshments?" His interpretation of the meaning of the communion service was not the same as mine!

Any given cultural or language form may be interpreted in such a way that a fair variety of meanings are derived from it. This principle may be diagramed thus:

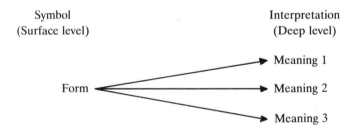

Figure 4. One form may be assigned multiple meanings

Yet a given meaning may frequently be stimulated by more than one form. The bride in a wedding ceremony may, for example, interpret the wedding as signifying that she "has arrived." Other women in attendance may, however, have found other cultural forms, such as the attainment of a career goal or the birth of a child, to have conveyed to them that same meaning. In church, frequently, older and younger groups experience the same feeling of reverence and devotion via quite different musical forms. Different language, likewise, is required to communicate the same message to different groups. The following diagram illustrates this point.

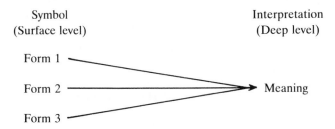

Symbol   Interpretation
(Surface level)   (Deep level)

Form 1

Form 2   Meaning

Form 3

Figure 5. Several forms may be used to convey the same meaning

Both of these principles are of obvious importance in our attempt to understand and effectively employ the communicational mechanisms at our disposal. The *first principle* assures that whenever we deal with an audience made up of people with different backgrounds and life experiences, there will be a variety of different understandings of what we say and do. And the greater the sociocultural distance between the communicator and the audience the less certain we can be they will understand the communicator's intent. An effective communicator, therefore, segments the audience (as Jesus did), choosing one group to reach well, allowing the others to get what they can. Pastors and/or church music directors may effectively choose one group one week and another the next. If this is done, though, they need to interpret what they are doing for the groups being ignored on any given occasion.

The *second principle* allows for variety in the presentation of messages. For many different wordings may be employed to say essentially the same thing. On the other hand, it points to the fact that groups of people prefer that certain forms be used if they are going to be reached. If, then, the forms that they associate with another group or another time and/or place are used, they are likely to reject the message because the forms are not "theirs." Young Americans frequently reject a Christianity couched in the music, preaching, and worship forms of another generation. This is not necessarily out of perversity. It may simply be that those forms convey to them paramessages concerning the fact that the system "belongs" to a group (their parents) that they have been carefully taught (in school and by peers) to reject.

If, therefore, a second group is to arrive at the meanings that come across to the first group, the forms/symbols used to convey them need to be just as much theirs as the forms used by the first group are theirs. This principle applies whether we are talking about the movement of messages, institutions, music, or other cultural forms from society/subsociety to society/ subsociety or from generation to generation. God's approach to nomadic Semites via their familiar patriarchal system, to the settling Israelites via a fairly flexible system of judges and prophets, to a later generation of settled Israelites (though grudgingly) via kings, and so forth is one demonstration of God's use of this principle. His appeal to tradition-loving people via tradition (commonly translated "law") in the Old Testament and to those influenced by the Greek devotion to grace via that concept is another of many biblical illustrations. See Paul's statement of the principle in 1 Cor. 9:20-22.

This principle underlies all effective communication from one group to another, whether via speaking, music, translation, or other means. This aspect of the second principle may be stated broadly: *If the same meaning is to be retained when communicating to another group, the communicator needs to change the forms employed from those appropriate to the first group to those specifically appropriate to the new receiving group.*

The corollary of this statement is the warning that *if the forms preferred by the first group are retained in presenting the message to the second group, the original meanings will be changed.* The paramessages conveyed by the use of their (i.e., the outsiders') vocabulary, their places, their music, and the like will hijack the message and make something else out of it. This is probably how the practices of the Pharisees (e.g., handwashing for purification and refraining from carrying loads on the Sabbath) that once meant devotion came in Jesus' day to be perceived by many (perhaps most) as signifying oppression. Older peoples' music and sermonizing, antique places and forms of worship, archaic Bible translations and the like, though once conveying properly devotional meanings, now convey meanings such as oppression to many contemporary youth.

This is why parachurch organizations, such as Young Life, that have learned how to use youth culture forms to reach youth are more effective in their specialty than most churches. They have discovered that *the forms used to convey the message to one group (the senders) have to be exchanged for the equivalent forms of the other group (the receivers) if the message is to remain the same.* Successful are the churches that are learning from them.

The Place of Language

Although, as contended above, the linguistic vehicles we use to convey messages do not *contain* their meanings, they still play a very important part in communication. For the forms of language are the most important of the cultural forms interpreted by the participants in communicational events. When cultural forms are used or interpreted communicationally, we refer to them as symbols. All communication proceeds via symbols. Hence the crucial importance of interpretation, since there are apparently no symbols that are universally interpreted (i.e., by all people in all societies) as conveying the same meaning.

Spoken language is the most important symbol system (or code) in human experience. It is not, however, the only one. Human groups have developed other symbol systems based on touch, pictures, instrumental (i.e., nonvocal) music, posture, smell, time, space, lighting, and the like. See chapter 9 for a discussion of certain of these.

Language is commonly defined as a system of arbitrary vocal "symbols" employed by the members of a community in socially approved ways for purposes such as communication and expression. The vocabulary of language is symbolic in that it stands for something other than itself. The relationships between linguistic symbols and the reality they represent are arbitrary in that there is no necessary connection between the sound of the symbol and the reality it represents. There is no part of reality that requires that the name given to it sounds the way it does. The names are given and maintained by the community of those who use them for as long as the members agree that those symbols should be used in that way. They are changed when the members agree that they should be changed.

Language, furthermore, is systematic and structured. There are six thousand or more distinct languages in the world today, each with its own peculiar symbol system and structure. To date, not one language has been discovered that is not carefully and tightly structured. For this reason we refer to language as a system.

To put it in a prescriptive rather than a descriptive way, if language is to serve us adequately, it needs to function as a kind of code into which members of the community can encode and from which they can decode messages.

> A language code ... must go together in a systematic way, or no two people could use the code. No one could possibly remember thousands of unique utterances. What is more, a language to be really useful must have the potentiality of endless generation of new expressions (Nida 1990:74).

But beyond these mechanical aspects of language lies the level of *meaning*. And it is that relationship that is relevant to our discussion here. I want, therefore, to make a series of statements concerning the semantic area of language that is based on the insights of modern semanticists and summarized aptly by J. C. Condon (1975).

The first of these statements is that *language is personal*. We have already emphasized this to some extent by pointing out that people's sociocultural situation, personal experiences, and the like strongly affect the way they attach meanings to the words they hear. We learn our language as persons from other persons in ways that are affected "by the training, whims, and historical accidents of our culture, community, and family" (Condon 1975:52). Note, for example, the different labels used by people speaking different dialects of English to apply to the same objects: napkin/serviette,

trunk (of car)/boot, tacks/drawing pins, wrench/spanner, soda/pop, bucket/
pail, sneakers/tennis shoes.

In spite of such group agreements, individual usage differs within each
community in accordance with the differences in the experience of the
members. Though we may refer to essentially the same objects by using the
same labels as most other members of our community, there will be minor
or major differences in our emotional attachment to those objects stemming
from our experience with them. Nevertheless, if we do not operate within
the range allowed by our community, we will not be understood. Most of
us, therefore, conform to that range at most times. It is, however, a range
not a point. Thus there is always room for "slippage."

The possibility of slippage, secondly, draws our attention to the fact that
language can never be precise. "Its very nature and purpose require it to be
more general than any single experience that might be described in the
language" (Condon 1975:80). A given label, therefore, must refer to the
item of reality in focus in such a way that any member of the community
can recognize what is being referred to and attach the meaning that their
experience suggests. Ponder, for example, the range covered by broad labels
such as "dog" or "tree," each of which covers a well-nigh infinite variety
of the kind of item that the society has agreed to categorize under that
label. *Thus the range of meaning covered by any linguistic label is that attached
to it by the members of the community, all of whom have experienced it slightly
differently.*

Though scientists and other specialists have found it possible by strictly
controlling the experiences of a limited community to narrow the range of
meaning covered by technical labels, ordinary language does not work that
way (Condon 1975:80). And for our purposes, we must remember that the
Bible was written in ordinary, nontechnical language. Furthermore, the
people with whom we seek to communicate participate for the most part
in ordinary rather than technical language.

A third important insight noted by semanticists is that *language requires
us to divide our total experience into parts, each of which is given a name*
(Condon 1975:52). Our language provides a kind of grid in terms of which
we tend to perceive reality. Since language is the product of a community
of speakers, the labels are attached to items and aspects of reality as that
community perceives them or, often, as those of a previous generation
perceived them, not as they actually are. *Language labels are attached to
perceived reality, not to objective reality.* For example, English speakers perceive five senses, eight to eleven basic colors, one kind of snow, and a
general category called ant. Many other societies perceive less than five
senses, three to five basic colors, many kinds of snow, and so many distinct
types of what we call ants that they refuse to lump them into a single
category. As we are taught our language, then, we are taught to perceive
reality in the ways that our forebears handed down to us. Indeed, *we tend*

to perceive those things for which we have labels and ignore those for which we do not have labels (Condon 1975:52).

Language is a remarkable vehicle for communicating what we want to communicate. But we do well to recognize the fact that *what we see and want to communicate is often severely limited by the language and culture into which we have been trained* (Condon 1975:52). For example, most of us in America have a very difficult time believing in the existence of spirits, whether angels or evil spirits, in more than an academic way. The term *spirit* has been passed on to us with an aura of myth, unreality, and even fairy tale about it. To suggest that some or all diseases may be caused by spirits is, therefore, to most Americans tantamount to selling out to an alien perception of reality. We have been taught our bias so persuasively that any other bias seems wrong. Such limitations, mediated by language, affect our interpretations of all reality, including that presented by the Bible.

A fourth important insight of semantics is that *we have many choices of what to call things in a language* (Condon 1975:52). There are usually several ways to say essentially the same thing. We have the kind of resources within our language to enable us to communicate nearly any relevant concept across the whole range of our community. It is, therefore, seldom good form to restrict ourselves to a single label for any given concept in a usually fruitless attempt to be precise. *The preciseness of a word is in direct proportion to the smallness of the community that uses it and the limitedness of the range of contexts in which it is used.* And it usually simply wastes time to attempt to define for people a precise label for a concept. We ought, rather, to define and elaborate the concept by the use of synonyms and alternative labels, some of which may be a part of the receptor's experience.

A fifth important semantic insight is the notion that vocabulary relates to meaning in such a way that *words operate on different levels of abstraction.* Whereas certain expressions refer rather specifically to a given item (e.g., my foot, the red truck), other expressions refer to much more general categories of reality (e.g., beauty, love, truth, justice). Both kinds of labels are symbols, but the one kind is specific and the other general. And as we speak, we commonly intermix the two levels of abstraction without warning to our hearers.

> High-level abstractions, including generalizations, are extremely useful, for they help to show order and relationships. When the high-level abstractions may be clearly related to sense-data experience, these words are both convenient and important. Such high-level abstractions also characterize some language habits at their worst, for they are the basis for stereotypes and evocative terms that mean nothing because they might refer to anything. The thoughtful speaker is aware of the many things that might be designated by his words, and thus speaks with caution and qualification.

Because high-level abstractions include the most highly valued terms in our vocabulary (beauty, love, truth, justice, and so on) and because such words represent so many ambiguous but deep feelings, we may seek to objectify the terms ... instead of labeling an experience, we may attempt to experience a label (Condon 1975:53).

Being specific is an important communicational art, and one that is often in short supply among Christian communicators. We often feel that because abstract concepts such as love and truth are mentioned so often people must know what such concepts mean. On the contrary, frequency of usage of abstract terms often lulls people to sleep, keeping them from really understanding the concepts to discover the meanings and applications to life that are intended. As pointed out in chapter 2, I believe God is in favor of specific, life-related communication, communication that functions primarily at the specific rather than the abstract end of the spectrum.

Implications of This View

The understanding that what messages mean is constructed by the receiver rather than inherent in the message is perhaps the single most threatening insight of contemporary communication theory for Christian communicators. For in keeping with several of the myths discussed in chapter 3, those who deal with communication from a Christian point of view tend to focus much more strongly on either the source of the message or the message itself than they do on the receptors. It is my contention, however, that not only does contemporary communication theory indicate that a change is necessary, but the very example of Jesus demands that we be receptor-oriented. In addition to recognizing the importance of receptors, we need to make explicit certain of the implications of this view.

The first implication is that in every communicational situation we can point to at least *three separate "realities"* or views of reality. The first reality may be labeled (a) *objective reality.* To distinguish this reality from the ones that follow we may label this one *Reality* or "capital R reality." This reality includes *all that actually exists or goes on* both external to and internal to the participants. Only God has an undistorted view of Reality, though a perceptive, uninvolved observer may come closer to seeing the interaction in this way than either of the participants.

All participants, however, have their own view or perception of this Reality. The participants observe such external indications of Reality as the looks on people's faces, people's reactions, the external context in which the interaction takes place, and so on. They also "read into" each situation a plethora of assumptions that come from such things as previous experience with this kind of situation, their attitudes toward themselves and the other participants, and how they feel at the moment.

On the basis of these observations and assumptions, then, the communicator perceives what may be labeled (b) *the communicators' reality.* A description of this reality would speak of the communicators' intent and their perception of the various components of the communicational situation. Their overall perception of self, receptors, message, setting, timing, and so forth would be prominent in such a description. The communicators' internal state (i.e., how they felt physically, psychologically, emotionally, and so forth) would also be in view as would such things as the security/ lack of security, confidence/lack of confidence that they feel at the time the interaction is taking place.

What we may call (c) *the receptors' reality is likely to be quite different.* How receptors perceive self, communicator, message, setting, and timing plus their internal state, security, and confidence are bound to be different from the communicator's in both minor and major ways. Thus the picture of the situation from the receiver's point of view will differ measurably from that in the communicators' mind. And both will differ from objective Reality.

It is that perceived reality, however, to which the participants respond. Receivers, for example, respond not to what the communicator says, but to what they believe the communicator to have said. Likewise, receptors respond not to the communicator as a person but to their perception of the communicator as a person. Furthermore, with respect to setting, time, message, and even their internal state, it is the receivers' perception of these to which they respond, not the actuality that an objective view would describe. It is out of their own reality, then, that receptors construct their meanings, since the "materials" they use come from their subjective interpretation of the situation, rather than from the "objective" details of the interaction. Meanwhile, communicators are restricted in their construction of meanings to their subjective (and different) perception of the communicational situation and of each of its components.

Meanings, then, "are the internal responses that people make to stimuli" (Berlo 1960:184) based on their perception of the stimuli from within their own reality. On the basis of these meanings both the reality from which we respond and the reality to which we respond are constructed.

A second implication of this view is *the close relationship between the process of communication and the ongoing process of the living of life on the part of the participants.* As in life, so in communication, each aspect is intricately interrelated with the myriad other aspects of the process. In any type of communicational interaction, therefore, the process is closely tied to the relationship between the participants.

Though it has been traditional to focus on the content of communicational events, the personal nature of the assignment of meaning requires that we give at least as much attention to the relationships between the participants. For *"Every communication has a content and a relationship aspect such that the latter classifies the former"* (Watzlawick et al. 1967:54). That is, the dynamics of the relationship between the communicators and the receptors provides them and any observers with information concerning how to interpret what is really meant by the utterances (and other symbols) employed. Watzlawick et al. illustrate their point by asserting that "the messages 'It is important to release the clutch gradually and smoothly' and 'Just let the clutch go, it'll ruin the transmission in no time' have approximately the same information content . . . , but they obviously define very different relationships" (1967:52).

Since all that transpires is interpreted and becomes part of the message as heard by the receptor, the importance of this relationship aspect should not be surprising. It is, however, very important to make ourselves continually aware of this factor since it is rarely in focus unless something goes radically wrong. To quote Watzlawick et al. (1967:52) again:

> Relationships are only rarely defined deliberately or with full awareness. In fact, it seems that the more spontaneous and "healthy" a relationship, the more the relationship aspect of communication recedes into the background. Conversely, "sick" relationships are characterized by a constant struggle about the nature of the relationship, with the content aspect of communication becoming less and less important.

It is not, therefore, simply the surface-level verbal (and other) symbols that are interpreted to produce the meanings of a communicational event. These are but the most obvious of a large number of items with which the communication game is played. *Indeed, often the verbal symbols conveying the content of the message are to the total message only what the tip is to the total iceberg.* Frequently, in fact, it is the components that belong to the underwater portion of the communicational iceberg that provide the clues that enable receptors to interpret the content portion of the message accurately. Such an underwater, relational phenomenon as the tone of voice used in the above examples concerning how to release the clutch, for example, is crucial to arriving at the correct understanding of the messages conveyed.

Such symbol systems as tone of voice, facial expressions, the use of space, time, lighting, and music are often employed along with verbal utterances to send messages (technically, *metamessages*) concerning how to interpret the verbal utterances. The lighting that accompanies an invitation for a young man to enter a lady's apartment or the distance that she stands from him when they talk or that she sits from him when they sit all provide powerful metacommunication concerning (a) her perception of their relationship and (b) how he should interpret her other verbal and nonverbal communications. Other aspects of this topic will be dealt with in the following chapters (see especially chapters 9 and 10).

A third implication of this view is that *those with similar perceptions of similar experiences are most likely to construct similar meanings*. Note the importance of similarity of perception (interpretation). There are many with similar experiences whose responses to those experiences are quite different. They are likely to come up with quite different meanings. The optimist, for example, believes that whatever happens will turn out well, while the pessimist believes that whatever happens is likely to turn out badly. Each would interpret a given experience quite differently. Thus, objective reality would say that they both had the same experience, but the subjective reality of each would label it quite differently.

There is, furthermore, often an important difference between the interpretation of a repeat experience and of an experience that one has not had before. Thus, our experience strongly affects our perception and, consequently, the meanings that we attach to subsequent experience. On the other hand, our perception of life in general and of any given experience within that stream strongly affects the way we participate in later experience.

The fact that people arrange themselves in groups within which they conduct most of their interpersonal interactions leads to the standardization by these groups of their interpretations of reality. Thus it is that groups agree strongly that given symbols are to be interpreted in one way and not in another. This raises the predictability of similar response to similar stimuli within a given group to a very high level.

The tighter the group, the lower the risk of misinterpretation of the communicational symbols used (see chapter 8). The greater the diversity and lack of closeness between the members of a group, the greater the likelihood that various members will interpret communicational symbols differently. Note that although membership in a group affects the similarity of the experiences of the participants, its greatest influence is on the similarity of the participants' *interpretation* of experience. *Perceptual reality is the construction of a group.* Objective Reality is not, of course, so constructed. That Reality is, however, a fact, whether or not our interpretation corresponds with it. One of our aims should be to learn as much as possible about all of the factors that contribute to the communicational situations in which we participate in order that our understanding will get as close as possible to the underlying objective Reality.

A fourth implication of this perspective on meaning is seen when we recognize that *not only groups but also individuals differ*. For even within the tightest groups there are at least slight differences in interpretation. One reason for this is that human beings are incurably *creative*. Another is that we continually make *mistakes*. Thus, certain members of every group will make major mistakes in at least some areas in their understanding of the group-approved ways of interpreting the communicational symbols they employ. And all members will make at least minor mistakes in this regard. Furthermore, at least certain members of any group will not be content with the same old customary ways of interpreting. They will insist on creating what they hope will become new traditions. And while these *opinion leaders* will be more creative than other members of the group, available evidence suggests that everyone indulges in some degree of communicational creativity from time to time.

This means that when you get right down to fine details, *no two people ever attach exactly the same set of meanings to any given symbol*, no matter how tight the group they are in. Even the members of a tight group accept *a range of allowable variation* in the interpretation of the symbols they use. Ponder, for example, the range of variation allowed within American society in the interpretation of the word symbol *my father*. The range would include perceptions varying from close to distant, warm and loving to cool and reserved. That is, we accept within our group that fathers can properly manifest the whole range of characteristics between these poles. We agree, however, that the ideal is for a father to be as close as possible to the close, warm, loving end of the spectrum. Indeed, if a father is so distant and cool that he is interpreted as projecting hatefulness toward his children, we would question whether he is in fact a father in any more than a superficial, biological sense. And if the person is female or someone else's father, our group would not agree that the label *my father* is properly applied to that person at all.

Thus, though the agreements of the group keep the label (symbol) from being totally arbitrary in the sense that it could apply to anything at all, *each symbol refers to a range of meanings rather than allowing a single possible interpretation*. When we compare various groups, we find that certain subgroupings within the American context would restrict the meaning of such a label as *my father* even more than we have just described. Some within our society might even side with many non-American groups in expecting (even requiring) that a father always be distant and reserved rather than close and warm. In these cases the agreement of the group, on the basis of which they interpret this aspect of reality, might well be to consider any father who acts warm and loving to be acting outside the range of allowable variation for that group.

The point is that even as two groups using the same symbol are likely to interpret that symbol differently, so even two people within the same group are likely to interpret any given symbol at least slightly differently. Again, the variables are actual experience on the one hand and perceptions concerning that experience on the other.

A fifth implication of this understanding of meaning concerns *how new meanings are to be stimulated by a communicator*. If receptors create the meanings to which they respond on the basis of their own perceptions of the communicational situation rather than on the basis of the directives of the communicator, how can a communicator stimulate change? The answer lies in what the communicator does in relation to the perception of the receptor. Something that is perceived by the receptors to be relevant to a need that they feel to be important, for example, has a fair likelihood of acceptance, provided the receptors do not feel that it requires an amount of effort disproportionate to the benefits they would receive from adopting the change.

Note that again the key factor is perception. A suggestion that will be genuinely helpful to the receptor is likely to be rejected if it is not perceived to be relevant. Likewise, something that the receptors perceive to be in their own best interest is likely to be rejected if it is perceived to require too much effort. And, of course, something presented in such a way that the receptors perceive no relationship between their needs and the suggested change is extremely unlikely to be accepted. Wise communicators, then, seek to pair their answers with the receiver's questions. This matter will be discussed in greater detail in the following chapters.

A sixth implication of this approach is the fact that *the determination of meaning requires that we get considerably beyond the surface-level structures employed to convey it.* Meaning is a deep-level phenomenon, even though it is symbolized by surface-level forms. And though the surface-level structures (such as language, music) are themselves complex and interesting, our primary focus must be on how they function to relate the depths of one person to the depths of another. This and subsequent chapters are intended to alert us to the nature of these depths and to what to do about them in the communicational process.

A seventh implication of this approach concerns the *nature of language*. We have often focused on the structural linguistic aspects of language to the neglect of the personal nature of this medium. As human beings *we "own" our language*, and there is very little else that we regard as more precious. This is one very important reason why it is incumbent on those who seek to communicate to us that they do so on our linguistic turf.

Partly because of the personal and societal nature of language and partly because of the structural limitations of even this most intricate of human creations, *language is not very precise.* The surface-level structures are only minimally able to convey the depth and breadth of human experience and creativity. They must continually be supplemented by adaptation and guesswork on the part of receivers if intended meanings are to get across.

One limiting characteristic of a language is the fact that in order to use it we are required to *categorize life and experience according to pigeonholes that have been set up by members of previous generations* whose experiences and perspectives may have been quite different from ours. One problem, evident in this book, that arises from such a fact is the lack of a nonspecific third person singular pronoun in English. Our language, though adequate for previous generations, in this regard hinders us when we seek, in keeping with modern sensibilities, to "de-sex" our statements. Thus we have to resort to techniques such as using "he/she" or the like, at least until our community develops a new set of pronouns.

Partly because of the diversity of groups within a language community and partly because humans are so creative, *a language ordinarily provides several ways of saying the same thing.* We can, therefore, avoid the boredom produced by always saying the same thing in the same way (if we care to). We can, likewise, produce nontechnical, nonacademic renderings of materials originally presented in another style. And we can do this in the kind of language most likely to be regarded positively by our hearers.

Even on the surface level, *certain words are more general and certain more specific*. We can, therefore, speak more abstractly or more concretely. This can, however, be dangerous (especially in Christian communication) if we gravitate more toward the abstract. We often speak of love, for example, without getting specific enough to deal concretely with its component parts such as respect, commitment, unselfish seeking of the best for a loved one, willingness to sacrifice, and the like (for more on this subject, see Kraft 1979a:139-43).

8

What Keeps People from Misinterpreting More Often?

You Know What I Meant

Under the right circumstances, each of the following utterances and gestures is readily understood:

"Did you bring it?"

"Right now!"

The nod of a head (resulting in a person's leaving the room).

"[Pilate] took some water [and] washed his hands in front of the crowd." (Matt. 27:24b)

"It's like the difference between a bundle of sticks."

"Isaac called Jacob ... and told him. ... "Go ... and marry ... one of your uncle Laban's daughters" (Gen. 28:1a, c, 2a, c, e).

"Here?" "No, over there."

It is, furthermore, possible to delete every fifth word in a text, give it to someone to read, and expect that that person will both understand the text and be able to fill in correctly most of the words.

How can this be?

Protective Devices Built into Human Experience

I have strongly emphasized the sovereignty of the audience in the communication process. I have implied or stated that the verdict concerning what is communicated is up to the receptor, that persons receiving the messages can do whatever they want with what is presented, that once communicators have spoken or otherwise presented the message it is out of their control, that messages are irretrievable, and that the receptor's interpretation will be the last word. I have contended that words do not contain their meanings but are assigned meanings by those who interpret them.

Such factors are frightening and disturbing at best, and may lead us to envision rather wild distortions of the results of our communicative efforts. Yet, though strange distortions do sometimes occur — distortions that do appear to be absurd when compared with the intended message — *it is amazing that a very high proportion of communicative activity is relatively successful in getting across what is intended.*

There are, of course, frequent misunderstandings. And these sometimes lead to conflict. But, when one considers the enormous volume of communication that goes on, the amount of serious miscommunication that occurs is comparatively small and usually the result of extraordinary rather than ordinary factors in the communication process. In considering conflict resulting from communication, however, one must distinguish between conflict that results from miscommunication and conflict that results from the fact that the receptor understood very well what the communicator intended. I would guess that a high percentage of the conflict that comes about between persons and groups is the result of *effective* communication rather than of ineffective communication.

Be that as it may, it is nothing short of remarkable, given the above characteristics of the communication process, that so much communication is so effective. What are the reasons for this?

The first factor to mention is the human propensity for *rule-ordered structuring of behavior.* Human beings and groups seem to have a deep-seated drive to produce and live by rules (agreements). When a group gets together to play a game, for example, the first discussion is designed to bring about agreement as to what the rules will be. Once these are agreed on, there is seldom any further discussion of them unless it should become clear that someone does not understand them or is not abiding by them. It is assumed by everyone in the group that there must be rules, that everyone must agree to them, and that effective participation in the game and in the interpersonal interactions surrounding it is dependent on adherence to those rules.

The fact that the agreed-upon rules are arbitrary seldom concerns anyone. People seem to know intuitively that if there were no such agreements there could be no game. Thus, people willingly engage in the fiction of accepting arbitrary rules as reality for the duration of the game and can usually trust each other to play according to those agreements.

It is, however, *necessary that all participants agree to the same set of rules.* In a basketball game, for example, all participants must agree that the line around the outside of the floor distinguishes between what is in-bounds and what is out-of-bounds. Likewise, everyone must agree concerning what is appropriate to do with the ball at any given time. If it is carried or dribbled or passed over the out-of-bounds line, everyone must agree that it is appropriate for the official to stop the game and to assess the proper penalty for the breaking of the rules.

All must agree concerning what constitutes a score and what the significance of that score is. It would not do for someone to compute the scores according to some other set of rules, even though alternate rules are thinkable (e.g., that each basket be valued at six points as in American football). In addition, all must agree to the presence and power of the officials. Those who disagree with these and the many other rules of the game either refuse to play the game or are disqualified.

All human behavior is governed in a similar way by rules that may be just as arbitrary as the rules of basketball. Cultural behavior, that behavior that we are taught from the beginnings of our semi-consciousness in the womb and which we habitually follow from birth till death, consists of such rule-ordered structuring. Communication behavior is, likewise, rule-ordered. This propensity for and commitment to rule-ordering, then, is the first characteristic of the human situation that leads to communicational understanding.

A second important characteristic is the fact that *humans organize themselves into groups.* To be human is to be part of one or more groups. Such groups, referred to in chapter 6 as *reference groups,* are characterized by rather strong agreement concerning what the rules should be and how they should be adhered to. These agreements are supplemented by equally strong agreements concerning what the penalty should be for those who break the rules. In order to survive, groups must strongly recommend and enforce within their membership such things as trust and positive regard, complementarity, interdependence, reciprocity, and, of course, agreement. If such characteristics break down, the group falls apart.

There is a sense of "we-ness" between the members of a group and a strong predisposition on their part to regard outsiders as "they." There is often a feeling of all for one and one for all within the group in response to any real or imagined threat from outsiders. And there is often a sense of cliquishness accompanied by feelings of superiority toward other groups.

While we would not say that all these characteristics are always admirable, this sense of "we-ness" is a powerful facilitator of communication. And the fact that humans tend to spend the vast majority of their time in interaction with other members of their own group greatly raises the percentage of communication that is effective. For it is within in-groups that receptors are most likely to trust communicators, to give them the benefit of the doubt, to attempt to understand them whether or not they have articulated their thoughts very well, and, in general, to do whatever is necessary to interpret communication both accurately and sympathetically. It is, furthermore, within groups of people who trust and are positively disposed toward each other that the kind of communicational interaction takes place that encourages feedback and adjustment. This gives maximum possibility for accurate understanding.

To return to the basketball analogy, we may liken the communicational rules employed by a given group to the rules employed in a given basketball league. Within that league, though the teams play by the same rules, each team (in-group) will approach the game in a slightly different fashion. One team may play rougher than another and be regularly penalized more frequently than the other teams. But that team still operates according to the same rules, even though it chooses to push at least one of these a bit further than do the other teams. Another team may base its strategy primarily on long shots in contrast to the other teams whose strategy favors shorter shots. Certain teams may be more aggressive than others. They will depend, perhaps, on their aggressiveness to compensate for a lack of ability. Others may possess more ability to score without the necessity of being overly aggressive. But, though each group uses the rules and any slack they allow slightly differently, they all play by the same rules.

Thus it is with communication. There are many groups playing in the same league, so to speak. These will be part of the same overall subculture. That is, their "league" consists of groups from the same socioeconomic level, consisting of people who share a very similar outlook on life — a common worldview. Though there will be differences that turn out to be minor when compared to differences between this "league" and another "league," these groups will share most of the same values. As with the basketball teams, each of these groups will use the rules of the game in a slightly different manner, but in general, since the agreements are high even between members of different teams, the ability to communicate even between teams is high.

Suppose, however, a basketball game was arranged between two teams, one of which was from a soccer league. Suppose, in addition, that the latter had no understanding of basketball rules and anticipated that the game would be played according to their soccer rules. When these teams get together, then, we find one team, the basketball team, advancing the ball by dribbling or passing with the hands, while the other advances the ball by passing with the feet. But each time the soccer team kicks the ball, the officials blow their whistles and stop the game, awarding the ball to the other team since kicking the ball is illegal in basketball.

The soccer team understands that the aim of the game is to score goals at the opponents' end of the court, since this rule corresponds with a soccer rule. But they are intent on scoring goals by kicking the ball under the basket rather than by throwing it through the basket. In addition to the rule that scores are made at the opponents' end of the floor, the soccer players understand the meaning of the out-of-bounds lines, the importance of the referees, and similar rules that are common to both basketball and soccer. But when the soccer team follows the rules of its game, it finds itself frequently penalized by officials intent on enforcing the rules of a different game.

A situation exemplified by imagining basketball teams playing by the same rules but with different styles illustrates fairly well the kind of thing that happens when groups from different subsocieties (but speaking the same language) attempt to communicate with each other. Often there is enough superficial resemblance between the external trappings of the communicational situation to give the impression that each group can anticipate that the other is using rules in the same way. In such communicational situations, the language often sounds nearly identical, but this masks the fact that underneath each group has a distinctive interpretation of the language. Facial expressions, likewise, may mean different things to different groups. Gestures, uses of space, intonation patterns, and similar variables also mediate different things. Thus there seems to be the same set of out-of-bounds lines, similar officials, similar positioning of the goal posts, and so forth. But enough of the rules are different that confusion abounds.

There is, however, an even greater communicational distance between the members of groups speaking different languages and conditioned by the agreements of radically different societies. Such interactions might be likened to the supposed basketball game in which one team was playing basketball and the other soccer.

Such facts make it obvious that the influence of group identity is of great relevance to the communicational process. It is not strange at all that we prefer our own group and that we experience tension and emotional stress when we have to function in a group other than our own. Culture stress (often called "culture shock") results from the insecurity people feel who know well the rules of one cultural game but find themselves in another game in which they are constantly unsure of whether obedience to the rules they know will result in an effective interaction or in being penalized for breaking some rule of which they may be unaware.

If we stay within our own groups, we ordinarily avoid such confusion unless someone changes the rules, as happens between generations in a rapidly changing society such as ours. Then we experience a kind of culture stress that Alvin Toffler has labeled "future shock" (see Toffler 1970). This fact results in adult groups and young peoples' groups regularly playing in different communicational leagues. Thus we have communicational gaps between generations even within socioeconomic classes and geographical groupings that one would otherwise predict would be relatively homogeneous. As these gaps widen in our society, the result is a division into groups characterized more by the homogeneity of age than of class, geographical proximity, or the like.

A third strong factor guiding communication toward effectiveness is *the power of habit.* Even before birth we have been learning to operate our lives reflexively (habitually) according to the cultural (including language) patterns and structures passed on and recommended by our elders to organize and carry out much of what we do. The adults who have lived their lives according to these cultural and linguistic guidelines have so indoctrinated and drilled us that we very seldom question the appropriateness or adequacy of the guidelines. We, therefore, change very little of what we have learned.

Indeed, our cultural perspective has been presented to us with such an aura of reality about it that we ordinarily simply assume that what we have been taught is the only valid way of understanding the world around. That is, we equate our subjective, culturally inculcated view of reality with objective Reality. We were taught in such a way that we became convinced that our society's way is the only right way long before we became aware that there was any other way. Though we do observe a certain amount of variety in the behavior that surrounds us, such variety is similar to that described above for those playing the same game by the same rules in the same league. That is, it is well within allowable limits and in no way approximates the kind of difference that exists between groups employing different rules and playing totally different games. We do exercise creativity by varying our performance from time to time but, with rare exceptions, always within the guidelines laid down by our society.

The relevance of this kind of recognition to our subject lies in the tremendous grip these customs have on us. The processes of training and habit formation are apparently so powerful that we seldom change or even question the validity of the habits we have developed or the rules those habits induce us to follow automatically. For *we follow the dictates of our society almost entirely by reflex, not by rationally thinking out each move.* Such cultural reflexes appear to be at least as deeply ingrained in us as the reflexes by means of which an athlete performs. And we can ordinarily trust people to respond according to those reflexes.

I have spoken above about the human propensity for ordering our lives by rules. Here the focus is on the habitual nature of the way in which we follow those rules. Those habits have the power to bring about conformity among the members of a group in the way they produce and interpret communication. Their influence is great on the automatic and largely accurate operation of communicational processes.

We interpret the way we do because we have been taught to interpret that way, and we have practiced it until we do by reflex habit what our group considers appropriate. The power of these customs, therefore, lies in the strength of the habits we develop to follow the customs. Although habits can be changed, this ordinarily involves so much work that change occurs quite slowly, even between generations. And this is true even in a society like that of the United States that has a reputation for changing quite rapidly. The strength of these habits, then, has a powerful positive influence in the direction of accuracy of communication, especially within groups. This power also extends to communication between groups and generations within the same society.

A fourth factor contributing to communicational success and closely related to the habitual nature of our cultural activities is the fact that *what we do and say has a high level of predictability or, more technically, redundancy.* One aspect of this redundancy is the fact that we tend to deal most of the time with familiar subjects and in a way that finds us frequently saying the same or similar things over and over again. The content of many conversations and a large number of books is, in fact, so highly predictable that it is often possible to get almost all of the important content in a conversation by listening no more than half the time. We can also fairly well master the content of certain books by barely skimming them. Indeed, speed reading courses are based on this fact.

Such predictability leads to the energy-saving propensity of human beings that we call *stereotyping*. Though there are many negative things to be said about stereotyping, a positive one is that stereotypes enable us to guess fairly accurately most of the time many of the things we need to know in order to interpret properly. Stereotyping at its best is merely the categorizing of people, places, times, things, and so forth in such a way that the factors held in common by the members of any given category are kept in focus and, in a communicational situation, do not need to be restated. Such predictability and the reflexive way in which we respond to it play an important part in our ability to accurately interpret communicational phenomena.

One important factor that leads to predictability is the fact that communicational events take place in *contexts. These contexts often convey at least as much information as the more visible features of the communicational event.* A receptor ought, for example, to interpret differently the use of the phrase *Jesus Christ* in a church service from its use by a carpenter who has just struck a finger with a hammer. The factor that enables one to interpret those words differently but correctly in the two situations is the knowledge of certain predictabilities attendant to each of those contexts. Words, phrases, sentences, and other vehicles of communication often have very wide ranges of meaning. The predictability of any given meaning for a given word in a specific context, however, narrows that range considerably, enabling interpreters to have a better chance at correct interpretation than would otherwise be the case (see chapter 10 for further discussion of the place of context).

A fifth factor that has much to do with our ability to interpret correctly is *the capacity of human beings to adapt or adjust to others.* There seems to be within us a drive to understand, a predisposition to make sense out of what others do and say. And we are ordinarily motivated even to go out of our way to bring this about. We frequently adjust even to poor attempts at communication by inferring what we think the person might be trying to say. Note how often we are able to complete each other's sentences.

There is a sense in which, despite the pressures for conformity laid on us by our society and group, we all differ from each other. Individuality seems to be a fact of life. This leads to communicational gaps between person and person even within the same tightly knit group. One important basis for this is the fact that we all have a different life history, leading to differences in the experience dimension of our lives. There are also differences at the perceptual and, therefore, at the interpretational level. Thus,

learning to adjust to people working from a different perceptual and experiential base than our own is absolutely necessary if we are to understand
and be understood at all. But adjusting to another person takes motivation,
desire, ability, and work. Not all persons have these characteristics sufficiently to enable them to make the effort required to bridge every communicational gap even within their own group. Yet most people at most
times seem to expend the necessary energy to adjust, thus making effective
communication their normal experience most of the time.

A sixth factor contributing to communicational effectiveness is the fact
that, in human communicational interaction, *we settle for approximations
rather than demanding preciseness.* In spite of the impressive array of sociocultural factors that press us toward conformity with the other members
of our group, there is precious little sameness either between persons or
between the things persons produce. It might be assumed, for example,
given the discussion concerning the cultural training that brings about
meaning agreements, that there is a greater degree of preciseness in the
interpretation of the symbols via which we communicate than actually is
the case.

The fact seems to be, as will be discussed in chapter 9, that *language
and the other vehicles by means of which we communicate are not very sharp
tools.* Words, for example, often cover wide areas of meaning and are frequently ambiguous. And the more widely words are used and the more
different people and groups that use them, the greater the area of meaning
covered and, therefore, the greater ambiguity of these words. But this lack
of preciseness is compensated for by the fact that those who communicate
with each other very seldom demand preciseness. If words can be likened
to darts, receptors seldom demand that those darts hit the bull's-eye as
long as they hit somewhere on the target.

The one exception to this general rule is *scientific or other jargon.* Such
language is developed by a relatively small group and used in very limited
contexts with fairly precise intent. The limitedness of the group and the
contexts in which these terms are used, then, plus the rather intense indoc-
trination with which they teach new members the meanings of the terms
they use make a higher degree of preciseness possible in this kind of language than in ordinary language. Ordinary language is much less precise
than technical language. And unless one is talking to scholars, Christian
communicators are well advised to refrain from using technical language.
As mentioned previously, the Bible and Jesus himself rarely, if ever, resort
to technical language in deference to their hearers.

The fact that people settle for approximation in communication rather
than demanding preciseness joins, then, with our ability to adapt, our drive
to understand, the predictability factor, and many other similar factors to
enable most communication to pass fairly effectively between participants.

So What?

This chapter has been designed to help us regain a bit of the stability
we may have lost as we considered the dire consequences of a communi-

cational process that leaves so much up to the receptors. It is indeed frightening to consider the possibility that those who receive communication from us can do anything they want with it. And we find enough examples of situations where receptors have deliberately misinterpreted messages to make us rightly fearful of their sovereignty. It is, therefore, helpful to point out that receptors do not always use the power at their disposal in destructive ways.

Nevertheless, it would be quite unfortunate if we allowed the discussion in this chapter to lead us to minimize the importance of the power wielded by receptors in the communication process. We should, rather, in full recognition of that power, seek to use factors such as those pointed out here to attain greater assurance that what we say and do will be correctly interpreted.

We can, for example, recognize that it is normal for people to play by the rules and to attempt to interpret accurately. If they are regularly interpreting inaccurately, then, it is likely that either they or we are breaking some important rules, whether by accident or by intent.

If the rules are being broken by intent, it is probable that there is some major group boundary between us. For those who intentionally misinterpret usually refer to those they misinterpret as "they" rather than as "we." In our attempt to communicate to them, therefore, either they will need to learn the rules of our frame of reference or we will need to learn the rules of their frame of reference. For Christians who seek to imitate Jesus, I believe the latter is the way to go. Groupness facilitates effective communication. And becoming a part of our receptors' group is the surest way of overcoming the problems inherent in attempting to communicate over the gap between an in-group and an out-group.

This recognition leads us to focus on the *importance of groupness for communication.* The trust relationship that groups engender between their members virtually assures that the members will grant each other a maximum of consideration, goodwill, and patience even when a communicator's attempts are not very expert. It is not by accident that God expects Christians to be organized into caring fellowship groups called churches. Nor is it strange that these groups tend to be sociological rather homogeneous. Apparently, God is willing to risk the many dangerous possibilities of such groups (e.g., cliquishness, exclusivity) for the sake of the many healthy, growth-producing possibilities that can be attained.

Given the human need for groupness, it is not surprising that any *communication (including Christian communication) is most effective within fairly homogeneous groups.* Attempts to communicate are, then, most likely to be misunderstood when representatives of one group attempt to communicate to those of another group.

To exemplify this fact, we may point to a major problem that arises when Christians seek to witness from their position as members of the Christian community to members of the non-Christian community. At conversion, we move from being members of a non-Christian group to being a part of a

Christian community. As we grow in Christ, then, we tend to grow more like other Christians and more different from our former non-Christian friends. This widens the communication gap between us and our former friends, making it increasingly difficult for us to relate to those former friends or other non-Christians. As mature Christians, therefore, we need to learn to communicate cross-culturally to reach non-Christians. Witness can, however, pass more easily to the members of a non-Christian out-group from those most recently converted from that out-group, since new converts have not yet lost the language and thought patterns of their former group. Assuring effective communication, then, means giving solid attention to factors related to group identity.

We must recognize the power of the habits and customs that we and others have been taught from birth, for the same habits that facilitate intra-group communication (e.g., putting "my" group first, associating only with "my kind of people") often need to be changed in the process of Christian growth toward maturity. Yet they are powerful and tenacious, and we need to be patient in dealing with them.

We do well, likewise, to give attention to the place of *predictability* in Christian communication. I have spoken previously of the ritual nature of preaching. It is predictability, often very much needed by the participants, that ritualizes preaching. There is usually nothing wrong with this, unless the communicators do not recognize it and, therefore, believe that they are doing something quite different. An understanding of this factor should make it possible for Christian communicators to better match their intent with the vehicles employed to carry it out.

An understanding of the *adaptability* factor contributes to our appreciation of the personalness of communication. People can adjust over rather wide gaps. The question is, though, How can we motivate receptors to go to the effort of making whatever adaptations are necessary to understand us? When we speak to people within our in-group, we can ordinarily assume that they will go to the effort of adapting. But when we speak to members of an out-group, the question of motivating them to adapt becomes a major one.

The discussion concerning the approximate nature of language should help us turn away from an excessive zeal for preciseness. It should motivate us to illustrate and repeat more in order to effectively zero in on crucial points, for these are the ordinary ways to sharpen understanding. The use of technical language with popular audiences is seldom a good idea. One might even question whether it is as effective as assumed with scholarly audiences. Perhaps we can learn a lesson from the fact that the Scriptures are in ordinary, nontechnical language — it is such language that suits God's purposes best.

9

The Vehicles We Employ

The Vehicle, Help or Hindrance?

The purpose of a vehicle is to convey something. A vehicle of communication is intended to convey a message. When such a vehicle does its job well, it either goes unnoticed or enhances the message. An inadequate or poorly suited vehicle disturbs, distorts, or otherwise hinders the free flow of the message. Note what the following vehicles do to the messages they convey.

"I'm not fat. I just have a husky stomach!" (Charlie Brown)

God so loves the world that he gives a damn about you.

When any Ephraimite who was trying to escape would ask permission to cross, the men of Gilead would ask, "Are you an Ephraimite?" If he said, "No," they would tell him to say "Shibboleth." But he would say "Sibboleth," because he could not pronounce it correctly. (Judg. 12:5b-6a)

"When John came, he fasted and drank no wine, and everyone said, 'He has a demon in him!' When the Son of Man came, he ate and drank, and everyone said, 'Look at this man! He is a glutton and wine-drinker, a friend of tax collectors and other outcasts!' " (Matt. 11:18, 19a)

David, wearing only a linen cloth around his waist, danced with all his might to honor the Lord. . . . Michal, Saul's daughter, looked out of the window and saw King David dancing and jumping around in the sacred dance, and she was disgusted with him. (2 Sam. 6:14, 16b)

Consider the problem that a single American girl continually encounters of where to place [herself on] the front seat of an American car when a male is driving. Does she sit in the middle? Close up? Against the door? Clearly there is a code here, and clearly it is based on communications and shared understandings about the girl's relationship to the driver. . . . Such codes are learned but not written . . . we are rarely conscious of them (Keesing and Keesing 1971:21-22).

Time talks (Hall 1959).

Space speaks (Hall 1959).

"God speaks Navaho!" (exclamation of a Navaho in response to the Bible in his language; see Wallis 1968).

"Can it be that our use of monologue in the church is the reason why none of your elders come to church?" "Of course, we've alienated them all" (part of a conversation between the author and some Nigerian church leaders).

Codes

Having surveyed the nature of the communication process and certain of the elements in it, we now turn to a consideration of the vehicles by means of which we communicate. There are at least *two types of vehicles to be discussed: codes and media.*

By *code* we mean "any group of symbols that can be structured in a way that is meaningful to some person" (Berlo 1960: 57). *Language is the most important communicational code.* But there are *a number of other important codes as well*, all based on what Smith calls "the twelve primary signal systems" (1984). These twelve signal systems are verbal, written, numeric, pictorial, audio, kinetic, artifactual, optical, tactile, temporal, spatial, and olfactory.

Either alone or in combination, the culturally prescribed structuring of these elements produces interpretable codes such as those we call music, graphic art, plastic art, drama, dance, gesture, tone of voice, eating together, flowers, sexual interaction, ritual, and the like. In addition to these more obvious codes, there are structural messages sent via codes of which we are often much less aware such as smell, touch, spacing, timing, coloring, temperature, lighting, and even silence.

When, for example, an American young lady seeks to communicate to a young man that she cares for him romantically, it is likely that she will make careful use of several of these codes. She will very probably use perfume to attract his interest via his olfactory perception. She will use a spatial code when she sits or stands near him. She will carefully time what she does and says. She is likely to punctuate her speech with frequent gestures and to use touch symbols at various points during their time together. In addition, they may dance, listen to music, eat together, observe graphic and/or plastic art, and the like. The young lady may quite consciously control much of such symbolism, as when she arranges the pictures on the walls of her apartment or chooses the music that will be playing as they talk. She may, however, be largely unconscious of much of what goes on in the mind of the young man as he attempts to interpret the nonverbal messages he believes she is sending. That is, there may be *a higher or lower degree of consciousness that one is using these codes and a greater or lesser degree of preciseness in the way they are interpreted.*

The context or situation in which a given code is employed will, of course, contribute greatly to the interpretation of the message channeled through that code. Such contexting makes use of time and space codes. Soft music played late in the evening after a dating couple have returned from a movie is likely to be interpreted quite differently from soft music played in church before a worship service. (See the following chapter for further treatment of context.)

In addition to our ability to interpret the time and space coding of the context, we can also often interpret the choice of code. The same grouping of words employed in the strictly verbal code of a sermon and in the combination (i.e., combining words and music) code of a song, for example, rarely, if ever, convey the same message. Nor do the words "I love you" said verbally, communicated by touch, or sent via a greeting card. The differences are not in the main message but in the fact that when *receptors interpret the main message they also interpret the code through which it has come.* The interpretation of the code via which a message is transmitted itself becomes a part of the message perceived. One who seeks to be an effective communicator dares not ignore the influence of the codes chosen on the message conveyed.

The first major requirement for a code, if it is to be helpful in the transmission of messages, is that it *facilitate the accurate interpretation of the messages transmitted.* A message is likely to be worthless if it is presented via a code that renders the message uninterpretable by the intended receptors. A message in a foreign language, for example, is obviously beyond the ability to interpret of one who does not know that language. So is a message via a code such as dance for those who do not understand that code or via a form of music that is regarded as objectionable by the receptors (see point 2 below).

As with all aspects of communication, *the use of codes is transactional and based on agreements between communicators and receptors* concerning the proper interpretation of the intended meanings. Differential conditioning between groups, then, is a major factor in the interpretability of codes. In American society, for example, women and men often interpret the personal space code differently. That is, a man may understand a woman who stands close to him in casual conversation to be sending a message inviting him to be more intimate with her, especially if she combines that use of space with smiles and other gestures of amicability. She may, however, intend no such message and wonder why she is so interpreted.

Likewise, it is common for the codes used by the members of a given generational group or social class to be interpreted differently by those of another generation or class. Clothing styles, hair length, music, and even life-style are codes frequently misinterpreted intergenerationally in American society. When, though, such codes are used by young people to communicate disaffection with and rebellion against the values of previous generations, the message read by the older generation may be quite accurate. Young people often know very well what codes to use to communicate such messages. It is not uncommon, however, for young people who use a music, clothing-style, or hair-length code merely to signal belongingness to the peer group to be misinterpreted by their elders as intending to send a rebellion message intergenerationally. Likewise, when a person of a lower social class buys a big car or an ostentatious home to communicate achievement to the peer group, the message is likely to be misread by those of a higher social class.

Though such problems of the differing interpretations of different audiences cannot always be neatly solved, code users need to choose their code carefully with considerations of interpretability and impact on the intended audience clearly in mind. In some situations, for example, the giving of flowers or sitting or standing too close signals something more or other than is intended. In other situations the use of words just cannot do the job, whereas the language (code) of flowers or space or even of silence is the right code to convey the intended message. In any event, *the right code is the one most readily interpretable by receptors as accurately conveying the intended message.*

A second (and closely related) code characteristic is the *need for an appropriate fit between the message and the code style.* In chapter 7 we dealt with language and meaning. We did not, however, deal with the effects on the message of different styles of the same language code if used with the same target group. It is entirely possible, for example, for a given message to be presented via a style of language judged by the receptors to be inappropriate to that message. Such would likely be the verdict if a sermon included large amounts of profanity or if a professor delivered a lecture in baby talk.

The principle is that when receptors perceive a lack of appropriate fit between the code used to communicate a message and the message itself, the incongruity of that lack of fit obtrudes into and radically alters the overall message. This is because receptors interpret the code and its fit with the message as parts of the overall message. The finer the tuning between the intended message and the language (or other) code used, the greater the likelihood of accurate interpretation on the part of the receptor.

Imagine, for example, a sermon entitled, "The God Who Gives a Damn."

If only the main message were interpreted, the title might be a very good one with greater impact than the alternative, "The God Who Cares." But many would judge this use of the word *damn* to be inappropriate at best and scandalous at worst. The negative impact on them would, therefore, negate the potential positive value of such a title because the ill-fitting code (from their point of view) obtrudes in a disagreeable way into the overall message.

In Charlie Brown's phrase "I just have a husky stomach," the code (i.e., the style of language) also obtrudes into the main message but in a way judged by most to be agreeable and clever. In that case the fit between main message and code also results in the hijacking of what might have been the overall message. But that hijacking is done by design in order to deliberately change the overall message from something pedantic to something more impactful.

Effective communicators learn to fit code to message in such a way that they guide receptors to interpret the main message plus the paramessages (including that of the code) to square with their intent. A pastor may, for example, find it advisable to use archaic language in certain church situations if the overall message would be enhanced thereby. Prayer or Scripture reading for elderly parishioners for whom contemporary language would sound inappropriate would be cases in point. In similar situations with young or mixed audiences, however, a pastor needs to consider whether the use of an archaic-language code is aiding or hindering the overall message. If the impression of such an audience is already that God is at least three hundred years behind the times, perhaps the pastor should deliberately use another style of language to alert the hearers to a countermessage.

The language code for sermonizing may not be so much archaic as impersonal and/or intellectual, giving the impression that God and his messengers are impersonal and/or academic. It is possible (and often done), for example, for the most relational topics such as God's love and concern to be presented via a code that totally obstructs a normal interpretation of those concepts. Preaching is, therefore, often interpreted as performance because of the code employed. Later in this chapter I will suggest a way out of this dilemma.

We now turn to a consideration of several codes other than language as message vehicles.

The first of these is *music*. As Berlo (1960:57) points out, "Music is a code: it has a vocabulary (notes), and it has a syntax: procedures for combining notes into a structure that will be meaningful to the listener. If we are to understand music, we need to learn the code."

Though most of us are as unaware of the technical aspects of the musical code as we are of the intricacies of our language, we all learn to use and/or interpret the code at some level. And expert communicators need to learn to use such a code expertly. For there are messages that are better gotten across via music than via other vehicles. And there are messages that are continually communicated via music that may need to be recognized and counteracted.

Among the latter, we need in church contexts to ferret out and counter the powerful musical messages concerning the irrelevance of God that spring from our hymnals whenever an outdated (or even objectionable, e.g., "a fountain filled with blood") analogy or metaphor is combined with a time-honored tune. And can we endorse the message "Listen to me, see how well I can sing/play this instrument" that comes so powerfully through the music code as used by many of our church musicians? If church communication is not simply performance and if we are concerned about such paramessages as (ir)relevance, we need to ascertain and often take steps to alter the interpretations of the music code whenever it is used.

It is hard to overestimate the impact of an attractive message put to a catchy tune that will stay in people's minds and be sung over and over, long after the occasion on which it is learned. Much of Jesus' teaching may well have been passed on in this way, since much of it is in poetic form (see Toyotome 1953). Likewise with the Old Testament, 40 percent of which is said to be poetry (Klem 1982). I wonder if church services aimed at sending people away with a growth-encouraging song in their heads might more closely imitate the scriptural fit between code and message than most sermonizing does?

Drama is another code or, perhaps, combination of codes that should be more often and more effectively used by Christian communicators. Large-scale productions dramatizing biblical or other events can be extremely valuable. That is, if the message is not hijacked and obscured by the performance dimensions of the presentation. In drama, as perhaps via no other code, it is possible to highlight the personal, living, experiential dimensions of Christian messages.

But not all church drama needs to be large scale. A pastor can often work out a very effective fit between the message and the drama code by playing the part of a biblical personage. "My name is Judas Iscariot," was the opening of one such presentation, spoken by a pastor dressed in Near Eastern garb. The message, then, was presented in the first person and was long remembered by those who experienced (not simply heard) it. I have heard of another pastor whose sermon "The Theology of Ecology" was punctuated by a communion table covered with trash. This was accompanied by a staged argument between two members of the congregation over the propriety of using the table that way. The point was made, then, when a small girl with a trash can appeared and silently cleaned up the mess, demonstrating at least one approach to part of the ecology problem.

A resourceful pastor in New Guinea even arranged for the police to stage a mock arrest while he was preaching about the arraignment and trial of Jesus. I have heard it suggested, however, that he may have overdone that drama a bit by not arranging for anyone to explain to the astonished congregation that, though this event was intended to be realistic, it was not real. Apparently they thought the arrest was real and both prayed for the pastor and attempted to find and get him released once the meeting was over. At that point, the receptors confused drama with real life and probably lost much of the intended impact of the message concerning the events of Christ's life in their concern for their pastor. With but slight modification, however, the intended message could have been preserved.

The dramatization of Scripture reading can often enhance the effectiveness of that part of a church service. One experiment of this nature involved an actor dressed like Luke sitting at a desk in the front of the sanctuary acting out the writing of a letter while an invisible reader read over the public-address system the prologue to Luke's Gospel. On another occasion, the sermon dealt with the handwriting on the wall of Daniel 5. As an invisible reader read verse 25, an invisible hand (with the help of an overhead projector) wrote on one wall of the sanctuary *mene, mene, tekel* and *parsin* (RSV), the words that puzzled King Belshazzar. Choirs can often dramatize the Scripture reading as well.

Eating together and other types of participatory activities (e.g., taking a date to a movie) can be powerful codes for conveying meanings such as fellowship, concern, willingness to sacrifice (e.g., if the meal is expensive), desire to be together, and the like. There seems to be a widespread (even cross-cultural) tendency for people to interpret eating together as invested with a kind of sacramental significance. This fact makes the Lord's Supper probably the most potentially meaningful of the codes regularly employed within Christianity, at least when it is practiced as a meal.

When, however, the Lord's Supper is practiced (as in most of Western Christianity) as a skeleton ritual with precious little resemblance to a participatory meal (or to any other part of *real* life), the communication value is radically altered. The excessive ritualization of such a code destroys its value by pushing the experience to an extreme diametrically opposite that of the example cited above, in which the pastor was dragged off to prison during the church service. In that case the value was damaged by enacting the drama in such a way that it was interpreted as real life.

In the case of the excessive ritualization of the Lord's Supper, the communication value is lost (or at least radically changed) when it bears no resemblance to anything else in the participants' experience. This means that our attempts to interpret the event via analogy with other life experiences are frustrated. But since we are taught that God commands us to do it, we tend to interpret the strange, unique thing as sacred and magical. That is, we interpret this meaningless ritual as we interpret any meaningless ritual (e.g., kissing grandma)—as required by the one in charge (in this case God) and entered into to please him rather than as a participatory experience.

As in the case of the dramatic dragging off of the New Guinean pastor, however, restoring the communication value of the Lord's Supper would not be a major undertaking. Since eating together already exists as a meaningful code within the society, all that needs to be done is to practice the Lord's Supper as a real meal (as the early church did). This would allow the sacramental significance of the activity to develop naturally from the associations between it and real life, on the one hand, and between it and the historical experience of Jesus with his disciples, on the other.

As it is, a church supper usually has more in common with the original Lord's Supper (both in form and in meaning) than the ritual as ordinarily practiced. *A ritual with no contemporary analogy is a dead code*, tending to stifle the receptors' ability to identify with the historical event that the ritual is designed to reenact. Though some receptors are able to creatively construct a meaningful experience in response to a dead code, most will not put out the great amount of effort involved. Unfortunately, both of the major Protestant rituals, the Lord's Supper (as usually practiced) and baptism, are dead codes. These (like poor Bible translations) are like bridges halfway across a river that require the receptors to build their own half from the opposite bank if they are to be able to make use of the part of the bridge that has been built.

Other codes such as *dance, graphic and plastic art, as well as smell, space, lighting,* and the like are often best used in combination with speech, music, or drama. Within restricted groups in which the members all agree on the meanings of dance movements or of the intricacies of graphic and plastic art, these codes can be extremely effective vehicles of communication. The less agreement between receptors and producers concerning what the elements of the code are intended to communicate, however, the greater the likelihood that the code will be seen as an end in itself (i.e., a performance or a ritual) rather than regarded as a means of conveying another message.

As suggested above, *ritual* is also a type of code, although its communication value is often quite different from that intended by those in charge. As with ritual language (e.g., greetings) the interpretation of what is really meant is arrived at by looking beyond the surface structuring of the ritual (or linguistic) behavior into the deep structuring of the interpersonal relationships of the participants. Worship ritual, for example, is best understood via an analysis of the motivations and relationships of the participants rather than via an analysis of the words spoken or sung and of the other surface-level behavior manifested. Since ritual is a dead code on the surface, the interpreter needs to look beneath the surface to discover the intersections between ritual behavior and the real lives of the participants.

People who participate in worship ritual together often, however, attribute different meanings to the forms employed. For some (probably a small minority), their knowledge of the historical background of the ritual provides them with the materials from which they construct a meaningful contemporary interaction between themselves and God, on the one hand, and their fellow worshipers, on the other. This may be for them roughly equivalent to the biblical or historical analogues from which the ritual has developed.

For those who do not know the history (and for many who do), though, the best they can do may differ widely from the original intent of the ritual. At best they may experience Sunday worship (including the sermon) as a generalized rite of consolidation with their fellow believers and with God. At worst they may regard the whole thing either as magical or as nonsense, since the church ritual is most nearly analogous to one or the other of these areas in the life of the participants in nonchurch contexts.

The Person as Medium

The second kind of vehicle used in the communication process is what we refer to as media. I will here deal with *two kinds of media: personal and extending.* The most important kind of medium used for purposes of communication is the person involved in the communication process. Beyond the person are technological devices that, like all technological devices, extend the person's ability to control at least to some extent factors such as space and time. I will deal with the person as medium here and with the extending media in the following section.

From what has already been said, it should be clear that the place of persons in the communication process is absolutely crucial. Persons create and send messages. Persons receive and interpret messages but in an involved rather than an uninvolved manner. And people identify so closely with at least certain of their messages that they may accurately be seen both as the vehicles of those messages and as their originators. There is a sense in which we can say communicators *are* the message that they seek to communicate, especially with respect to messages such as those that Christians attempt to communicate. For those messages are expected to affect lives. And *life is affected by rubbing against other life.*

There are, of course, messages that communicators attempt to convey that supposedly require a minimum of personal involvement on their part. Conveying a news report or a scientific fact, for example, is not ordinarily thought of as requiring the involvement of the reporter in the facts passed on. Yet, even in such reporting there is an interpretive dimension in which the interpreter selects what is passed on and the way in which it is passed on. This shows a personal involvement with material where we might not have expected it. We would say, then, that *communicators are always involved with their material in such a way that some part of the receptor's interpretation of the message is an interpretation of the person of the communicator.* A message delivered is never left untouched by the deliverer. Likewise (and just as relevant to the point), a message received is never left untouched by the receiver.

Messages intended to *persuade* other people are, however, affected to a much greater extent by the person of the communicator than are purely informational messages. It is with respect to this kind of message that perceived incongruities between the words delivered and the behavior of the deliverer are most damaging. For the message of a person's life seems usually to carry more weight than the message of a person's words. A professor of mine used to say, "Do what I say, not what I do." He seemed to recognize within himself an inability to live the way he recommended that others live. We chose, however, to follow neither his words nor his example. We would only take information from him, and that largely because we were being graded on it. Though this man's life was not a bad one, it does seem to have been a sad one.

Far different was his advice from that of the apostle Paul, "Imitate me, then, just as I imitate Christ" (1 Cor. 11:1). My professor was not taking Jesus seriously. For our Lord, in recognition of the truth of the principle I am here articulating, both saw acceptance of himself as synonymous with acceptance of God, and acceptance of us his followers as synonymous with acceptance of himself. In Matthew 10:40, Jesus stated the principle as follows, "Whoever welcomes you welcomes me; and whoever welcomes me welcomes the one who sent me." Then, in Luke 10:16b as he sent out the seventy-two he said again, "Whoever listens to you listens to me; whoever rejects you rejects me; and whoever rejects me rejects the one who sent me."

It is probably safe, then, to suggest that, at least with respect to life-affecting messages, *communicators are a major part of the messages they deliver.* There needs to be congruence between the behavior and the statements of those who would communicate effectively. Can love, for example, be learned from an unloving person? Or spiritual vitality from a spiritually ill person? Or faith from a doubting person? Or joy from a complaining person? Or wisdom from a fool? The answer is, Only occasionally—and then only when receptors engage in a disproportionate amount of adjustment and reinterpretation to make the message come out differently at their end.

There are structures such as teaching and preaching that effectively isolate most of the communicator's behavior from the view of the respondents. Teachers and preachers may, if they choose, relate only those portions of their experience that show their behavior in the most favorable light. We are particularly susceptible in contemporary mass society to experiencing a large number of communicators in this very partial, almost depersonalized way. Their reputation coupled with the few things they select to recount to us are often all that we know of them. How they live at home, how they treat those close to them, how (or if) they really practice what they preach are often rather totally hidden from us. We, therefore, frequently develop very unrealistic expectations for such people and are terribly disappointed if we find they do not measure up to those expectations. Such a problem is, however, at least partly the responsibility of the pastors or teachers who communicated themselves only partially and often unrealistically.

At the other end of the spectrum is the kind of person who we experience at close range day in and day out in life involvement. That person's behavior in areas such as faith, hope, love, spiritual vitality and the like is impossible to hide. That person is a life-changing message for us, either for good or for ill. Jesus, in his adoption of life involvement as his strategy, became for those close to him a twenty-four-hour-a-day message concerning the nature of God and how humans should relate to God. I believe his approach is normative for those who would effectively communicate his message.

Not only are individual persons important vehicles of the messages we seek to communicate, but groups of persons also function as communicational media. The commitment of a group such as the church to the cause of God is the most powerful possible message concerning that cause. The church as vehicle is, then, God's continuing message concerning God's nature and cause. As such, a church is a message for good or for ill. And with respect to groups as with respect to individuals, the message of the personal medium is much more powerful than the message of the words conveyed.

Extending Media

By extending media we mean those vehicles that extend the possibility of communication beyond the ordinary space-time limitations of those who seek to communicate. The three major types of extending media in focus will be: (a) *print;* (b) *radio/cassettes;* and (c) *television/film.* Each of these is "nonpersonal," a device or technique that stands between the person who seeks to communicate and the ones who receive. Depending on how they are used, they may also be *impersonal,* damaging rather than enhancing any relationship that might be established between the participants.

There appear to be three major factors involved in influencing the effectiveness of the transfer of messages from one participant to the other(s). These are: the skill of the communicators in their use of the medium; the intensity of the need felt by the receptors for the messages being sent; and the amount of competition for the attention of the receptors.

This third factor interacts with and often overrides the other two. If there is little or no competition for the attention of the receptors, many messages communicated poorly even in the face of little felt need may get across quite well. For example, in areas of the world where little information from the outside world is allowed or available (e.g., in countries under totalitarian rule, rural Africa), inexpertly presented messages of any kind coming from outside may be "gobbled up" by information-starved receptors. In areas where there are a great many sources of information, however (e.g., in Europe and America), the same presentations would likely be turned off or avoided in favor of other sources with greater appeal to the receptors. Unless, of course, the receptors felt a great need for those messages.

Where many sources of information are available, considerable skill is usually required to effectively advocate behavioral change via extending media, unless the receptors feel a strong need for change. To merely communicate information ordinarily requires much less skill, unless the receptors are negative toward the information itself, the communicator, or the means by which the information is conveyed. In either case, the degree of skill required of the communicator is proportionate to the felt needs of the receptors. If that felt need is high, little skill is needed and almost any medium will serve the purpose. If the felt need is low, choosing the right medium and using it with great skill are crucial to the success of the venture.

Extending media, like all others, are interpreted by receptors in such a way that their attitude toward the medium becomes an important part of the overall message. We must, therefore, ask again what these media are best at; how well any specific use of them suits the goal, content, and context of the communication; and how adaptable each is to serve purposes other than that to which it is most suited. (See Rogers 1983:19ff., 273.)

Since about 70 percent of the world's population is not literate (Klem 1982), *print* is not very useful in many areas. And even among literate people, I believe it is a highly overrated vehicle of communication. It is not at all surprising to me that Jesus did not write. Print tends to reduce communicators either to nonpersons or to whatever the reader imagines them to be. It also demands great psychological sophistication on the part of the readers to construct from print what they feel the author intends and then to react to it from their own point of view. Among the fairly limited group of those who have developed such psychologically sophisticated reading skills, however, print media can be quite effective, especially when the felt need for the information conveyed is high.

Print is most successful at *preserving* in bare bones fashion information coming from another time or another place. But such information becomes set, like a still photograph, and loses all life except what a clever reader can resupply. Material in print can, though, be disseminated widely and be subjected to close, repeated analysis.

Print truncates communication, on the one hand, but makes it more widely available, on the other. And when combined with examinations and grades, even such truncated communication can be effective in influencing people's thinking. The great prestige that messages in print still have in our society, of course, has much to do with such influence.

The wide dissemination of printed materials, however, often takes them well outside the bounds of their intended audience and the original context from which must come much of the information necessary to interpret them (see chapter 10). This characteristic of printed material greatly increases the possibility of misinterpretation. The fact that printed material can be gone over and over and dissected minutely can also lead to problems. Printed materials are of different kinds. Some materials are informal, some formal, some poetic, some technical.

To treat an informal or even a formal letter as if it were a technical, scientific treatise in which something crucial hangs on the precise interpretation of every word constitutes a serious mishandling of the material. Yet Bible students regularly make this mistake. One might ask the question, Were Paul's letters, the Psalms, Jesus' parables, and the book of Revelation really intended to be dissected in this way?

Print, like public media, is better at disseminating information and, therefore, in raising receptors' awareness than at bringing about behavioral change. This is not to say that behavioral change never results from reading. Indeed many, due to the fit between their own felt needs and the message of the Scriptures (or of other books), have made significant behavioral change in response to reading. This, of course, depends on one's reading ability. Given an ability to read, print, like any other medium of communication, is most successful when the author deals with a need that receptors actually feel. Books, magazines, newspapers, and the like — if they are to be most effective — should, therefore (like other types of communication), be directed to specific audiences in relation to specific problems.

Written materials directed to specific people in specific contexts in a relevant and deeply life-related way hold the greatest potential for getting beyond the mere conveying of information to the affecting of motivation and behavior. Biographical materials are among the most effective kinds of writing, especially if they enable readers to identify with the subject. Fictional materials can also have a powerful impact if they are presented in believable, true-to-life fashion and if they line up with the receptors' felt needs.

The Bible consists of high-impact literature — largely biographical with many true-to-life fictional stories (e.g., parables) — and is constantly addressed to the real felt needs of its readers. Good biographical and true-to-life fictional writing often approximates the impact of drama for those who read well.

Radio and cassettes have an advantage over print in that the presentation is vocal rather than written. It is usually easier, for example, for a receptor to be drawn into the action of a drama presented vocally than one presented in writing. Unlike print, however, radio presentations cannot ordinarily be listened to over and over again for close analysis. The use of cassettes solves this problem. (See Sogaard 1975 for an expert treatment of the value of cassettes.) Like print and lectures, these media are particularly effective at disseminating information and heightening awareness. They are, like lectures, somewhat more effective than print in conveying an emotive quality, however.

They are nonpersonal (though not impersonal), in the sense that listeners cannot see the person speaking. These media seem, however, to engage the listeners' imagination to a greater extent than other media. And this fact makes them comparatively more effective than other media for most purposes. For example, repeated listening to the same communicator plus the imagination of the listener can invest the person with a very attractive personality—sometimes even more than that derived from listening in person to a lecturer. This fact can result in very high impact and influence if the messages are relevant. If, however, the hearer knows personally the one on the other side of the microphone, the impact can be even more powerful.

Radio and cassettes are capable of a variety of uses. When lectures or sermons are conveyed via these media, the limitations of monologue (see chapter 5) come into play. That is, radio and cassette lectures suffer the same limitations as other lectures when used to attempt to motivate people to change. The fact that these media can "create" a more attractive personality for the communicator, however, may give them greater impact than the same lecture given in person might convey.

Discussions, debates, interviews, and the like, especially if done creatively, can also have their impact enhanced by the imaginations of the listeners. In these, as in all else presented via radio or cassette, the key is the creativity of the presentation. Uncreative presentations can deaden the hearers' imaginations just as surely as creative presentations can stimulate them.

Radio stations in the United States are getting a lot of "mileage" these days through "talk" programing. These are programs in which listeners are able to ask questions and/or make comments directly to those behind the microphones via telephone. This approach, if handled by an able and creative host, is very effective in at least partly overcoming one of the major drawbacks of extending media—the lack of immediate feedback. Though only a limited number of callers can actually speak with the radio host, their interactions often enable listeners to identify with the host and in this way feel their needs being met to a greater extent than would ordinarily happen via radio. Even cassettes of such radio and telephone interactions can be helpful to those not able to hear the original interaction.

The way advertisers are able to use radio to sell their products illustrates well the effects of creativity. They have found radio a good medium for utilizing the power of suggestion as a means of moving people toward new options. Unfortunately, Christian broadcasters have seldom been so creative. In areas where people have a choice of what to listen to, uncreative Christian programing tends to attract only those who already agree with the message being presented. Those who disagree turn the program off. Christian radio broadcasting has proven its effectiveness as a device for consolidating already-held Christian positions but has been much less effective in winning people to new positions.

As noted above, exceptions to this generalization occur in parts of the world where radio is new or serves a kind of lifeline function as virtually the only connection with the outside world. In such situations the stimulus provided by new information, especially that from a respected source, combines with the receptors' felt needs to produce high impact for change. Also, as with all public and media communication, the potential for high impact can be increased enormously if, in addition to the communications via the media, there is person-to-person contact between the source and the receptors.

Television, video, and film have most of the advantages and disadvantages of radio plus a visual dimension. They are particularly good for presenting drama and involving the viewer in the action taking place on the screen. Documentary-type programs appealing to the interests of the audience can also be very effective via these media. Worship services come across well for the highly motivated, though it often takes very high motivation to stay interested in the preaching part. For the highly motivated learner, videos can be used profitably, especially if they are used along with written materials.

There is high potential for a kind of *pseudopersonal* involvement between communicators and receptors through these media if the presentations are done in such a way that boredom is avoided. When lectures are presented, such things as eye contact, appearance of sincerity, and other attractive personal mannerisms can produce relatively high impact even for life change if the viewer is open to the message. Enough variety needs to be present to fight boredom, however, or major segments of the audience will "tune out."

As with all extending media, these media are only as effective as the fit between what is presented and what the medium is good at. Visual media are particularly suited to drama and entertainment and much less suited to lecture-type presentations, except for highly motivated viewers. In such lecture-type presentations, there may be a considerable enhancement of the viewers' feeling of personal closeness to the speaker, however. This comes by virtue of the fact that most of the pictures are close-ups, giving viewers the feeling that they are sitting closer to the speaker than would be possible if they were actually present at the event being filmed. Beyond this advantage, however, lectures on film suffer most of the same limitations as lectures not on film. And it is easier to get bored with a lecture on film than with one attended in person.

Though drama can be effectively presented via these media, it suffers communicationally if it is not really well done, with considerable attention to every detail of setting, costumes, gesture, and the like. And doing drama on film with adequate attention to such details is usually a very expensive proposition. In comparison, drama presented via radio/cassette requires much less attention to detail and, in addition, seems to have greater appeal to the hearers' imagination than visual presentations. In countries like the United States, where the prestige of TV is much higher than that of radio, Christian communicators may feel the extra expense and effort are required just to get an adequate hearing. In places where radio is the medium of choice, however, the extra effort and expense are seldom justified. And even in America, when the aim is to reach Christians, radio, is usually a better choice, since many American Christians listen frequently to radio, especially in their automobiles.

A pervasive problem with visual media derives from the fact that they are so widely used for entertainment purposes. Since the medium of communication is interpreted along with the messages being presented, the unconscious expectation of entertainment tends to intrude into the interpretation of any serious presentation. That is, those accustomed to expecting entertainment when they watch these media often find it very difficult to maintain a proper attention level and respond appropriately to serious material. As public television stations have discovered to their dismay, serious presentations are seldom widely watched unless external factors, such as widespread interest in the issues addressed, motivate people to watch them.

In the United States, Christian preaching (or other programing for that matter) is seldom watched or listened to by those not already convinced. In parts of the world where there is little or no competition from secular programing, however, the situation is quite different. (See Engel 1979 for more detailed treatment of this subject.)

The *credibility of communications via mass media is high in the minds of average Americans*. So is the credibility of persons who have a broadcast or who have written a book. This is probably because most assume that there is more quality control than actually exists over what is broadcast or published. But when preachers or authors who are slick enough to raise the necessary funds can get access to these vehicles whether or not they have anything worth communicating, one must question the basis for such credibility. It is hard to escape the impression that many Christian communicators are using these vehicles simply to enhance their own credibility (and even their fortunes) rather than to genuinely help those to whom they appeal. And the price, especially for television, often seems unjustifiably high when compared to the results.

From time to time there is discussion of the potential impact of Christian television personalities on American politics. Those who study media audiences tend to conclude that their influence is fairly minimal. The question in my mind is, however, whether the activities of such people do, in fact, affect the behavior of their viewers more than the results of audience research would allow for. If so, why?

As I see it, the basic communication principle that such television personalities exploit is the fact that whenever a body of receptors feels a need virtually any communicational means will serve fairly well. These speakers compensate for the weakness of television as a medium of persuasion by appealing to a set of needs felt by a fairly homogeneous audience that tends to be quite fearful of the world in general and of American secular society in particular and quite open to promises of spiritual solutions from convincing leaders. The credibility enhancement provided the television personalities by their ability to use (and to increase their use of) television seems to be a major factor in their ability to sway their audience and to gain their financial support.

Although there may be a modicum of behavioral change brought about in the receptors by such communication, the major impact would seem to be the consolidation of the group and the enhancement and deepening of commitments already important to them. The television phenomenon, then, becomes the rallying point for this group, the symbol of their group identity, and the means for raising the funds necessary for keeping the television programs going. Given the felt needs of this group and the intensity of their fear of secular approaches to the problems involved, such communicators need do little more than maintain their credibility and visibility to assure themselves of a hearing.

Perhaps my attitude toward the use of extending media in Christian communication focuses too much on the negative side of things. This is because I know they will continue to be used, and I'd like them to be used with more awareness than we often find. For there is a one-sidedness to extending media that is frightening and often (consciously or unconsciously) exploited. For most audiences, media communicators do not have to prove they really have anything to contribute as long as they sound or look sincere or write persuasively. There is no opportunity for immediate feedback requiring adjustment and, therefore, great possibility (a) for communicators to believe that what they say must be correct merely because it is they who have said it and (b) for receptors to uncritically accept whatever is said on the assumption that the communicators must be trustworthy or they would not be allowed to present such a message via television, radio, or print.

Even as I sit here and write, the thought frightens me that people might accept things I say uncritically and damage their ministry thereby. My fear that those who use such media will mislead extends to an awareness of my own tendency to pass on uncritically things whether or not I can prove them, simply because it is unlikely that I will be challenged on such issues.

Beyond such fears, however, my cautiousness concerning Christian use of extending media derives from at least three sources: my respect for the personalness of God's relationship and interaction with us; my respect for the media themselves; and a sense of disappointment over what now exists in much of how Christians use the media. For there would seem to be too much commitment to putting into the mass media what already exists (and is often found wanting) in the churches. Yet the potential is there for creatively producing materials that are specifically suited to these media and to the audiences they serve.

It is a shame, for example, that drama, a vehicle admirably suited to both audio and visual media, is often looked down on (or at least underutilized) by Christians who say they would like to reach non-Christians. Contemporary music and dance, vehicles that the world uses with great effectiveness, are often most condemned by those who profess to be most concerned about winning non-Christians. The conviction that God has ordained monologue preaching and that he wants all good preachers to get their sermons onto radio/cassette and/or television/video seems to be so pervasive in such circles that little of genuine merit and high potential for constructive life-change gets created. Yet one radio drama, such as the Pacific Garden Mission's long-running "Unshackled" or the Lutherans' "This Is the Life," is probably worth more communicationally than hundreds of sermons, both for non-Christians and for Christians. Perhaps Christian "soap operas" ought to replace many preachy Bible studies. And the gospel message via Christian rock over a secular radio station probably says more intelligibly about Christ to certain audiences than all the sermons ever delivered. Even for Christians, as Charles Wesley has taught us, more teaching is gotten across via music than from the pulpit—if the musical vehicle is appealing to the audience.

The power of messages sent via the extending media is both great and fearful, but the potential for misuse is high. Media must be used with maximum concern for the impact on the receptors of the messages so channeled, lest the personalness of the true Christian message be compromised by the lack of personalness of many (perhaps most) messages presented via extending media. Much more serious attention must be given to suiting the presentation of the message both to the intended receptors and to the strengths and weaknesses of the medium chosen. In this regard the audience-analysis researches of Engel (1979) and his former colleagues and students at Wheaton College need to be taken much more seriously.

As mentioned above, the Bible, though in print, is the kind of literature that maximizes the fact that God's communicational activity is person-oriented and focused on behavioral change. It is a life-related casebook (see Kraft 1979a:198-202) rather than an impersonal, intellectual, academic textbook (like most written expositions of the Bible). It thus demonstrates by its nature, even in a mass-medium format, the kind of approach to communication that God endorses by enhancing the ability of receptors to respond personally and behaviorally.

My one desire for those who use mass media, whether electronic or print, would be that they *learn to use their media the way God in the Bible uses print*. This would involve a considerable reduction in the use of those vehicles that depersonalize and intellectualize the message (e.g., monologue, dead ritual, academic and technical writing) with a corresponding increase in the use of vehicles that increase personal interaction and identification and that stimulate behavioral growth (e.g., life involvement, live ritual, drama, biographical casebook-writing). In addition, the combination of public or media communication with more personal methods, such as life involvement and small group dialogue, can go a long way toward maximizing the best aspects of each technique.

Translation as Communication

There is one additional vehicle, usually presented in print form, that can well be treated here, especially since it is both so widely used and widely misunderstood in Christian circles. *Many have a very mechanistic view of Bible translation.* They do not see translation as it should be seen, as a form of communication, but rather as a mechanical process for preserving as much as possible of the ancient text on which our faith is based. Furthermore, they tend to see this preservation as largely related to the linguistic forms of that text rather than to the meanings that God intended to convey through those forms. They get too tightly tied to the vehicles through which God transmitted his messages and often end up with translations the meanings of which are hijacked by archaic, overliteral, overtechnical, or otherwise obstructive language.

Translation is, however, properly seen as a form of communication by means of which messages once presented in other languages in other times may come to be understood in as nearly equivalent form as possible in new languages and different times. A good translator is a good interpreter of the original meanings into contemporary language for the purpose of stimulating an effect today as equivalent as possible to that originally stimulated by the original communicators (see Nida and Taber 1969; Kraft 1979a).

The purpose of translation is not a mechanical one. And translators who simply translate word for word rather than concept for concept are not being accurate, they are being irresponsible. We would not tolerate that kind of "translation" on the part of one who was attempting to interpret a lecture or conversation by a speaker of a foreign language. A literal translation, like any other poor communication, allows the vehicle of transmission to so obtrude into the transmission that the meanings constructed by the receptors are affected negatively and often badly altered.

A perception of irrelevance is, for example, a frequent response to Bible reading, not because the material is irrelevant, but because it is translated badly. Should we blame young people if they reject Christianity because they feel it to be generations if not centuries out-of-date? Or should we blame the translators and users of poor translations who have done their job irresponsibly? The linguistic and other vehicles used by God to communicate his messages in the original contexts were as relevant as the messages themselves. They fit God's goal, the content of his messages, and the contexts in which his messages were presented. We should imitate God in this.

With respect to Bible translations, the God of today is not honored by a translation that gives the impression that he has been dead for centuries (such as the King James Version). Nor is he honored by translations that give the impression that only scholars can understand him (such as the American Standard Version, New American Standard Bible, Revised Standard Version, and to some extent New International Version). The Bible was originally in the language of the common people, language that required no academic degrees, no knowledge of history to understand. Translations in that kind of English (e.g., the Good News Bible, Phillips' New Testament, the Living Bible, and the New English Bible) fit God's messages most effectively into the vehicles that are today most like those he originally chose. Christian communicators do well to imitate God in their use of Bible translations as well as in every other aspect of their attempts to communicate his messages.

The Main Point

Since the vehicle employed is interpreted along with the other aspects of the communication in the construction of the meanings, communicators must give solid attention to the fit between the intended message and the vehicle chosen to convey it. *Vehicles are not good or bad in and of themselves.* But when the fit is bad, an inappropriate vehicle—like Saul's armor on David—virtually assures that the battle will be lost. Communicational vehicles must, therefore, be studied with a view toward ascertaining just how they affect messages. And some of the vehicles (notably preaching and mass media) frequently employed by Christians are to be suspected of often obtruding into and distorting the messages entrusted to them.

10

The Part Played by Context

Five Settings for Witness

Imagine yourself presenting the following message to an appropriate group of receptors in several settings, which we shall spell out below.

The Message. The receptors should seriously evaluate the direction in which their lives are moving and consider the invitation of God to change their perspective and to commit themselves to him.

Questions to ask as you imagine each setting:

1. How would I introduce the subject in that setting?

2. What kinds of perceptions will be in the receptors' minds concerning me, my message, and the appropriateness of the message to that place and time?

3. What kind of vocabulary should I use?

4. What may I assume concerning the receptors, given the fact that they have come to that place at that time?

5. What are the advantages and disadvantages of that setting for presenting this message, and how may they be utilized or overcome?

Setting One. You are in church on Sunday morning. Though the congregation is small, you are standing behind the pulpit with a carefully prepared set of notes in front of you. The congregation has just sung a hymn and now looks expectantly toward you for the sermon. Imagine how you would answer the above questions.

Setting Two. Change the scene in your mind. Keep the message the same, but move with a few friends to a table in a dimly lit restaurant with soft music playing and scantily clad waitresses scurrying from table to table serving drinks and meals. Now how would you answer the above questions? What assumptions are likely to differ, and how should you adjust to those differences?

Setting Three. Next move your participants and message to a private home in an urban setting in which the neighborhood is engulfed in a riot. It is nighttime. Police and fire sirens, gunfire, and the explosion of small bombs can be heard from where you sit, and the reflections of nearby housefires dance on the walls. How would your communicational interaction proceed in such a setting in the face of imminent tragedy? How would you answer the above questions? What assumptions would guide you?

Setting Four. Now flash to another home setting. There is no apparent emergency in this suburban home. The group is a family including middle-aged, affluent parents and their teenage children. They are nominal members of your church, and you have called on them unexpectedly out of concern for their spiritual well-being. What answers would you give to the above questions to enable you to deal effectively with this situation?

Setting Five. Finally, imagine yourself presenting your message via the lens of a television camera transmitting via TV screens to an unknown audience. How would you deal with the above questions in that circumstance? What should differ when an impersonal vehicle comes between you and your audience?

The Influence of Context/Setting

Is the message presented in each of these contexts really the same message? Yes and no. The communicators' intent is that the message be the same, and they would likely use much of the same vocabulary in each situation. But if the presentation in, say, the restaurant were exactly the same in form as in the church, there would be so much static created that the result might well be perceived as quite a different message.

The reason is, of course, that the context or setting is a complex kind of vehicle that, like the vehicles treated in chapter 9, affects the message as it conveys it. Or to put this another way, receptors interpret in such a way that the information derived from the context influences the way in which they understand the main message. Such information frequently enhances the main message. Often, however, it is perceived as distorting it.

Receptors interpret contexts as well as messages sent within those contexts. And communicators depend on the context to supply a good bit of information that they, then, do not need to explain. If a person suddenly exclaims, "Look at those trunks!" they depend on the receptor's ability to interpret the context to provide the unstated information concerning just which kind of trunks are in focus. If the setting were a railway station, the receptors would look for one kind of trunk. At the beach they would look for another kind, while near the elephant pen at the zoo they would look for still another kind. In each case it is the physical context or setting in which the statement is made that enables the interpreter to understand the command correctly.

In each of the five settings in focus above, we also have the influence of a physical setting affecting the interpretation of the message. The most radical influence of context is seen in the riot situation in which both communicator and receptors are likely to perceive that their conversation and even their lives may be terminated at any time. The urgency of the situation, then, impinges strongly on their consciousness as they talk and deepens the level of their interaction. The communicator is likely to choose the words more carefully, to focus on the main point more, and in all ways possible to dispense with formalities and niceties in order to get the major points across in the shortest possible time. The receptors, then, will likely evaluate the message more highly than in a less disrupted circumstance, since they will assume that only very important matters will be raised by a communicator whose life is in danger. Is it a different message? Yes and no.

In church this message is so predictable that we can speak of the sharpness of the message being blunted by the fact that it occurred in that context. The message is expected, predictable, a part of the commonly agreed-on stereotype of messages that occur in that context. But what about in the restaurant? The message in that context is unexpected enough to attract attention. But it might also be judged to be quite inappropriate unless, of course, the receptors had raised the issue and the discussion never exceeded the bounds of private conversation (i.e., never became a public presentation). If, however, the communicator raises the matter without the permission of the receptors and/or deals with it inappropriately, the witness of love might well be interpreted as an exhibition of arrogance and condemnation.

People interpret by looking for the expected. When the unexpected occurs, they are forced to work harder at the interpretation process. They often look for subsurface motives and conclude that those of the communicator are much like their own would be if they were speaking that way in that context. Such an interpretation, however, does not ordinarily lead to openness on the part of the receptor if the setting seems inappropriate.

As noted in chapter 9, people ordinarily expect entertainment from television programs. This is not surprising, given the preponderance of television usage for this purpose. This is probably the reason why only the most entertaining of Christian efforts gets much of an audience and those who do tune in are almost entirely Christians already (see Engel 1979). *The medium often shouts, "Inappropriate!" even as the preacher whispers, "God loves you."*

How Do Contexts Establish Meaning?

Contexts/settings, like other vehicles, and the words, gestures, and so forth that flow through them, mean something because they are interpreted to mean something. And, as with all other symbols, the interpretations are those agreed on by the community of interpreters. There is nothing in the objective differences between, say, the church and the restaurant that compels the great difference in meaning attributed to a given message delivered in those settings. The compulsion lies in the people who attach their socially conditioned subjective interpretations to those contexts.

The context of a communicational event, then, becomes a major component in the participants' interpretation of its meaning. That is, some portion of the information that is the raw material for communicational interaction is derived from the context. As illustrated above, the kind of information available is "extracted" from the context, provided the context is interpretable by the receptors. Children or foreigners who have not yet learned the social agreements concerning the inappropriateness of Christian witness in a bar would probably not derive the kind of information that would disturb them if such a witness were made in that setting. Nor might a recent convert who has not been conditioned (as have large numbers of American Christians of older generations) to be negative toward that kind of music, dance, attire, and so forth.

Contexts, like words, gestures, and the like, both facilitate and restrict the messages they are used to convey, again on the basis of social agreements. As with all other vehicles of communication (see chapter 9), they serve best when they are least noticed. And they are least noticed when they are considered to be most appropriate. Receptors intuitively interpret the fit between message and context as either appropriate or inappropriate, either facilitating the flow of the message or interfering with it. When a context is perceived as interfering with a message, the overall message that comes through is quite likely to be different from the one intended.

We may assume such to be the case if a Christian message is presented in a bar (unless in a conversational style and at the invitation of the receptors). In the riot situation envisioned above, the feeling of appropriateness might well be enhanced by the context. Though if the communicator were perceived to be talking when they should be doing something else, the perception could go the other way as well. The suburban home context could, likewise, either enhance or disrupt the flow of the message. If, however, relational components are added to the situation, such as a good personal relationship between the communicator and the receptors plus a feeling on the part of the receptors that the communicator really cares, the chances are greatly increased for the effective communication of Christian messages in that setting. The influence of television on Christian communications was discussed in chapter 9.

With respect to the church service, another factor comes into play. There is no doubt about the appropriateness of the church context for the message we have designated. But the fit between that context and that message is often too predictable, too expected, for the combination to carry much impact. Predictability has a stifling effect on communication if one focuses on the information value of the message only. But if we recognize that people need the security of predictability (such as that expressed in habit and ritual) at least as much as the challenges that come via new messages, we are better prepared to evaluate such a situation realistically.

In a church situation the context ordinarily overrides the sermon, as it were, and turns the latter into a part of what can (and should) be a very meaningful ritual by means of which group solidarity and commitment are expressed and reinforced. In that case, as in many others, the context contributes more to the overall interpretation of a communicational event than does the message itself.

Another way of dealing with this factor is to focus on the difference between the amount of information derived from the message itself and the amount derived from the context. The proportions differ from event to event, from setting to setting. In greeting rituals, for example, it is considered strange (even impolite) for one to respond to "How are you?" as if the question were really asking about the details of one's health. As native speakers of English, we reflexively interpret the context information telling us that this is a ritual. So we answer, "Fine," whether we feel fine or not. The intent of the interaction is not in the words at all, but in the context. This is what Edward T. Hall calls a *high-context* situation (1976:91ff) in which a participant needs to know the meaning of the context even more than the meaning of the verbal message in order to participate effectively.

A *low-context* situation, then, is one in which the bulk of the information necessary for accurate interpretation is on the surface of the message itself. Little, if any, understanding of the context is required of the receptor. An extreme example of low-contexting of a message would be the way a parent or teacher might construct a message for unindoctrinated children because it is assumed that they know little or no background information and, therefore, need everything made explicit. High-contexting assumes that the communicator and the receptor are already on the same wavelength and that, therefore, the receptor needs very little contextual information made explicit.

Marriage partners and close friends frequently high context much of what they say to each other. Say, for example, a wife's first words to her husband as he returns home at the end of a day were something like, "Did you bring it?" She is assuming he will remember whatever they had been discussing several hours previously and be able to answer her question without the need for further information. That is a high-context question, since it requires that the recipient be able to fill in the necessary information to interpret the word "it" from his memory of the context within which the discussion of the item referred to took place.

High contexting often occurs among people who are used to interacting primarily with the members of their own in-group. Christians, for example, use a large number of words and phrases with quite specific meanings, assuming that others will understand them in the same way we do. Among such are *sin, the cross, to be saved* or *born again, to accept Jesus as one's personal Savior,* and multitudes of others.

In relating to people outside our in-group, we often assume too much concerning the amount and type of contextual information available to our hearers and fail to (a) use the receptor's language and (b) adequately explain expressions that work fine within our in-group but become uninterpretable, high-context symbols when used outside of it.

The Bible, couched as it is in the languages and cultures of other peoples who lived in other times and places, contains much high-context material. The task of the biblical interpreter is, therefore, to attempt to discover the cultural agreements in terms of which the original communicators and receptors interpreted both their contexts and the messages they presented and received within them. Our task as interpreters of the Bible is helped by the fact that the biblical authors deal mainly with areas in which human experience (including its contexts) is quite similar from society to society. But there are still many (noncrucial) matters that are not clear to us because we cannot seem to unpack enough of the information buried in the ancient contexts. (See below and Kraft 1979a:134-43 for further discussion of the implications of contextual factors in biblical interpretation.)

Unwary interpreters are often led astray by attempting to understand a biblical utterance as if it were spoken in their context rather than in that of another people in another society. This is what the young lady did who began to pray sitting on her bed with the sheet pulled over her head after reading 1 Corinthians 11:5, 13 in the King James Version. So also generations of Western interpreters have focused on the sex issue in the David and Bathsheba story (2 Sam. 11-12), rather than the issue of how a powerful person uses power. The latter issue is clearly the focal point for the original participants (see Nathan's parable and prophecy in 2 Sam. 12). When, however, we read an account such as this, we automatically interpret it as if it had happened in our own cultural context. So we supply contextual information from our context rather than from that in which the event occurred. And the author's intended meaning is missed and/or distorted.

To focus on the place of contexting within a given communicational situation, note the story of the woman at the well in John 4. In verses 5 and 6a, the author low-contexts by explaining where Jesus was (in Sychar in Samaria, sitting by Jacob's well). He assumes (in high-context fashion) that Jacob, Joseph, Samaria, Judea, and Galilee are known to the hearers, though he explains (in low-context fashion) that Joseph was Jacob's son and that Samaria was on the way from Judea to Galilee. He does not explain, however, why Jesus "had to go through Samaria" (v. 4), contrary to the ordinary practice of the rabbis, or why the woman came to the well at noon, contrary to the ordinary custom. These are high-context items probably either clear to the original hearers or judged by the author to be irrelevant to his point. When Jesus asks the woman for a drink, then, we (interpreting from the perspective of our cultural experience) might well wonder why he didn't dip the water out for himself. The author doesn't explain, since all his hearers would have known (a) that a man does not ordinarily dip water for himself and (b) that he probably had no pot or bowl with which to dip. The author does explain, though, that the woman was surprised because Jesus broke the taboo against interaction between Jews and Samaritans. And so forth.

The point is that some of the information needed by the interpreter/ receptor lies in the message, while some lies in the context. In a high-context situation or a high-context utterance within a situation, then, the majority of the necessary information is derived from the interpretation of the context, with a lesser amount derivable from the message itself. In a low-context situation or utterance, a major part of the necessary information is made explicit in the message itself. The following figure is one way of depicting these facts. The "seesaw" line is intended to show that when the information from one source is high, then that from the other source is correspondingly lower.

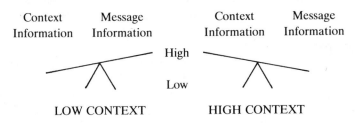

Figure 6. High Versus Low Context (see Kraft 1979a: 140)

Contexts still mean, then, what they are interpreted to mean. But the part context plays in a given communicational interaction differs with respect to both the type and the quantity of information it contributes to the interaction. The context may be judged to be appropriate or inappropriate to the message. If appropriate, the fit between message and context ordinarily facilitates communication, though the higher the predictability of the relationship, the more likely the interaction is to be interpreted as ritual (e.g., greetings) rather than as stimulus to change.

Certain contexts restrict or otherwise inhibit the flow of certain messages. Wise communicators evaluate the fit between their messages and the potential context and refrain from attempting to wed those messages to the wrong setting.

Those matters that both communicator and receptor assume without stating them may be spoken of as *information embedded in the context or implicit information.* When we communicate, we expect our receptors to know or deduce such information. When a translation from another language and culture is well done, it makes explicit as much of this implicit information as is necessary to enable the contemporary receptors to understand substantially as the original receptors did. If this is not done, the contemporary receptors will supply the necessary information from their own culture (rather than from the original culture) and interpret wrongly.

Receptors will always supply enough implicit information to enable them to make sense of the communication, whether that information is accurate to the original author's intent. That implicit information will, then, be interpreted along with the explicit information presented in the message and constructed into the meanings internalized. As discussed above, then, the percentage of information embedded in the context is sometimes higher, sometimes lower than that carried by the message. Wise communicators learn to arrive at and employ whatever balance is appropriate for their receptors.

Choosing and Using Contexts

If the fit between message and context is so important, *what considerations should enter into the way we choose and use contexts?* Can we afford to allow this aspect of communication to simply happen? If we do, we may have given up much of our ability to guide the communicational events in which we participate.

With respect to choosing a context, I would like to raise the question of "ownership." Certain contexts are perceived as "belonging" to people. The church belongs to God, the pastor, and the church members, doesn't it? Can an outsider, one with no commitment to any of these "owners," feel at home there? What does a feeling of being surrounded by other people on their turf do to the communication?

There are, of course, several kinds of contexts and several degrees of ownership. I have so far focused largely on physical contexts. These are easily possessed by groups and even by individuals. There are also, however, nonmaterial contexts (or frames of reference) such as language, culture, even social class, and the like. These and even individual words are frequently perceived as belonging to those who use them.

There is a communicational difference between an interaction that takes place on our turf and one that takes place on theirs. Imagine the difference in the perspective of the above-mentioned suburban family when the pastor visits them at home from when they attend "the pastor's" church. The pastor is perceived to be in control in "his" place but a guest in their home. The power relationship is different, even though for some the pastor's status would tip the scales even in their home. Nevertheless, the message embodied in the fact that a person of high status visited them on their turf is usually a powerful one, as long as that person does not act (as, alas, some pastors do) as if even a parishioner's home belongs to the pastor.

There is, likewise, *a communicational difference between interactions that use the receptor's preferred language or vocabulary and those in another language or one pervaded by jargon.* Pastors and other Christians often try to witness to non-Christians in language (often theological language) that belongs to Christians rather than to those we seek to win. People have a kind of possessiveness toward their familiar way of speaking, an attitude toward the linguistic matrix in which the communication is couched that regards it as either "ours" or "theirs." And this attitude pervasively affects whatever communication takes place in that matrix. The use of in-group language with those of another group is seldom attractive to them.

Whether it is the linguistic or the physical context, people tend to respond best when they feel flattered. With perhaps a few exceptions it is the use of the receptor's language that will be perceived as flattering. Wise communicators learn the preferred vocabulary of their receptors and make judicious (i.e., not showy) use of it to win a positive response from them.

With respect to *physical context,* however, there is more than one possibility. I have alluded to the fact that people of lower status often respond favorably when visited by people of higher status. I would also predict a favorable response if higher-status persons invite their receptors to their homes. Between people of equal status, though, I would expect communication (especially that aimed at Christian witness) to be more favorably perceived on the receptors' turf. In any event, both perceived proprietary rights and status relationships need to be carefully analyzed if such factors are to be effectively employed for communicational purposes.

The public or private nature of the physical context is another factor of relevance to communicational effectiveness. One problem with church communication is that the facilities are perceived as *public and, therefore, cold.* Private, warm facilities are perceived more favorably as settings for small group or individual communication. A public place such as a restaurant may also be perceived as warm, especially if the booth or table is perceived as private. The private, warm activity of eating together also plays an important part in the perception of that kind of public setting.

God made use of such factors as these when he chose to communicate with humanity on human turf, in human language, and mostly in warm, private contexts. Something important was added to Jesus' message to Zacchaeus by the fact that Jesus was willing to use Zacchaeus's home (as well as his language) as the context (Luke 19:1-10). Likewise with Jesus' relationship with Lazarus, Mary, and Martha. The uninhabited places and mountains were carefully chosen by our Lord as contexts amenable for instructing those close to him. Public places with a mixture of audiences were, however, adequate for making announcements of condemnation (e.g., Matt. 23). *Jesus chose the context to suit his communicational purpose.* Christian communicators can and should study these aspects of Jesus' ministry and imitate them.

We are not, however, always free to choose the most amenable context for the messages we seek to present. Often we are forced to make do with a crowded room when we would have preferred one with more space, a formal setting with fixed seats facing front when an informal setting with movable seats would have been better, a noisy setting in a public place when we desire quiet and privacy. At such times questions of use and possible adaptation arise.

The trick is to keep oneself from being captured by physical and/or nonphysical contexts that cause the interaction between context information and message information to be inappropriate and that (see below) cause static in the minds of the receptors. Do we, for example, allow ourselves to be perceived as distant and cold because we position ourselves behind a desk, table, or pulpit rather than planning our use of the physical context in such a way that we will be perceived as close and warm? Or do we allow ourselves to be perceived as irrelevant and scholarly because we regularly employ "theological" words such as justification, holiness, conversion, belief, and the like rather than contemporary, popularly used terms that would more effectively communicate the biblical concepts? Or have we adopted an inflexible, formal or performance style of speaking that contexts our messages quite inappropriately in nonformal (and probably most formal) interactions?

As Hall points out (1959, 1966), "space speaks." So does furniture. They speak because they are interpreted by receptors. Rooms, furniture, distance, height, posture, and the like are to be used by communicators to enhance their efforts, not to be allowed to cripple them. Wise communicators give solid attention to the type of setting in which they work, including the arrangement of furniture, the distance between themselves and their receptors, their posture, and so forth. An otherwise fairly formal setting can be quite deformalized if the communicator sits on a table or stands beside or in front of a podium rather than standing behind the table or a pulpit. Such use of the spatial context is likely to enhance the communication. Most counselors now recognize that sitting with nothing between counselor and client is more effective than sitting with a desk between them. Even many doctors have discovered that sitting by a patient's bedside has a more positive influence on the healing process than standing above the patient. See Hall (1959, 1966) for more detailed treatments of these factors.

Detechnicalizing the language we use can enable us to make more effective use of the linguistic context. Given the place and importance of receptors in the communication process, it is nothing short of foolish for us as Christian communicators to tie ourselves to technical or antique language on the assumption that biblical concepts can only be communicated adequately via certain English words and phrases. It is not those English words and phrases that are "biblical" but the concepts that underlie them. And being true to the God who poured himself into the effective communication of the biblical message demands that we use the contexts and vehicles at our disposal to bring those concepts to our receptors.

We should not require people to learn a "sacred" vocabulary that is not their own. When that is done, the paramessage that comes across (and, unfortunately, often obscures the main message) is that there is sacredness or magic in the technical and/or antique words and phrases that are used. Jargon words and phrases such as justification, blood of Christ, salvation, born again, be saved, and the like often obscure more than they reveal because they tend to be revered as if they are valuable in and of themselves rather than used as vehicles for messages that lie beyond themselves. Such reverence for words produces context features that tend to direct the interpreter's attention away from the relevance and applicability of the message and toward the ritual nature of interactions that employ such noncontemporary and nonpopular vehicles.

Queen Victoria's complaint about William Gladstone, one of the greatest orators of nineteenth-century England (referred to in chap. 5), reflects a perception that the style of presentation was inappropriate to the nature of the interaction. When this happens, such contexting has the same kind of distorting influence on the main message as the misuse of space or language. Effective communicators learn to suit their style to the situation. Many pastors, teachers, and others used to speaking in public, however, like Gladstone, develop a preachy or pontificating manner that they employ even in interpersonal contexts. This is detrimental to their ministries.

Context and Biblical Interpretation

Interpreting the Bible is as much a communicational matter as any of the other areas we have been dealing with. Two dimensions of this subject are important to us.

The first concern is to observe, analyze, and learn from the way communication took place within biblical contexts. Chapter 2 and subsequent references to God's communicative activities provide a start in this direction (see also Kraft 1973a and b, 1979a and b). Much more can, however, be done.

One assumption underlying this volume is that we in our day ought to attempt to imitate in our communicational activities the dynamics that we observe in biblical contexts. There are, I believe, communicational as well as spiritual reasons why one after another of the biblical personages (whether prophets, kings, apostles, or our Lord himself) had great impact on those to whom they addressed their messages. We are also expected to be dynamically equivalent (see Kraft 1979a) communicators in our day. This whole volume is aimed toward that result.

The second concern stems from the question, *What part do the biblical contexts play in the communication interruption process that takes place when Americans read or hear the Bible read?* This problem is, of course, technically labeled hermeneutics. It is, however, subject to the same rules applicable to any other communicational activity.

The cultural contexts of the Bible are at least as important to biblical interpretation as are the words and sentences. The problem is that we don't have as much information as we need concerning the contexts to make sure interpretive judgments. One difficulty is that much of what we would like to know is lost in the mists of history. Another is that biblical interpretation is a cross-cultural problem, like that faced by those who communicate with people of other languages and societies. We are, therefore, not in on the agreements that provided the basis on which the original participants arrived at their interpretations, unless we have learned the biblical languages and cultures.

The principles relating to the importance and use of context information in biblical interpretation are the same as those we have been discussing for communication in general (see Kraft 1979a:134-43 for a more detailed treatment of this important area).

Noise or Static

Contexts typically contain distracting or disrupting factors. These factors are often referred to as "noise" or "static." Noise may be transmitted by communicators as paramessages while they are transmitting the central message; result from other activities going on in parts of the context external to any of the interactants; or be internal to the receptor. In any case, such noise and static often play a significant part in the interpretation of communication.

When a communicator wears loud or very informal clothing in a formal situation, the receptors are likely to be distracted from the main message by an impression of inappropriateness. A tone of voice perceived to be inappropriate (e.g., a "preacher's tone," shouts when the subject matter calls for calmness, or laughter when gravity is appropriate) often becomes static, as do an accent, mispronounced words, strange postures, incongruous gestures, and the like.

There are, furthermore, likely to be factors in the external setting that constitute noise. The hum of an air conditioner, the hammering of workers, passing traffic, bells or sirens, children crying or fidgeting, a radio playing, even silence or the consciousness of another's presence can function as static. Often the simple fact of a given person's presence functions to restrict such factors as topics discussed, language used, or other aspects of the interaction. In addition, people who frequently move, speak, or otherwise draw attention to themselves and away from the main message produce static. I have spoken of warm and cold space. These and other characteristics of the spatial context can cause static if they are judged to be inappropriate to the interaction. When the furniture is arranged strangely or the communicator stands too close to (or too far away from) the receptors, static is likely to be perceived.

Many things are going on inside the receptor as well, and these often intrude into communicational interactions as noise. A receptor may have a pressing concern and be unable to squelch the tendency to ponder or worry over that concern while supposedly listening to a message. Or a receptor may not be feeling well.

Whatever the cause, again the receptor's perception is key. *For noise or static is in the mind of the receptor.* Nothing is noise that is not perceived (consciously or unconsciously) as noise. On the other hand, anything is noise that is perceived as disruptive of the communicational process. Although communicators cannot control everything that may be perceived as static, wise communicators do all they can to control at least the first two kinds of noise listed above.

If such control is ineffective, not infrequently the intended message is hijacked and the receptors come away with something quite different from what the communicator intended. Note, for example, what happens when singers who intend to communicate a message in the words of a song submit to the temptation to present the song expertly rather than communicatively. They might have been both expert and communicative. But if they give major attention to perfection of musical presentation, they will in the process make the words so subservient to the music that the resulting message communicates more concerning the expertise of the singers than of the intent of the lyrics. Pastors who submit to the temptation to be oratorical and/or to regularly use flowery language are likewise showing off rather than effectively communicating the message indicated by their words. In such cases it is the static created by the style chosen that changes the event from one focused on communication (as ordinarily construed) to one focused on performance (which, of course, is another kind of communication).

Application

Considerations of context are extremely important in the communicational process. Learning to observe, analyze, and adapt one's communicational efforts to the realities of the contexts within which one participates should, therefore, be a major focus of anyone who seeks to be an effective communicator. Though it is not possible to control all contextual factors, communicators are frequently able to gain greater control via careful analysis and to adapt effectively to many factors that lie beyond their control.

Jesus was a master at choosing and controlling the contexts in which he communicated. In entering human existence as a Jewish peasant, born to a devout Galilean carpenter, he, of course, chose a large number of the factors that would surround him. His ministry, then, is characterized by innumerable additional choices of place, time, and people to provide the matrices within which he functioned. He did not simply submit to chance. He took control of contextual factors as well as of all other parts of the communicational process. He regularly matched physical, social, linguistic, and other contextual factors to the messages he sought to convey. We who seek to imitate Jesus' example would do well first to study and then to follow his approach.

11

How Does an Effective
Communicator Operate?

Jesus, an Effective Communicator

Jesus chose his audience and in choosing "deselected" those of other groups. Once a woman from one of these other groups came to Jesus to ask him to heal her daughter. Jesus tried to dismiss her because she was not from his chosen audience, the Jews. "The woman was a Gentile, born in the region of Phoenicia in Syria. She begged Jesus to drive the demon out of her daughter. But Jesus answered, 'Let us first feed the children. It isn't right to take the children's food and throw it to the dogs'" (Mark 7:26-27).

John the Baptist and Jesus had different life-styles and, therefore, appealed communicationally to different groups. Jesus, however, was frustrated because the people of his day refused to respond to either style. They were, he contended, like groups of children playing who refuse to respond to each other's music. Then he says:

> When John came, he fasted and drank no wine, and everyone said, "He has a demon in him!" When the Son of Man came, he ate and drank, and everyone said, "Look at this man! He is a glutton and wine-drinker, a friend of tax collectors and other outcasts!" God's wisdom, however, is shown to be true by its results (Matt. 11:18-19).

Communicational effectiveness does not always result in the acceptance of the communicator's message, for receptors have wills and frequently choose to reject what they understand. When the message is understood, the communicational process is technically complete, though the goal of the communicator may or may not have been accomplished. In the passage that follows, note Jesus' success in bringing the rich young man to understand his message. But the story ends sadly when the message is rejected.

Once a man came to Jesus asking, "What good thing must I do to receive eternal life? . . ."

"Keep the commandments if you want to enter life. . . ."

"I have obeyed all these commandments," the young man replied. "What else do I need to do?"

Jesus said to him, "If you want to be perfect, go and sell all you have and give the money to the poor, and you will have riches in heaven; then come and follow me."

When the young man heard this, he went away sad, because he was very rich. (Matt. 19:16a, c, 17b, 20-22)

Throughout Jesus' ministry, his messages are characterized by their appropriateness to the situations within which he was working and especially to the people with whom he was dealing. He could be harsh with those who insisted on rejecting him no matter what he did, as in his tirade against the Jewish leaders in Matthew 23 with its oft-repeated refrain, "How terrible for you, teachers of the Law and Pharisees! You hypocrites!" (v. 13a, 15a, 23a, 25a, 27a, 29a).

But with other audiences he was more often winning and even tender, as with the various people he healed (e.g., John 5; Mark 10:46-52), the woman at the well (John 4), the woman taken in adultery (John 8:1-11), Thomas (John 20:24-28) and Peter (John 21:15-19). This last passage exemplifies not only Jesus' tenderness but his great ability to use questions to lead his receptors to understand what he wants to get across. He used this technique both with his disciples as a means of leading them to discovery and with his enemies to silence them (e.g., Matt. 12:18; 21:23-27).

Guiding Communication

After all we have said concerning the influence of receptors on the communication process, it may seem hopeless to speak of any ability on the part of communicators to guide that process. We certainly cannot speak of our controlling the process, for as communicators *we can seldom guide the activity from out in the open.*

A good analogy may be of a young lady who guides, even controls, her courtship without her suitor knowing what is happening. She simply learns how to work subtly, to guide without ever directing, to work from the background rather than the foreground, to compliment her suitor by appearing to be totally dependent on him rather than challenging him by asserting her independence, to state conclusions by asking questions rather than by making assertions, and overall to appear to be totally concerned with her suitor at the expense of her own interests while, in fact, she totally pursues her own interests, but indirectly. Such an analogy says much to those who would be effective communicators, for the process of subtly guiding gives one a large amount of control over the situation.

The goal is, of course, that the receptor come to understand the message in essentially the same way that the communicator intended it. Ideally, this will take place as a part of a continuing process of interaction between communicator and receptors, a process that gives adequate opportunity for feedback and adjustment. The extent that such close interaction is not possible diminishes the extent that the communicator will effectively guide the process. The more important it is for communicators to guide the process, therefore, the more they should strive to obtain ideal conditions for the interaction. As we have seen, the mere presentation of information does not require much interaction. But *persuasion, especially if the receptors are at all cool or negative toward the message, requires as ideal a situation as possible.*

The most general thing that can be said is that effective communicators do their best to employ the kinds of principles of successful communication set forth in this volume. If I have accurately portrayed Jesus' example, it also follows that effective communicators imitate Jesus in his communicational efforts. I have attempted to present these principles from several perspectives. In what follows I attempt to summarize what has already been said for the sake of communicators who seek to effectively present the gospel message in a winning way to those who are not necessarily already inclined to accept that message.

The first thing effective communicators do is, like Jesus, *segment their audience.* By segment we mean to identify that group within a potentially larger audience as those to whom we will address our message (Engel 1979:45-46). The fact that Jesus did this comes out clearly in his interaction with the Syrophoenician woman recorded in Mark 7:25-30. When the lady asked for help, Jesus' answer sounds callous. Jesus is not, however, showing unkindness in verse 27. He is, rather, merely indicating that she is not a part of his primary audience and that any time spent with her is at the expense of time spent with those whom he had specifically come to reach.

Choosing an audience is a very difficult thing for American communicators to do. We have been carefully taught that we should be fair to everyone. And to us, being fair means making whatever we have available to everyone. Thus we are reluctant to be specific to one segment of our audience lest we be unfair to the other segments. There is, however, an example to imitate in Jesus' approach, not just in this one instance but in at least two aspects of his overall strategy.

In the first place, *he chose to be incarnated among a specific people in a specific geographical location at a specific period of time.* And though his message was for all peoples in all times, he faithfully restricted his activities to the group that he had chosen. Though he and the Father could have arranged his ministry so that he would flit from place to place, thereby reaching peoples of many languages, societies, and geographical locations, it is unlikely that he traveled more than about two hundred miles from his boyhood home.

In the second place, *Jesus chose to restrict himself largely to interactions with the common people* rather than attempting to reach all segments of Jewish society. He chose to be raised as a peasant in order to reach peasants, to speak the Galilean dialect for the sake of reaching those who spoke that dialect, to refrain from attending the approved educational institutions because the members of his primary audience would have difficulty identifying with a communicator on the other side of that kind of educational gap. True, many Jewish leaders were attracted to him, and some became his followers (John 12:42), but these were a kind of by-product, the result, on the one hand, of an attractive communicator with an attractive message and, on the other, of sincere, needy people who were willing to adjust, even over a frame-of-reference barrier. *Jesus aimed at a specific group.* So did the apostle Paul (see 1 Cor. 9:21-22). So should we.

A second principle is that once we have chosen our audience *we can best guide the communicational interaction from inside the receptors' frame of reference.* Unless the message is within the receptors' frame of reference (context), there is no guarantee that they will even be able to interpret it correctly. I have spoken in chapter 10 about the importance of contexts. That discussion, particularly the part concerning the personal attachment of people to context, is relevant here. Communicators who seek to effectively guide communicational interaction need to operate on turf that puts the receptors at ease. If it is their turf, well and good. If it is another context or frame of reference, they need to feel at home at least to the extent that their interpretations of the context do not intrude into the main message in a negative way. Contexts familiar to receptors ordinarily add a positive, often warm, note to whatever communication goes on within them. This fact should be recognized and taken advantage of by communicators.

At this point, perhaps a word should be said concerning the matter of *manipulation.* There is a sense in which all persuasion, indeed all interaction, is manipulative. People end up doing things they never intended to do as a result of persuasion and other kinds of interpersonal interaction. Changes that are made by receptors of their own free will, however, even if the result of persuasive communication, are not perceived as the result of manipulation. This term is reserved for changes made under the influence of a communicator whom the receptors perceive to have some kind of power or authority over them. Such may well be considered by the receptors to be the result of manipulation. And when something is *perceived* as manipulation, it *is* indeed manipulation.

Communicators should do their utmost to protect the receptors' right to choose for or against what they are recommending. This is the only loving thing to do. For love is wanting the very best for the receptors, whether or not they do what we want them to do. We should treat receptors in communicational situations like we would like those who communicate to us to treat us (Matt. 7:12; see Griffin 1976 for an excellent treatment of this matter).

When we speak of the importance of the communicators' guiding the process of communication, we are not recommending that they manipulate the receptors. We are recommending that if we are to be effective communicators we need to learn how to *manipulate the circumstances* of the communication itself so that all that is done contributes to, rather than detracts from, our receptors' understanding our intent as accurately as possible. Though there is a fine, perhaps invisible, line between manipulating circumstances and manipulating people, I believe the cause we serve and the message we bear demands that we do our utmost to bring about understanding.

Understanding does not, however, automatically mean acceptance by the receptors. Jesus' interaction with the rich young man (Matt. 19:16-22) provides a good scriptural example of understanding that resulted in rejection. Unfortunately, many people either accept or reject the gospel because they don't understand. Many accept it on the basis of false expectations because the communicators have manipulated the communicational mechanisms at their disposal in such a way as to mislead the receptors. Many have, however, rejected it because the communicator was not sufficiently in control of the mechanisms to be able to eliminate harmful paramessages that led the receptors away from the message. Jesus manipulated the mechanisms in such a way that the rich young man saw clearly what the implications were. And, because he understood them, "he went away sad."

A third principle to follow if we are to communicate effectively is that *we need, insofar as possible, to control the vehicles in the communicational interaction.* In chapter 9, I attempted to make explicit some of the important factors in this area. The language employed is, of course, crucial. The receptors need to hear it as their language. Personal style, including the use of clothing, furniture, space, personal illustrations, and the like, is, however, no less important. Though it may take some time and experimentation for one accustomed to traditional forms of church communication to learn some of these techniques, it is well worth it.

One caution must be noted: With vehicles and contexts, as with messages themselves, we are able to make effective use of them only when permitted to do so by the receptors. Thus, if we are accustomed to interacting with a particular group in a formal way, we should not be too quick to adopt less formal vehicles of communication all at once. If our audience has become accustomed to a certain style of language and a certain set of dress patterns and we wish to change them, the changes should be made gradually and one at a time. In this way, by the time our style of dress and language has become informal, our audience will have gotten used to it and granted the necessary permission to interact with them in that way. If such adjustments are done too quickly, it is easy for the receptors to interpret the changes as fakeness rather than as growth. Such an interpretation hijacks the message.

In considering the need to control the vehicles we use, it is important to recognize that we should employ different vehicles for different audiences. The effective communicator should have more than one style, just as effective repairpersons have more than one tool in their toolboxes. When, then, we choose the audience or the group within the audience that we seek to reach, we can use the vehicles judged to be most appropriate for conveying that message to that group of receptors.

For some audiences it would be very unwise to use informal language, dress, and posture. For other audiences it would be very unwise to use formal language, dress, and posture. Whatever the situation, the vehicles employed should not be interpreted by the audience in focus to call any attention to themselves. They should, rather, by remaining out of the receptors' consciousness, enable as free a flow as possible of the main message.

In a similar vein, communicators who would effectively guide the communicational interaction must give solid attention to *presenting both their person and the message so that they are within the receptors' range of tolerance.* This is often, initially at least, largely a matter of using words, phrases, and communicational style that enable the receptors to feel the communicator to be "one of them." The underlying factor is a demand for communicators to demonstrate their trustworthiness in ways the receptors can properly interpret.

For example, I was once asked by a very conservative congregation to conduct a series of midweek lectures concerning Bible translation. After completing the first lecture and appearing a week later for the second, the leader pointed out (in private) that I had not mentioned "the blood of Christ" once in the previous week's lecture. His suggestion was that I "get it in" at some point during this week's lecture. The fact that I did not use that phrase constituted "noise" in the communication channel that disrupted the ability of that group to hear what I was saying. I could probably have solved the problem if I had merely used that phrase and perhaps certain others. Hearing those "in" words would have enabled them to relax and listen without interference from the "noise" of mistrust.

For, as with most subgroups in a society, these people identified those who were "with" them (as opposed to those against them) by their use of certain phrases. But what they quite legitimately sought was more than the use of a word or two. *They were asking, Can we trust you?* Are you one of "us" or one of "them"? Perceiving this, I decided to tackle the matter head-on by taking time to give my personal testimony. This satisfied their need, answered their question, and moved me well within their range of tolerance so that they could relax and trust both me and my message. After that they responded very well, even to sensitive subjects. My first lecture was, however, only acceptable to them when they reflected back on it after I had demonstrated my trustworthiness in the second lecture.

Very often, however, the demonstration of trustworthiness requested will need to be communicated in some other way than as a part of the messages in focus. A pastor who from time to time does menial work with the people, for example, often achieves higher credibility and trust than one whom the people never see doing such tasks. The pastor I grew up under gained enormous trust and credibility with us by frequently playing softball with us. The fact that we knew him as a human being (i.e., out of the stereotype) rather than simply as a pastor meant a lot to us.

The name of the game at this point is *credibility*. And credibility is like a bank account (see Griffin 1976:126). When we start the process of communication, our hearers may grant us a large or small amount in that bank account. Communicators with big reputations are often granted quite a large amount of credibility capital with which to work. Others will have to settle for less. And some will find themselves in considerable debt, possessing no discernible credibility with their hearers.

During the course of the communicational interaction, the credibility capital may be increased or spent. Dealing with sensitive issues when one has little or no credibility is likely to result in communicational bankruptcy. Those who have very high credibility at the start or who gain high credibility as they proceed may, with the permission of their receptors, deal with a wide range of sensitive issues and still come off with their credibility bank account in good shape.

With many audiences, there are certain issues with which even the most credible communicators dare not deal if they are to retain effective contact. It is, however, the responsibility of communicators to use, even risk, whatever credibility they may have if such be necessary in order to effectively communicate the message they are called to communicate. Credibility is not simply to be amassed, as one would amass a monetary fortune, without ever making use of the resources for purposes that lie beyond the simple collecting of those resources. Credibility is only as valuable as the use to which it is put. And it may, of course, be misused.

Communicators need to build credibility from whatever point the receptors allow them to enter their range of tolerance. They should use vehicles and contexts acceptable to the receptors they have chosen. Once they have entered that range of tolerance, then, they need to give constant attention to the accumulation and disbursement of their credibility. Ideally, in this process, the receptors' range of tolerance will be widened (if it starts out narrow) to the point where the communicator can effectively deal with a wide variety of messages with some assurance that the receptors are likely to correctly understand them. If, however, the communicators squander some of that credibility, it is possible that the receptors will narrow their range of tolerance and tune them out.

To be effective, communicators need to constantly monitor the process taking place throughout the whole interaction and, if necessary, adjust their presentations to regain any credibility they may have lost. For example, I was making a presentation once concerning communicating via music. At one point I was asked a question on an issue over which I knew my opinion differed with that of most of the audience. As I pondered my answer, I calculated whether it would be profitable to give them my true feelings as opposed to skirting the issue; if so, whether I had enough credibility with that audience to enable me to give a "straight" answer; how much credibility I was willing to spend; and whether I would have enough time before the end of my presentation to regain whatever credibility I might lose. I judged that my credibility was high, that it would indeed be profitable if I stated my true convictions, and that there would be enough time to recover and to leave them with a positive impression of me and my message. I answered "straight," lost some credibility, made my point, but was able to regain at least most of the credibility I lost. And many felt the point I made was valuable to them, even though it contradicted what they had previously believed.

A sixth important principle for guiding communication is *relevance*. Relevance is closely related both to credibility and to the receptors' range of tolerance. Credibility applies to both messages and messengers. Relevance, however, focuses entirely on the messages as received. For ready acceptance within a receptor's range of tolerance, messages need to be credible. *To be credible, messages need to be relevant.*

As already noted, relevance is just as much a matter of the receptors' interpretation as any of the other aspects of the communicational process. And what a communicator considers to be relevant may differ greatly from what the receptors consider to be relevant. To effectively guide the communication, therefore, communicators need to study their receptors in their normal life to discover what their felt needs are. One pastor of my acquaintance did this quite effectively by taking part-time employment in the kind of factory that most of his parishioners worked in. He thereby engaged in the kind of participant-observation research that anthropologists and other perceptive students of human behavior engage in to find out where their receptors are. He could then construct his messages on the basis of concrete insight into what he discovered to be relevant to his receptors' lives. Such a strategy is particularly important to pastors who have received the majority of their training in schools rather than in the context of real life.

It is relevance to felt needs that, at the message level, enables communicators to get within the range of tolerance of their receptors. The continued demonstration of that relevance, then, functions like credibility to enable receptors to widen their range of tolerance. It is, however, very important for communicators to monitor the receptors' felt needs, since the process of communicational interaction on the basis of felt needs commonly results in two ongoing processes. First, certain of the original felt needs get solved. Then, deeper needs are brought to the surface—needs not originally in focus in the interaction either because they were not felt or because the receptors were not open about them. Communicators need, therefore, to alter their messages to deal with the new felt needs rather than to continue to deal with those needs previously felt but now solved.

Unfortunately, much Christian communication has not taken account of this fact. We find, therefore, many Christian communicators dealing only with the very early stages of the Christian life and seldom, if ever, getting to the real meat of the Christian message. Two things then happen: (1) The audience for whom those messages are relevant keeps changing, since the messages always deal with the same subject matter. It is as if a communicator could only talk baby talk. Thus, only those who consider baby talk relevant to their needs would be attracted. New groups who consider baby talk relevant would need to constantly replace those groups who leave because they have outgrown the need for it. (2) There are in most churches a certain number of those who should have outgrown baby talk but who consider it the only appropriate kind of talk for church settings. They regard such an approach to the gospel as a required sacred ritual that is in and of itself the only proper thing to do in church. They no longer look for relevance for themselves in church. They evaluate pastors and other Christian communicators on the basis of whether they use the proper sacred words, phrases, and customs (such as an invitation at the end of every service) rather than on the basis of whether they speak to the genuinely felt needs of their receptors.

Effective communicators who genuinely seek to communicate something worthwhile as well as to communicate it effectively seek to discover the felt needs of their hearers and to present biblical messages that those hearers will perceive as relevant to their felt needs. In this way the credibility of the messages is built up along with the credibility of the messengers. Furthermore, the sincere concern of dedicated Christian communicators for the good of their receptors is demonstrated in a truly Christian way.

Finally, it is appropriate to reiterate *the specificity principle*. This principle proceeds logically from the relevance principle and from all else that has been said in these pages. Christian communicators are effective when they not only choose a specific audience but when the content of the message is presented in such a way that it is specific to the receptors in focus. *God deals with actual people, not just with people in general.* The people whom Jesus dealt with had names, occupations, homes, and aspirations. Jesus, therefore, dealt with each of them as specific persons, not as general categories. And his messages were both better understood and more impactful because of his specificity.

To effectively guide communication, then, wise communicators (1) choose their audiences, (2) enter and work within the receptors' frame of reference, (3) control the vehicles employed in the communicational interaction, (4) present both self and message within the receptors' range of tolerance, (5) give maximum attention to attaining, maintaining, and creatively using their credibility, (6) seek to be relevant, and (7) seek to be specific.

Relating to Receptors

A persistent problem that is particularly difficult when there is a status gap between communicator and receptor is the matter of how communicators should relate to the receptors. As should be completely obvious by now, *I regard the ideal relationship as that of a fully human communicator relating as a person to a fully human receptor.* Church leaders often relate in what one author has termed a "station-to-station" (i. e., status-to-status) manner with their receptors (Loewen 1967). Such a relationship, though often comfortable, hinders the effective communication of a person-to-person God. That kind of an understanding of and relationship to God is best conveyed by a person-to-person relationship.

Often, however, it is not so much the fault of pastors, teachers, or other church leaders that there seems to be a distance between them and the receptors. The basic problem is, rather, the receptors' perception concerning how they should relate to persons in such positions. Such receptors often relate station-to-station even though the leader would prefer a person-to-person style. The questions are: (1) How can a communicator break out of such a station-to-station relationship? and (2) Who should take the initiative?

With the precedent of God's activity to guide us, I believe the initiative should always be taken by the communicator. As a means toward accomplishing this, I would like to suggest five practical steps.

1. The first step that we need to take as communicators is to *try to understand our receptors*. This is an obvious step but not always as easy as it sounds. We are often called upon to try to communicate to people who have been deeply affected by experiences we just do not understand or who have adopted life-styles of which we do not approve or who for one reason or another we just don't like. So understanding, really understanding, their life, their points of view, their biases, their reasons for what they are and do may be a tall order.

We often try to understand people from other groups in terms of the meanings their behavior would have if it were a part of the context in which *we* live, rather than in terms of the meanings the behavior conveys within *their* contexts. The behavior of certain Christians is, for example, a considerable improvement over that of other members of their reference group, even though it might not conform to our expectations. This fact needs to be understood and such receptors given credit for it.

Furthermore, the kind of training provided for pastors and other church leaders, both professional and lay, is often quite counterproductive for the real communicational tasks to which we are called. Such training is typically almost completely intellectual, based on the reading of books. The task we face, however, is almost completely that of attempting to understand persons who are primarily concerned in their day-to-day living with nonintellectual matters. We need, therefore, *to learn how to study people even more than how to study books*. The first problem we face is to try to really understand our receptors.

2. On the basis of such understanding, we are able to take the second step, which is that of *empathizing with our receptors*. To empathize with a

person is to try to put oneself in that person's place, to attempt to enter that person's world and see life as that person sees it. Empathy starts with asking a question such as, "If I perceived the world the way that person perceives it, how would I think and act?" The empathizer then sits next to that person (literally or figuratively, cf. Ezek. 3:15) or, as an Indian proverb puts it, walks a mile in his moccasins. Empathy is as important to effective communication as it is to expressing love. Church leaders should be totally involved in empathy for both purposes.

3. Beyond understanding and empathy, the third step is the attempt to *identify with our receptors*. Identifying with another person puts us with that person within their frame of reference. This is what the apostle Paul was speaking of in 1 Corinthians 9:19-22 when he talked of becoming a Gentile to win Gentiles. Such identification is not shallow or fake. It involves us, rather, in becoming more than we have ever been before. As I have said elsewhere:

> There are dimensions to most of us that we have never really probed. And identifying with another person or group, genuinely entering into his frame of reference, challenges us to probe another of these unprobed areas. One of the amazing things about human beings is that we can become bicultural. We can, by entering into the lives of other people, become just as real in that context as we are in our normal context. It takes more work, it takes a lot of learning, a lot of modifying. However, when we find our efforts paying off to the extent that people remark, "you are just like one of us," we begin to realize that it is very much worth it (Kraft 1979b:25).

4. Proceeding from understanding, empathy, and identification is the fourth step, *actual participation in the life of our receptors*. Many church members see their leaders only in terms of their life in the church. They, therefore, often have very little understanding of the other aspects of those lives. Many parishioners are amazed, for example, to find that their pastor can work with his or her hands. Their understanding can be expanded, however, if the pastor participates with them in a variety of activities perceived by them as genuinely human. Participation with one's parishioners in play is often at least as valuable as participating with them in work. As mentioned above, several of us in the youth group in which I grew up have been indelibly affected for good by a pastor who regularly spent time playing with us.

5. Within and beyond such activities lies the fifth stage of which I'll speak, that of *self-disclosure*. At this stage, communicators really give themselves to those whom they seek to reach. I define self-disclosure as

> the practice of sharing one's innermost feelings with those with whom one participates. It is not the kind of questionable practice that some

indulge in when they share intimate details of their inner life in their public presentations. It is, rather, the sharing of one's innermost feelings with those within the receptor group with whom one has earned intimacy. At this level, the confession of faults, doubts and insecurities becomes a valid part of one's testimony rather than a disqualification of one's right to speak convincingly. . . . Becoming a genuine, credible human being to our receptors takes us beyond understanding, empathy identification and participation to this kind of self [disclosure] (Kraft 1979b:26).

Genuine reaching out for a relationship with our receptors, then, starts with understanding them and ends up with giving ourselves to them. In the process, we identify with them and participate in their lives. And through our self-disclosure and self-giving, we enable them to identify with us. Thus the communicational circle is complete, and they are enabled to imitate us as we imitate Christ because they see us at close enough range to know what imitating us is all about. Such a procedure cannot, of course, be employed with large groups. But it would be sad if, because we could not do it with everyone in a group, we refrained from doing it with anyone. Selecting an audience to identify and participate with and then giving ourselves to that group, even though they are a part of a larger group, is far better than not interacting closely with anyone.

Working with Social Structure

I have at various points noted the nature and influence on communication of the sociocultural matrix within which we operate. Without this matrix there would, of course, be no communication. Yet not all aspects of that sociocultural setting can be regarded positively by Christians. Satan works through the communicational structures as well as through the political, social, economic and all other structures within which we operate (John 5:19b). The question, then, is what our attitudes should be toward these structures. Should we reject them lest our message be contaminated? This would not work since we have no alternative structures. Should we, then, endorse them since we have no better structures? Such an approach would be going too far in the opposite direction.

My suggestion is that we be realistic concerning these structures, recognizing that we must use them even though they are infected by being widely used for purposes contrary to the purposes of God. But we should, claiming God's protection, use them with better motives than those that characterize non-Christians who use them. We should, furthermore, use them for purposes that so transcend the ordinary use of these vehicles that our use may even ultimately result in the altering of the vehicles themselves.

An example of what I am talking about is the fact that *those with power, prestige, and reputation are more frequently listened to than those without such*

154 HOW DOES AN EFFECTIVE COMMUNICATOR OPERATE?

qualifications. Though there are powerful people who ought to be listened to, it is often the case that an undue amount of attention is paid to them while other, more sensible but less recognized voices are ignored. This seems unjust. Can Christians possibly use such a social structure in a more Christian way for Christian ends?

I believe we often can. If we have personal prestige, can that not be used for Christ? A Christian approach to such structures would, however, be to win a hearing rather than to demand it. A Christian approach seeks to politely invite people to listen and respond on the basis of how credible they perceive the communicator and the message to be. Christians should not demand a hearing even though they have a close relationship to God, the Source of all power.

Although the cultural structuring gives precedence to those with power, the Christian ought to follow the example of Jesus in this regard. Jesus turned his back on the power and prestige that he could have demanded as a legitimate entitlement of his position as God. He chose, rather, to *earn* his way in association with human beings, using (and eventually succumbing to) those who controlled the structures in order to accomplish purposes that lay far beyond the way the structures were ordinarily used.

Another type of illustration is that of the so-called *homogeneous unit principle* (Wagner 1981; Kraft 1978). Statements of this principle simply point out that people choose to group themselves into collections of like-minded people. Any given church, therefore, like any other viable organization, is made up of people who either aspire to be or are already members of the same socioeconomic class and who, in addition, often share many other common perspectives and interests. Such groups often turn inward to such an extent that they tend to become cliquish and quite unconcerned with those of other groups around them. The question is often raised whether such groupings are pleasing to God.

I would make the point that, though there are notable problems with such social structuring, we have no option but to recognize that human beings are this way and to work with such groupings. However, we need not be enslaved by such structures simply because we work with them. In recognition of the damage done not only to Christians but to the Christian message by our actual or potential cliquishness, we need to expose Christian groups to other groups with like commitment to Christ but with different approaches to worshiping and serving him. These others are our Christian brothers and sisters, and we must learn through experience with them to love and accept them even if there are points of disagreement between us. The homogeneity in which we exist, therefore, becomes a means for enabling us to transcend our cliquishness.

A third point at which we can work with the social structures in order to transcend them relates to *opinion leaders*. In every segment of society there are those whose opinions carry more weight than the opinions of others. This is not always fair, even in Christian groups. And woe be to pastors who find themselves on the outs with powerful opinion leaders! Yet wise communicators will recognize that this pattern can often be worked with. They therefore seek to discover who the opinion leaders are in the group and to work with and through them to communicate their ideas.

I know an older pastor who discovered that the leaders of his denomination would not accept new ideas from one as old as he. So he developed a strategy in which he would bounce his ideas off some of the younger leaders in hopes that they would see the merit of the ideas and adopt them themselves. As it turned out, this frequently happened, leading to the adoption of many of the older man's ideas by the denominational leaders. Usually, though, the ideas were not adopted immediately, for it seemed necessary for the younger pastors to mull over each idea long enough so that they came to believe it originated with them rather than with someone else.

When they presented the ideas, however, they presented them as their own rather than those of someone else. The opinion leaders with whom they interacted, then, accepted the ideas as the creations of the younger men, thereby validating the strategy of the older man. The latter was often frustrated by the fact that he seldom got the recognition he deserved for originating the ideas, but he was quite pleased to see so many of his ideas implemented because he had learned to use unjust structures in such a way.

A fourth area that has frequently been in focus throughout these pages and that might be considered problematic is that of *felt needs* or *group preferences*. The question that this area raises is whether or not it is proper to feed people's perceived needs for fairly trivial things in order to gain their permission to deal with more substantial matters. A similar question would be whether it is proper to appeal to selfish motives in order to win people to the Christian way. This is, of course, often done. When I was young the primary approach to non-Christians seemed to be to warn them of an impending eternity in hell if they did not accept Christ. For what I now judge to be rather selfish reasons, I myself responded to such an invitation and am very glad that those who presented the message did not refuse to witness for fear my motives might be less than pure.

In dealing with this particular problem, two facts become apparent: (1) There would seem to be no such thing as a pure motive on the part of any human being; and (2) the motivating principle around which human beings wrap their lives would seem to be self-interest. If these statements are true, our criteria for using such structures are largely limited to the validity of the goals we seek and to the usefulness and ethical nature of the structures that we employ in attaining those goals. Appealing to a person or group's self-interest simply to feed that self-interest might be judged as a sub-Christian use of this communicational structure. Appealing to a person or group's self-interest as a stepping-stone toward leading that person or group to transcend that selfish purpose by committing themselves to a higher cause might, however, be judged to be a use of the structure that transcends its less desirable features. To be ethical and Christian our means must be loving, both from our own and the receptor's point of view.

Learning to Communicate More Effectively

The ability to communicate, like any other human activity, is learned. Some learn the principles of effective communication very well as they grow up. Others are not so fortunate. Some who learn to communicate well in certain situations regularly bomb out in other situations. The problem is that whatever we have learned in this area, as well as in all other areas of our behavior, has become habit. When, therefore, we discover a need to learn different techniques, we face the great difficulty of unlearning the old habits. Nevertheless, difficult though it may be, new habits can be learned if our motivation is high enough, if we work hard enough at it, and if the rewards are sufficient both to encourage us in our task and to keep our motivation and effort high.

It is hoped that this volume will provide you with enough insight into the communicational process to enable you to *more accurately analyze any communicational situation you observe or participate in*. This analysis is the first step toward greater communicational effectiveness. We perceive largely what we have learned to perceive. If we have not learned to perceive in communicational events the kinds of things that will help us to be more effective communicators, it is unlikely that we will reach our goal. Learning to perceive analytically is thus an important first step.

Since as humans we are totally immersed in communicational events, the materials to analyze are never far from us. Each casual conversation, whether involving ourselves or not, each lecture, each advertisement on radio or television, each book, each song, and all the gestures and glances and body postures and use of space that accompany such events are all valid subjects for communicational analysis. That is our data, and the principles set forth in this book are intended to provide the perspective from which the analysis is made.

A second point I would like to make concerning how we are to learn to communicate more effectively is that *we should learn to study the Bible from a communicational point of view*. Our commitment to the God of the universe is a commitment to the Originator of the principles we seek to study. It is also a commitment to learn from what he has revealed to us in his Word. As pointed out early in this volume, I believe that his revelation of himself includes a revelation of the way he uses and expects us to use the communicational principles he has put into the universe. Without denying that the primary purpose of the Bible is to record the revelation of God's messages, we can confidently assert that there is also much there concerning his communicational methods. At this point, I am recommending that we look at the communicational data in the Bible from the perspective developed in this book in order to gain the kind of insight that will enable us to do a better job of handling God's messages in God's preferred ways. (See Gibbs 1985, Engel 1988, and Webber 1980 for additional help in this area.)

Once we have analyzed both ordinary communicational events and those in the Bible from this point of view, we can look at Christian communication with new understanding. Then the hard work begins. For as we gain such understandings, we become more aware of the necessity of exchanging our old communicational habits for better ones.

Recognition of the importance of receptors in the communicational process demands that *we learn to pay much more attention to their interests and concerns than may have been true previously*. Much of the training that pastors and other Christian leaders have received tends to be source- or message-oriented. By this I mean that those who write and teach on preaching usually give the impression that the message from God as perceived by the communicator from the text of the Scriptures is and should be the primary focus of the Christian communicator.

The discussions of preaching I remember left me with the impression that the key ingredient in a sermon should be the expository proclamation of an authoritative word from God. Much less focus was put on the need to tie that message in with the interests of the people in the congregation. We were to devote the major portion of our presentations to taking the receptors back into biblical times. Toward the end of each message, of course, we ought to make some attempt to apply it to contemporary times. But the application seemed to be a less significant issue than the exposition of the Word designed to help them understand it. (See Chartier 1981, Lewis and Lewis 1983 for more on this.)

Had I at that time known enough to analyze the Scriptures communicationally, I would have noted that *Jesus seldom started with Scripture in his interactions with people. He started instead with their concerns, their felt needs, and led them from those to the God who could meet them*. What he did was to bring the message of God to them, not simply take them back to another message aimed at another group of people in the past. He spoke messages from God that relevantly addressed topics of pressing concern to them. Yet topical preaching is considered by many teachers of homiletics the least desirable kind of preaching!

Furthermore, we were taught that the crucial part of a sermon is the outline of topics to be dealt with. This outline, we were led to believe, shows the real content of the sermon. To help keep people's attention and to elucidate difficult points, we would need to introduce illustrative material from time to time. But the message content, not the illustrations, was considered critical to get across. Had we known enough to analyze Jesus' approach to communication, it would have become clear to us that *he spoke illustratively rather than from a logical outline*. He realized that analogies, much more than straight statements (propositions), are the most effective carriers of potent messages from human being to human being (see Gibbs

1985). Since learning that fact, I have been forcing myself to illustrate much more thoroughly than ever before, with a corresponding increase in the effectiveness of my communicational efforts.

Another habit that many Christian communicators need to replace is that of being overformal in the way they handle the Christian message. Given the fact that formality is sometimes good and often imposed on us by circumstances beyond our control, I believe it is worth noting that Jesus was seldom formal in his presentations. Increasing the amount of illustrative material is, of course, one important step toward deformalization. So is a move toward greater personalization of the message.

Jesus, of course, personalized his messages largely in deed rather than in word. His total life was much more visible to his receptors than ours usually is. We may, therefore, have to compensate to some extent by verbalizing more of our experience than he did. We need, however, to be careful that our self-disclosure is not motivated simply by a desire to show off.

Self-disclosure as a communicational device is intended to assist the messages we bring rather than to hijack them. Its use as a technique should be balanced in at least two ways: (1) We should discuss our failures, difficulties, and uncertainties as well as our successes; and (2) when we show our difficulties, we need to be careful to also discuss the ways in which we, as fellow strugglers toward Christian maturity, are working with God toward the resolution of those problems. Learning to judiciously allow people to see within us can be a powerful means both of deformalizing our communicational interactions and of enabling our receptors to profit by enhancing their ability to identify with us. Such a technique often results in a considerable amount of life involvement, even though it is only a token effort on the part of the communicator.

We need, further, to learn to *take more time in our presentations to transmit less information and to give greater attention to illustration and application of the information to the life of the receptors.* Our American attachment to information has produced an information glut. Many of us have in response developed "informational indigestion." Our constant exposure to so much information keeps us from adequately processing it in our minds and applying it to our lives. The situation reminds me of the farmer mentioned earlier who did not want to learn how to handle his crops better until he had caught up with what he already knew.

I believe that most of us need, not more information, no matter how fascinating that might be, but more application. Our training procedures (both secular and religious) and our overdevotion to information-based sermonizing within the church are powerful factors mitigating against the development of better habits in this area. I have, however, experienced at least one preacher who had developed an effective alternative. As I recall, he never sought to develop more than one point in any given presentation. And the way he developed that point was always by presenting illustration after illustration, application after application of that single point. I remember trying to take notes on his messages and experiencing only frustration. The points he sought to make, however, were made very effectively.

We need to develop the habit of regularly involving receptors more completely in the communicational process. One approach would be to develop creative techniques by means of which receptors can be encouraged to produce and send feedback they know will affect the presentation of our messages. Some church leaders have developed feedback sheets that are available to the members of a congregation on which they are encouraged to write their responses to sermons and lectures. Others have developed small group interactions that follow sermons and thoroughly discuss in a less formal setting the topics raised by the monologue presentation.

An even more creative idea is the conducting of small group sessions on the sermon topic prior to the delivery of the sermon. Such sessions become for pastors a trial run during which they become aware of alterations that ought to be made if the points are to be gotten across effectively. For the receptors, such sessions become both opportunities for input and for participation in the building of the pastor's message. Such opportunity provides stimulus and greatly enhances the communication value of the message both for those who assist and for the rest of the congregation.

Another technique designed to increase the participation of the receptors is to use more questions. Many communicators, including Jesus, have increased their impact enormously by developing the fine art of leading people to make their own discoveries by pointing to key answers through questions rather than through statements (see Gibbs 1985). Such a procedure is both stimulating and complimentary from the receptors' point of view. It is stimulating because it points the receptors in a direction without carrying them all the way there. It is complimentary because the use of such questions implies that receptors are intelligent enough to draw correct conclusions without having everything spelled out for them.

In using this technique, it is frequently advisable to ask questions with fairly obvious or easily deducible answers. Sometimes it is good to ask questions we intentionally do not answer even implicitly in order to stimulate at least the more creative members of our audiences to grapple on their own with important issues. Jesus seemed to do this quite often. There is, apparently, great communicational power in a question such as, What do *you* think about this?

In these and perhaps other areas it is possible and advisable to replace communicationally counterproductive habits with habits that are more productive. As pointed out above, this will often be a difficult task. It will require insight, determination, and a great deal of experimentation. There are likely to be frequent failures as we experiment, but the satisfactions are great when we achieve success.

12

Communicating for Life Change

Christian Newness

What happens when people become Christian? And what is the difference between a Christian perspective and a non-Christian outlook on life?
The apostle Paul deals with these issues by speaking of newness at the deep
level of a person's being: "When anyone is joined to Christ, he is a new
being; the old is gone, the new has come" (2 Cor. 5:17).

Such newness "is done by God" (v. 18a). But it has an important human
dimension as well, for it requires that those so changed "from enemies into
[God's] friends" give themselves to "the task of making others his friends
also" (v. 18b). We, then, are to communicate "for Christ, as though God
himself were making his appeal through us. We plead on Christ's behalf:
let God change you from enemies into his friends!" (v. 20b).

Our mandate as Christian communicators is clear: We are first to experience newness ourselves (vv. 11-16), being "ruled by the love of Christ"
(v. 14b) and then to "plead on Christ's behalf" (v. 20b) for others to join
us in that newness. The newness is, however, a deep-level change. It
requires what philosophers of science term a *paradigm shift* (Kuhn 1970;
Barbour 1974), a radical change in perspective (see Kraft 1979a). Jesus
called this being "born again" (John 3:3b). And Paul points out that it
involves viewing the human world around us from God's point of view (2
Cor. 5:16).

Such a change takes place at the deepest level of human experience, the
worldview level. Communicating to people for change at this level provides
would-be communicators with the greatest possible challenge. Communicating for life change means aiming to bring receptors to newness of being
in their worldview assumptions, values, and commitments.

Worldview Assumptions, Values, and Commitments

The more we learn about human beings, the more we learn of the depths
of human assuming, valuing, and committing. Any discussion of commu-

nicating for life change requires that we probe some of these depths before we turn to a consideration of the strategies that might prove most effective in bringing about deep-level change. Though there are several ways in which this material can be analyzed, I will opt for an analysis that focuses on worldview as the deep-level assumptions, values, and commitments in terms of which people govern their lives.

These worldview assumptions, values, and commitments may be likened to a window through which human beings look out on reality. This may be the window or mirror through (or in) which we see dimly referred to by the apostle Paul in 1 Corinthians 13:12. Our worldview, like every other aspect of our culture, is taught to us from birth, and so convincingly that most of us never question that our view of reality is the only accurate one. Our deep-level worldview perspectives provide us with our understandings of both the personal and the nonpersonal universes around us. By being taught such perspectives, we learn who in the personal universe fits into the "we" category and who into the "they" category. We learn the differences and similarities between human beings and supernatural beings, men and women, adults and children, persons of one social class and those of another, leaders and followers, and so forth. We learn not only what groups there are but what groups there ought to be and how they should function. We learn where we fit into the world, both individually and groupwise.

We learn such basic perspectives largely via observation plus trial and error, with occasional verbal instruction. As children, we are very good at such learning and do it largely unconsciously, perceiving that our elders consider it very important and that we may not survive if we do not learn. Before long we come to focus on those things that our society focuses on, value those things that people of our society value, and respond to our universe as others in our society respond to it. At the deepest level, we come to agree with the adults of our society concerning the nature of both personal and nonpersonal universes, their organization, and dynamics. These perspectives we receive and believe to be absolute.

Most of these basic perspectives are at the deepest level of our psychology, adopted and followed unconsciously, and most of us go through our lives without ever questioning the majority of them. Basic assumptions such as the belief that human beings and supernatural beings are qualitatively different (a belief, by the way, not shared by people of all societies) or that time is structured more like a line than a circle or that the universe is to be conquered rather than submitted to are very deep and provide us with the perspectives in terms of which we perceive and evaluate the reality around us.

There are, then, perspectives that are closer to the surface (many of which are just as unconscious) that allow for alternatives, one of which is usually taught as superior to the others. Examples might be right- and left-handedness, the ways people eat and sleep, different styles of religious worship, perspectives on peoples of other languages and nationalities, and the like. Such basic perspectives provide the windows through which we view reality.

We not only view, we evaluate. And we commit ourselves psychologically to what we value most highly. We have deep-level commitments to such aspects of our life as our own self, our group, our family, our job, our God, our nation, our worldview, and the like. These commitments are to things that we value most deeply, often to groups or ideas or persons for whom we would die. At the surface level are commitments we would consider much less vital, perhaps even trivial. We prefer and, therefore, develop some kind of commitment to a brand of toothpaste, a style of automobile, kinds of clothing, housing, and grooming, geographical areas, types of food, and the like. Typically, nearly all the members of a society will share most of the same deep-level commitments. Closer to the surface there will tend to be variation, some people committing themselves quite superficially to items that others are much more seriously committed to. Take, for example, variations in the commitments of various members to a given club. For some, their commitment may be practically a life-or-death matter, while for others the value they place in and the commitment they have to the club might be quite small.

The Nature of the Change Process

Having said this concerning the general characteristics of worldview, it is important to outline the nature of the change process before we turn to the communicational dimensions of our subject. The first thing to recognize is that, in general, *it is much easier to convince people that they should make changes in those things that are closest to the surface, whether perspectives or commitments.* It is much easier, for example, to convince people that they should switch to another brand of toothpaste than to get them to really believe that it is spirits rather than germs that cause disease. Yet advertisers pour millions of dollars into producing commercials designed to win people over to their brand of toothpaste in recognition of the fact that even inducing such surface-level changes is a sizable task. How difficult, then, must it be to induce people whose primary commitment is to themselves to replace that commitment with a faith allegiance to God?

A change is initiated whenever a person or group adopts a new perspective to which a commitment is made. If an advertiser analyzes bath soaps in such a way that viewers become convinced that the kind of soap they have been using is inferior to the kind being advertised, a new perspective is developed. The viewers may (or may not) commit themselves to using the new brand. I once made such a change in commitment, from one kind of cold medicine to another after reading an article in a publication I trusted. The author contended that the only valuable medicine in the product I had placed my faith in was aspirin. And since, the article contended, the price of aspirin was considerably less than the price of the medicine I had been using, I could both save money and have just as good medical results if I simply used aspirin. I, therefore, changed my perspective and my allegiance from my previous medicine to aspirin.

The new information I received led me to reinterpret both my behavior and the faith I had placed in my original medicine. I took a new view of my situation and ultimately decided to develop a new habit. The process I went through seemed to involve: (1) a new perspective; then (2) a reinterpretation; followed by (3) a new commitment that, when acted on, led me to develop; and only then (4) a new habit. This, I believe, is a typical sequence in the change process. It is preceded by new information leading the receptor to analyze a belief or behavior that may or may not have been conscious previously.

I will attempt, below, to provide a brief analysis of certain aspects of the middle-class, Anglo-American worldview (assumptions, values, and commitments). I hope to lead the reader to recognize at the conscious, analytical level certain things about Anglo- Americans. For those of us who belong to this social grouping, these recognitions are intended to provide us with a new perspective on our worldview understandings on the basis of which we may wish to change some of our interpretations, commitments, and habits. For those not a part of this social grouping, this information should help you to understand us better and, hopefully, to suggest how you may go about analyzing your own worldview.

The nature of the change process is what Loewen has discussed under the label *resocialization*. In three excellent articles published in 1968 and 1969, Loewen summarizes and applies socialization research to the bringing of new members into the church. He points to the fact that newcomers to a society (or a church) go through a three-step process in which they successively seek (1) gratification or satisfaction, (2) social approval, and (3) self-approval (1968b:147). Appealing to persons and groups in terms of their search for such satisfaction is, thus, crucial to guiding them into the change process.

Note the importance of the group to the change process. It is group approval (and its extension, self-approval) that led to the learning and confirmation of the members of the group in their original perspectives and allegiances. The strength of the group advocating the new perspectives and allegiances is, then, crucial to the change process. Such a fact speaks to the great importance of the church in the process of change from non-Christian to Christian.

With this outline of the concept of worldview (for more see Kraft 1989) and of the nature of the change process (for more see Kraft 1979a), we may proceed to specific application of the principles in Anglo-American contexts with special reference to the communication of Christianity to this group of Americans. We will first look at a generalized view of certain Anglo-American values, then turn to a consideration of unresolved needs to which Christian communicators may appeal.

Anglo-American Worldview

Though many have helpfully described various aspects of Anglo-American worldview (see Arensberg and Niehoff 1971; Bellah et al. 1985; Kraft 1989; Stewart 1971; Kluckhohn 1949), we still wait for a truly comprehensive treatment. Perhaps our underlying perspectives and allegiances are just too complex to analyze neatly. Here, then, I simply point to four worldview-level "core values" that are typical and should be helpful in alerting us to the kind of deep-level perspectives with which we must deal when attempting to communicate to this group of Americans. These four areas are closely interrelated and sometimes overlapping. They are also assumed rather than reasoned and believed implicitly by those who hold them.

The first of these basic perspectives may be labeled *the American way*. As Anglo-Americans we, like most other peoples, believe that our way is the best way. We believe, furthermore, that our powerful position in the world is in some sense a justification of the superiority of our way. We believe in democracy, individualism, freedom, capitalism, pluralism and the like, all defined very idealistically. We believe that people are created with equal opportunity, that rulers ought to rule by permission of the people, that common people can make proper judgments, that people have a right to believe what they choose to believe, that everyone has a right to the good life, that everyone should go to school, and several other such things.

We have, furthermore, so absolutized our point of view that we believe that our version of the American way is not only specifically good for all Americans but that it is good for the rest of the world as well. We have, therefore, devised several schemes by means of which to export our ideology and institutions. Unfortunately, many mission organizations have had more success in exporting the American way of life than in communicating the essentials of Christianity.

A second worldview perspective that characterizes us may be labeled *scientific humanism*. We believe that the world and the various forces within it (including those forces that bring about sickness and death) can be controlled by human beings. *Science is our true religion*, scientists the priests and prophets that we take most seriously and we see our school system as the hope for both America and the world.

Middle-class Anglo-Americans tend to believe that human beings are basically rational (rather than emotional or willful) and virtually perfectible if we can get enough knowledge and information to them. We, with the Greeks, believe *the basic problem with humans is ignorance and the solution more information*. We are secular and naturalistic to the core. Religion is seen as private, personal, and irrelevant.

Schools, literacy, and mass media are therefore highly exalted as techniques for moving us all toward perfection. We recognize problems at both practical and technical levels but believe that it is only a matter of time until these problems are conquered. If people cannot get along with each other, we start organizations such as the United Nations and set up schemes to communicate via satellite to every corner of the world. *Our faith in human ability to correct and control is virtually boundless.*

We believe in *progress*. To us, change is a good thing. We interpret history evolutionarily, as if all history to this point were a steady movement from inferior societies to our own society, the most ideal that history has ever known. This concept used to be articulated in the statement, "Every day in every way we are getting better and better." Two world wars have muted the optimism of that statement, but the belief in progress is still very much with us. So we still look to a brighter future.

Ours is a future-oriented society in which we expect children to outdo their parents so that there can be a great big beautiful tomorrow. We advocate change rather than stability, conquest rather than holding positions already achieved, moving into the new rather than consolidating the old. And we are so ignorant of history's lessons that we cannot conceive of a day when our "superior" way of life will not be in the ascendancy.

We romanticize individualism. (See Bellah et al. 1985.) We believe that the good of the individual is more important than the good of the group. We all have our rights as individuals and should not be told by others what to do. We believe that common people are by definition capable of thinking, voting and making decisions in rational, competent ways. People can be expected, therefore, to have reasonable even if different approaches to life. We believe that effort pays off and that anyone can make it to the top if he/she only tries hard enough. We value competition because it pushes us on to conquest.

We worship success and fear failure above anything else. We want to be free from coercion of any kind, even from laws that are designed to keep us alive (such as speed laws). We are shallow in our commitments, superficial in our relationships, lest we sacrifice some independence and admit that we are not all sufficient. We demonstrate and complain about considerable personal insecurity but would rather die than sacrifice one bit of our individualism to gain greater security.

Unresolved Needs in Anglo-American Society

Such are some of the deepest assumptions, values, and commitments of those of us who are middle-class Anglo-Americans. But there is more to the story. *Things have happened recently that push us to question our commitment to such values.* Whereas once we saw the American way as absolute, we are now aware of other ways, some of which seem to be working better than our way at many points. Questions arise. Areas that once looked either black or white now look gray. We are faced with many equally valid options and are crippled as we try to choose between them because our basis for choice seems to have disappeared. Things are moving so fast that, as Alvin

Toffler (1970) contends, we suffer from culture shock (he calls it "future shock") even within our own society.

We once believed: we could not be defeated in war, but we could not win in Vietnam. We once believed that everyone really wanted to become like us. But world events do not bear out this assumption. We once believed that if things were wrong in the world, especially if people turned against us, we simply needed to exert our power to make things right again. But it's becoming more and more obvious that we are no longer in control. Meanwhile, internally we are lonely. Many have gotten to the top but at the expense of personal relationships with both fellow workers and their own families. Many have played the game and never gotten to the top but have still alienated fellow workers and their own families. We thus face the future confused, demoralized, and lonely. What of that progress and that scientific humanism in which we have placed our faith?

The problems of American society in general, of course, bear fruit at the individual level, producing widespread individual confusion, demoralization, insecurity, loneliness, extreme competitiveness, superficiality in interpersonal relationships, and a wide variety of moderate-to-severe psychological disorders. If we are looking for felt needs as bases for the effective communication of the gospel, there certainly are plenty. In the paragraphs that follow, I deal with several of these.

Americans deeply long for security. Our commitment to and involvement in rapid change has robbed us of the stability that a healthier society would provide for its people. Most societies provide at least enough tradition so that people can be psychologically comfortable. Typically, the society dictates how people are to relate to others so that they don't have to negotiate a new relationship every time they meet a new person. Our society, however, often does not do this, so that we meet every new person and enter into every new interpersonal interaction with the necessity of negotiating a relationship as best we can.

Most societies assign people enough of the statuses and roles that they will occupy during their lifetime to enable them to be fairly secure from the beginning of life to its end. Typical of our society, however, is the fact that it promises marriage to everyone but then requires everyone to achieve it and allows many to fall by the wayside not having attained marriage and blaming themselves when it was really the society that was at fault. Likewise, our society promises that all who work hard enough can get to the top of whatever field they enter. The society cannot keep its promise in this area either.

Such raising of expectations that are then not fulfilled leaves people profoundly insecure and often madly seeking security in ephemeral things like wealth, fame, or the simple attraction of attention by less honorable means. Sometimes people seek security by converting to whatever cause comes along or by attaching themselves to some prominent person or group. Whatever the symptoms, it is clear that the search for security is an important factor in the lives of many Anglo-Americans (and other Americans as well).

Closely related to the security factor, secondly, is the *need for consistency in the expectations society has for us*. Our experience is that very often we are expected to fulfill simultaneously two or more mutually exclusive sets of expectations. Commonly, wives are expected to be sexpots who are totally devoted to homemaking, totally devoted to motherhood, and often totally devoted to a career all at the same time. Husbands are often expected to be as totally devoted to the home and parenthood as they are to their jobs. Young people are expected to follow a multitude of often conflicting guidelines laid down by parents, teachers, church, and peer group. The expectations are simply too diverse and demanding. Furthermore, those who impose the expectations usually lack both understanding of what they are doing and consistency in application.

A third felt need, also closely related to the first, is *the need for some kind of reasonable resolution of the deep cleavage between the ideals of our society and our actual behavior*. The ideal is for a woman to get married. The actual situation dictates that she may not pursue her desire openly but must wait to be found. The ideal is that we treat everyone as we would like to be treated. The actual is that in order to get where we want to go, we must compete viciously with anyone who also seeks that position. The ideal is that a young man spend as much time as possible with his wife and children. The actual is that he must at that period of his life devote himself as totally as possible to his job in order to assure a reasonable future for his family.

Fourth, it is deeply demoralizing to Anglo-Americans to discover that *the way we have been taught is neither absolute nor always right*. It is nothing less than frightening for many of us as we grow up to discover that so many areas of life are murky gray rather than crisp black or white. For we were generally taught that only one way is the right way, all other ways are wrong. When, then, we see others, both within and outside our society, living by other standards and getting away with it, we find it deeply demoralizing.

Younger generations, in an attempt to reconcile such diversity with the "one right way doctrine," have ended up absolutizing pluralism. Tolerance for the views and practices of others, no matter how strange they may be, thus becomes a major tenet of the contemporary "right way." And a new set of inconsistencies and contradictions is added to an already unmanageable approach to perceptual reality.

A fifth area of felt need centers around *the discrepancy between the real American religion, scientific humanism, and the Christian traditions in which we have been raised*. The schools teach one thing and the churches another. We have the feeling that all truth should be one and that, therefore, there should be agreement between religion and science, but they seem so far apart. And the Christian option seems so far out-of-date, both to non-

Christians and to a distressing number of Christians. So we are confused and tempted to abandon the least relevant.

In a sixth area of need, *many people are feeling increasingly powerless and in need of spiritual answers to at least certain of their problems.* The feeling is widespread that there is something more "out there" that is influencing or could influence human affairs. Many, even in "secular" society, are becoming disillusioned with science and are searching for a spiritual reality beyond the material.

Some have begun to experiment. And a disturbing number of them are finding a spiritual connection with Satan through New Age types of involvement. Within Christianity, some are finding spiritual reality in charismatic experience. But most secular people and most Christians continue to live with their dissatisfactions rather than to explore new options. And, though many churches are moving into spiritual power, most still show so little that it would occur to few to look for it there.

Finally, we need deep friendships. Much of what we experience tends to alienate us from each other and to keep us from the warmth and support of genuine human caring. We move from place to place so often that we hold ourselves back from deep friendships. We see independence and individualism as ideal, so we turn away from relationships that require dependency or interdependency, lest our individualism be sacrificed therein. And in the process we often become "things" to ourselves as well as to the society around us.

These are some of the pressing felt needs produced in middle-class Anglo-Americans by the realities of life within this society. It is to people feeling these kinds of needs in this society or to those feeling the equivalent needs in other societies that we are called to communicate Christianity.

The Appeal of Christianity

Given this situation, what, if any, appeal does Christianity have? As I see it, those expressions of Christianity that remain tradition-bound and static have no appeal. Tradition-bound, static Christianity is saying to the world: "God is out of date." And the world replies, "Your God may be saying correct things, but he is not saying them *to* anyone. He does not know where we are and doesn't seem to be interested in finding out. If he has no more time and concern for us than that, why should we waste our time with him?"

But Jesus did not come to found a tradition-bound, static institution. He did not even come to start another religion in a world that already had religious indigestion. Jesus came to bring abundant life (John 10:10b). And life as we experience it is dynamic, creative, always moving. So is the Christianity that we see in the New Testament. That Christianity was in touch with people and the concerns they actually felt. It was contemporary, making no attempt to drag them back into previous centuries. Though it used institutions, it refused to be captured by them. It both spoke of and lived God's life genuinely among human beings who knew that God cared because his people cared.

Unlike most Anglo-American versions of Christianity, biblical Christianity was vital in the spiritual dimension as well as at the human level. It connected with those who sincerely sought both knowledge and power (1 Cor. 1:22, 24). It required the Holy Spirit as well as human ingenuity. It imitated the closeness between Jesus and the Father spoken about in the first chapter of this book. It saw and connected with the spiritual reality that lies behind the observable acts of God in the human context. What we call miracles were normal because Christians took seriously the power and authority Jesus had given to his followers (Luke 9:1, 2) and believed him when he said "whoever believes in me will do what I do" (John 14:12). They imitated Jesus in ministry, integrating healing into their own lives and their communicational activity just as he did.

Can this be done in twentieth-century America? Or are things so bad that we must, as Francis Schaeffer (1976) recommends, retreat to a previous age when our society was not so pervasively affected by relativism? Personally, *I refuse to side with those who recommend retreat.* I believe that God can still work in the world and that he is not crippled by our kind of world. But, with God, we must deal with the needs actually felt by our receptors. It is a distortion of God's intent when we, his fellow laborers, allow people to perceive him as unconcerned with their problems, unwilling to struggle with contemporary issues and concepts, and really only interested in dealing with people who have a special liking for theology, ancient history, and dead languages.

I have presented in this book an understanding of communication that is based on a philosophical concept labeled *critical realism* (see chapter 7 concerning three realities and Barbour 1974). This position attempts to reconcile the differences between reality as it is and any human perception of that reality by suggesting that we need always to distinguish between the two.

Many conservative Christians have, however, assumed that Christianity is committed to another position, labeled by Barbour *naive realism.* That position claims that an informed observer can see reality directly, as it really is, objective and undistorted by any subjective perspective. Conservative Christians often feel that they have committed themselves so fully to God that his revelation is clear to them. Anyone who disagrees with them is simply wrong (see, for example, the writings of Lindsell, Schaeffer, Henry, and others of the conservative right).

Such people see critical realism as a threat to the essence of Christianity. They consider this position an intrusion from the world to be fought against rather than an insight from God to be embraced and utilized by Christians. Obviously, I do not agree. I believe this perspective is both possible to accept, even for conservative Christians, and extremely helpful in our attempts to present Christianity in our society. Although pluralistic Americans have often adopted so much relativism that they have relativized God, matters are not helped by going to the opposite extreme and absolutizing any given human understanding of God or his Word. It is the absence of a balanced critical-realist position that leads to either extreme, for without such a position we "either absolutize human institutions or relativize God" (Nida 1954:282).

If we take a critical-realist position toward biblical revelation, though we hold to the inspiration and authority of the Scriptures, we refrain from absolutizing our (or any other) human interpretation of those Scriptures. We state that God has indeed revealed himself to us, but we are limited to our Spirit-guided perceptions of that revelation. We cannot, and God does not expect us to, claim any absoluteness for our understandings of his revelation, even though we ask for the Holy Spirit to guide us in our interpretations. The best we can claim is that God knows the limitations within which he has chosen to work and that, therefore, *the perceptions he leads us to, though never absolute, are adequate for his purposes.*

Furthermore, we can from a critical-realist position claim that there is a Reality, even an absolute God, beyond our perception of reality. *Admitting that we never see that Reality objectively does not force us to deny its existence.* Thus, I believe, it is possible to be critical-realist Christians. We find, furthermore, that such a position helps us both in our attempts to witness to the growing numbers of people who see reality in this way and in our attempts to understand what God is doing and how he is doing it.

A second illustration of the possibilities available to us for working within the present situation is the larger matter of *what is absolute and what is relative.* As we have seen above, the critical-realist position allows for a Reality beyond our perception plus the nonobjective perception of that reality by human observers. If there is an absolute God in the universe, as we contend, then he would be a part of that objective Reality that lies beyond our ability to see it objectively. Though we cannot see him directly, we can postulate his existence on the same basis that we can postulate the objective existence of any aspect of reality that our perceptions seem to give us. We ought not, however, to absolutize our perceptions of him even though we are committed to them and to the assistance we have received from the Holy Spirit in guiding these perceptions toward greater accuracy (John 16:13).

If we recognize that there can only be one absolute in any given system, then we can make our peace with much of relativity. In a system such as the universe, the One who created and sustains it alone can be absolute. All the rest, in that it is derived from his efforts and sustained by his power, is related or relative to him. In the universe, then, God alone can be absolute.

Even the rules and principles in terms of which the universe operates have been devised and are sustained by him. We may, therefore, refer to them as *constants*, though not as absolutes. Such constants, especially in ethical areas, are prominent in the Bible, and it is, we believe, incumbent on Christians to observe them because they come from God and observance of them constitutes an expression of our commitment to him. I believe, however, that we lose nothing while gaining considerable understanding of the way things actually are when we admit that even here we are obeying our perception of his commands rather than an objective understanding of them. Thus, when there is a difference of understanding of these commands between Christians, we are able to relate to each other in love rather than by criticizing and hating our brothers and sisters.

We can, furthermore, accept the fact of cultural diversity as God seems to have accepted it throughout the Bible (1 Cor. 9:19–22). As he endorsed no culture or language but willingly worked through whatever vehicles were appropriate for the group with which he was working, so can we. We can, I believe, accept (without endorsing) the validity of any cultural way of life, even though recognizing that all ways of life (including ours) are pervasively affected by sin and influenced from the background by the enemy called the "Ruler of This World" (John 14:30; 1 John 5:16). The Golden Rule can then be applied at the cultural level as well as at the individual level and understood for what it is, a command to accept as valid the diversity we see around us both in individuals and in cultures and to express love and concern toward each approach to life, whether or not we totally approve of it.

Cultural relativity as well as perceptual relativity is, therefore, a position that Christians can live and work with rather than one we must oppose. We must, however, be clear on the difference between cultural relativity (which God endorses) and ethical relativity (which God condemns). The former accepts the validity of cultural systems as Paul did in 1 Corinthians 9:19-21. The latter involves a refusal to abide by the ethical norms of one's own cultural system (whether native or adopted). It was for ethical relativism that Jesus continually scorned the Pharisees (e.g., Matt. 23:3ff.). They (and countless contemporaries) simply did not take the principles they claimed to live by seriously enough to abide by them. And God found them wanting by their own standards. (See Mayers 1974 for a valuable discussion of this important distinction. See also Kraft 1991.)

What I am advocating is what Nida calls *biblical cultural relativism*, or relative relativism. I prefer (following Mayers) to call it *biblical cultural validity*. Nida (1954:52) contrasts this biblical position with the naive realism of Islam (and many conservative Christians) as follows:

Biblical relativism is not a matter of inconsistency, but a recognition of the different cultural factors which influence standards and actions. While the Koran attempts to fix for all time the behavior of Muslims, the Bible clearly establishes the principle of relative relativism, which permits growth adaptation, and freedom, under the Lordship of Jesus

> Christ. . . . The Christian position is not one of static conformance to
> dead rules, but of dynamic obedience to a living God.

(See Kraft 1979a:124–31 for further discussion of this important issue.)

A third secular understanding that has been widely misunderstood by Christians is the position that *religion is a matter of faith whereas science is a matter of fact.* In this case, I believe, both Christians and non-Christians misunderstand the nature of the problem. It is indeed true that religions are based on faith commitment to assumptions that cannot be proven. What is often not recognized, however, is that science is also based on such positions. *Any position that assumes that God does not exist is just as much a faith position as one that assumes that God does exist.* Furthermore, positions such as the belief that visible things are more real than invisible things, that disease is caused by germs rather than by spirits, that the rate of decay of organic matter was the same thousands and millions of years ago as it is now, that human beings developed from lower forms of life, and a myriad of other such unprovable assumptions regularly used by scientists are all based on faith.

Indeed, many of the faith positions taken by scientists (such as the one that says the world got here by chance) take much more faith than a faith position that postulates God as the Originator and Sustainer of the universe. When religion and science are compared, therefore, the comparison is between two sets of faith positions. And, as good scientists recognize, the problem in discussing such matters is not that we take faith positions but that we are frequently not open enough to state what our assumptions are. *It is becoming more and more apparent even to scientists that proof of anything can only be approximate and based on unproven assumptions.*

A fourth problem area in which I believe there is hope is that of *tradition and change.* We are a part of a society that strongly advocates change as ideal in many areas of life and, as a corollary to that position, is critical of those sectors that advocate the perpetuation of tradition, especially tradition that appears meaningless to contemporary secularists. Unfortunately, the church has tended to fall into the habit of maintaining ancient traditions rather than moving with the society in its devotion to change. Consequently, we have gotten caught in the practice of retaining forms from the past that are now interpreted as conveying meanings other than those originally intended. Though we would not want to be uncritical of our society's headlong rush toward changing everything, it is indeed unfortunate that we have not perceived the fact that *essential Christianity (that shown in the New Testament) sides with the advocates of change against the advocates of tradition.*

What We Seek

What we seek is the kind of Christianity that is equivalent in its dynamics in today's society to the Christianity we see in the pages of the New Testament. This is what I have described as *dynamic equivalence Christianity.*

Whenever and wherever the Church has turned from venturesomeness and retreated into static forms of expression it has lost its
dynamic. In the institutional Church today most people would probably point to such areas as theology, organization, and worship as
dead areas. The reason is not hard to find—"establishment" Christianity (the party in power) has tended to content itself with indoc-
trinating new generations and new cultures into forms of Christianity
that are no longer culturally appropriate. Established Christianity has
feared to alter the forms lest in so doing the content should be lost.
By so doing, however, it has unwittingly assured that the content
would be largely lost.

The dynamic of Christianity, however, is not in the sacredness of
cultural forms—even those that God once used. The Christian
dynamic is in the venturesomeness of participating with God in the
transformation of contemporary cultural forms to serve more adequately as vehicles for God's interactions with human beings. What
we seek is a Christianity equivalent in its dynamics to that displayed
in the pages of the New Testament. But we often fear to let loose
from the old familiar forms. We may recognize the need for a new
dynamic but our cultural conditioning often mitigates against our
engaging in the kind of experimentation that might lead us to discover
it (Kraft 1979a:382).

If, in recognition of the essentially dynamic nature of Christianity, we
gave ourselves to the kind of creativity and risk (see Kraft 1979a:18-21 for
a discussion of this aspect) that we see in New Testament Christianity, we
would be in a much better position to communicate to the society around
us.

And the resources at our disposal are impressive. There is a sovereign
God who answers prayer. There are turned-on persons who live the best
kind of Christianity. There are Christian groups (called churches) that genuinely care and will respond to a challenge of relevance. There is relationship to God enabling us individually and corporately to appropriate his
power for constructive, goal-oriented life change. There is the tremendous
power of loving acceptance to attract people and to provide the matrix for
personal change in the right direction. All these and many other assets
provide genuine Christian commitment with high appeal to those who are
looking for something better than they now experience.

But Christianity involves converting, both for outsiders and for insiders.
It involves constant, lifelong movement in the direction of God and God-
likeness (see Kraft 1979a:240-45). And such converting cannot leave certain
American values unchanged. For although God is willing to start where
Americans are, he is not content if we continue to be crippled by simply
continuing in our commitment to the values in which we have been trained.

If, for example, our society advocates a naturalistic approach to life,

Christianity sees *a supernaturalistic dimension to everything*. If our society encourages self-centeredness, Christianity seeks to move us toward *God-centeredness*. If such things as commitment to the American way, scientific humanism, progress, and individualism are primary to us, Christianity seeks to lead us to elevate *commitment to God* and his cause to the primary place among our commitments. If as Americans we are given to independence, Christianity advocates *interdependence* (psychological and spiritual) with God and other Christians. If American society teaches us that "my rights" should be paramount, Christianity turns our focus toward the *service we can render*. If American society teaches security in money and position, Christianity teaches *security through a relationship with God* and his people. If American society teaches that we should compete with our neighbors to get the best we can for ourselves, Christianity teaches that we should *love our neighbors* and seek the best for them.

Christianity offers deep intimate relationships with God and other humans in place of American superficiality in relationships. Christianity advocates love and understanding across generations and other social gaps in place of American competitiveness and antagonism. Christianity offers a world controlled by an all-powerful, loving God, even when we least understand what is going on, in place of a world under the fickle control of fate or of bumbling human beings. Christianity is a way that transcends the American way and will be here when the latter is simply a historical rumor.

Christianity requires change, even though it advocates starting with perspectives and needs that are already a part of the society. In Christianity there is both acceptance of what is and hope for something better. When, therefore, we seek to communicate for that something better, we must not be captured by traditions that would render God's message impotent. This book is intended to assist us in this regard.

Bibliography

Arensberg, Conrad M., and Niehoff, Arthur H. 1971. *Introducing Social Change: A Manual for Community Development.* 2d ed. Hawthorne, NY: Aldine Publishing Co.

Baehr, Theodore. 1986. *Getting the Word Out.* San Francisco: Harper & Row.

Barbour, Ian G. 1974. *Myths, Models, and Paradigms: A Comparative Study in Science and Religion.* New York: Harper & Row.

Barr, James. 1961. *The Semantics of Biblical Language.* London: Oxford University Press.

Baumann, J. Daniel. 1972. *An Introduction to Contemporary Preaching.* Grand Rapids: Baker Book House.

Bellah, Robert N., R. Madsen, W. M. Sullivan, A. Swidler and S. M. Tipton. 1985. *Habits of the Heart.* New York: Harper & Row.

Berlo, David K. 1960. *The Process of Communication: An Introduction to Theory and Practice.* New York: Holt, Rinehart and Winston.

Bishop, David S. 1977. *Effective Communications.* Cleveland, TN: Pathway Press.

Chartier, Myron R. 1981. *Preaching as Communication: An Interpersonal Perspective.* Nashville: Abingdon Press.

Condon, John C. 1975. *Semantics and Communication.* 2d ed. New York: The Macmillan Co.

Craddock, Fred B. 1978. *Overhearing the Gospel.* Nashville: Abingdon Press.

Dance, Frank E. X., and Larson, Carl E. 1972. *Speech Communication: Concepts and Behavior.* New York: Holt, Rinehart and Winston.

Dodd, Carley H. 1991. *Dynamics of Intercultural Communication,* 3rd ed. Dubuque, IA: Wm C. Brown.

Egan, Gerard. 1982. *The Skilled Helper.* 2nd ed. Monterey, CA: Brooks/Cole Publishing Co.

Engel, James F. 1979. *Contemporary Christian Communications: Its Theory and Practice.* Nashville: Thomas Nelson.

———1988. *Getting Your Message Across.* Bloomingdale, IL: Media Associates International.

Fore, William F. 1968. "Communication for Churchmen." In *Communication— Learning for Churchmen.* Ed. B. F. Jackson, pp. 11-100. Nashville: Abingdon Press.

Fuglesang, Andreas. 1982. *About Understanding.* Uppsala, Sweden: Dag Hammarskjold Foundation.

Gibbs, Eddie. 1985. *The God Who Communicates.* London: Hodder & Stoughton.

Grieve, Alexander J. 1962. "Preaching." In *Encyclopedia Britannica.* Chicago: Encyclopedia Britannica.

Griffin, Em. 1976. *The Mind Changers.* Wheaton, IL: Tyndale House.

————1982. *Getting Together*. Downers Grove, IL: InterVarsity Press.

Hall, Edward T. 1959. *The Silent Language*. Garden City, NY: Doubleday & Co.

————1966. *The Hidden Dimension*. Garden City, NY: Doubleday & Co.

————1976. *Beyond Culture*. Garden City, NY: Doubleday & Co.

Hayakawa, S. I., with Hamalian, Leo, and Wagner, Geoffrey. 1964. *Language in Thought and Action*. 2d ed. New York: Harcourt, Brace & World.

Henry, Carl F. H. 1976. *God, Revelation and Authority*. Vols. 1 and 2. Waco: Word Books.

Hesselgrave, David J. 1978. *Communicating Christ Cross Culturally*. Grand Rapids: Zondervan Publishing House.

Hiebert, Paul G. 1976. *Cultural Anthropology*. Philadelphia: J. B. Lippincott.

————1978. "Conversion, Culture and Cognitive Categories." In *Gospel in Context*. Vol. 1, 24-27.

Keesing, Roger M., and Felix M. 1971. *New Perspectives in Cultural Anthropology*. New York: Holt, Rinehart and Winston.

Kittel, Gerhard, ed. 1967. *Theological Dictionary of the New Testament*, Vol. 3. trans. Geoffrey W. Bromiley. Grand Rapids: Eerdmans Publishing Co.

Klem, Herbert V. 1982. *Oral Communication of the Scripture*. Pasadena: William Carey Library.

Kluckhohn, Clyde. 1949. *Mirror for Man: The Relationship of Anthropology to Modern Life*. New York: McGraw-Hill Book Co.

Kraft, Charles H. 1973a. "God's Model for Cross-Cultural Communication — The Incarnation." *Evangelical Missions Quarterly* 9:205-16.

————1973b. "The Incarnation, Cross-Cultural Communication and Communication Theory." *Evangelical Missions Quarterly* 9:277-84.

————1978. "An Anthropological Apologetic for the Homogeneous Unit Principle," *Occasional Bulletin of Missionary Research* 10:121-26.

————1979a. *Christianity in Culture*. Maryknoll, NY: Orbis Books.

————1979b. *Communicating the Gospel God's Way*. Pasadena: William Carey Library.

————1981. "The Place of the Receptor in Communication." *Theology, News and Notes* 28:13-15, 23.

————1989. *Christianity With Power*. Ann Arbor: Servant Books.

————1991. "Receptor Oriented Ethics in Cross-Cultural Intervention." *Transformation* 8:20-25.

Kuhn, Thomas S. 1970. *The Structure of Scientific Revolutions*. 2d ed. Chicago: University of Chicago Press.

LaSor, William S. 1961. *Great Personalities of the New Testament: Their Life and Times*. Old Tappan, NJ: Fleming H. Revell.

Lerbinger, Otto. 1972. *Designs for Persuasive Communication*. Englewood Cliffs, NJ: Prentice-Hall.

Lewis, Ralph L. and Gregg. 1983. *Inductive Preaching*. Westchester, IL: Crossway Books.

Lindsell, Harold. 1976. *The Battle for the Bible*. Grand Rapids: Zondervan Publishing House.

Lingenfelter, Sherwood G., and Marvin K. Mayers. 1986. *Ministering Cross-Culturally*. Grand Rapids: Baker.

Littlejohn, Stephen W. 1978. *Theories of Human Communication*. Columbus, OH: Charles E. Merrill Publishing Co.

Loewen, Jacob. 1967. "Role, Self-Image and Missionary Communication." *Practical Anthropology* 14:145-60. Reprinted in Loewen 1975, pp. 412-27.

———1968a. "Socialization and Social Control." *Practical Anthropology* 15:145-56. Reprinted in Loewen 1975, pp. 223-86.

———1968b. "The Indigenous Church and Resocialization." *Practical Anthropology* 15: 193-204. Reprinted in Loewen 1975.

———1969. "Socialization and Conversion in the Ongoing Church." *Practical Anthropology* 16: 1-17. Reprinted in Loewen 1975.

———1975. *Culture and Human Values: Christian Intervention in Anthropological Perspective.* Pasadena: William Carey Library.

Mayers, Marvin K. 1974. *Christianity Confronts Culture: A Strategy for Cross-Cultural Evangelism.* Grand Rapids: Zondervan Publishing House.

McLaughlin, Raymond W. 1979. *The Ethics of Persuasive Preaching.* Grand Rapids: Baker.

Mortensen, C. David. 1972. *Communication: The Study of Human Interaction.* New York: McGraw-Hill Book Co.

———1973. *Basic Readings in Communication Theory.* New York: Harper & Row.

Newbigin, Lesslie. 1986. *Foolishness to the Greeks.* Grand Rapids: Eerdmans.

Nichols, Sue. 1963. *Words on Target.* Richmond: John Knox Press.

Nida, Eugene A. 1954. *Customs and Cultures.* New York: Harper & Brothers. Reprinted, Pasadena: William Carey Library.

———1990. *Message and Mission: The Communication of the Christian Faith.* Rev. ed. Pasadena: William Carey Library.

Nida, Eugene A., and Taber, Charles R. 1969. *The Theory and Practice of Translation.* Leiden: Brill.

Rogers, Everett M. 1983. *Diffusion of Innovations.* 3d ed. New York: The Free Press.

Schaeffer, Francis A. 1976. *How Should We Then Live? The Rise and Decline of Western Thought and Culture.* Old Tappan, NJ: Fleming H. Revell.

Schramm, Wilbur, and Roberts, Donald F. 1971. *The Process and Effects of Mass Communication.* Rev. ed. Urbana: University of Illinois Press.

Smalley, Gary and John Trent 1988. *The Language of Love.* Pomona, CA: Focus on the Family.

Smith, Donald K. 1984. *Make Haste Slowly: Developing Effective Cross-Cultural Communication.* Portland, OR: Institute for International Christian Communication.

Sogaard, Viggo B. 1975. *Everything You Need to Know for a Cassette Ministry.* Minneapolis: Bethany Fellowship.

———n.d. "Applying Christian Communication: Book I—Media in Mission." Unpublished manuscript, Pasadena, CA: School of World Mission, Fuller Seminary.

Stewart, Edward C. 1971. *American Cultural Patterns: A Cross-Cultural Perspective.* Chicago: Intercultural Press.

Stott, John R. W. 1982. *Between Two Worlds.* Grand Rapids: Eerdmans.

Toffler, Alvin. 1970. *Future Shock.* New York: Bantam Books.

Toyotome, Masumi. 1953. "Poetic Images and Forms in the Sayings of Jesus." Ph.D. dissertation. New York: Columbia University.

Wagner, C. Peter. 1981. *Church Growth and the Whole Gospel: A Biblical Mandate.* New York: Harper & Row.

———1988. *How to Have a Healing Ministry.* Ventura, CA: Regal Books.

Wallis, Ethel. 1968. *God Speaks Navajo.* New York: Harper & Row.

Watzlawick, P. Beavin, J., and Jackson, D. 1967. *Pragmatics of Human Communication: A Study of International Patterns, Pathologies, and Paradoxes*. New York: W. W. Norton & Co.
Webber, Robert E. 1980. *God Still Speaks*. Nashville: Thomas Nelson.

Index